THE SAFE INVESTOR

THE SAFE INVESTOR

INVESTOR

*How to Make Your Money Grow in a
Volatile Global Economy*

TIMOTHY F.
McCARTHY

This book is dedicated to all those hard-working people who provided for their families, broke out of poverty, and are now trying to preserve and grow their nest eggs.

THE SAFE INVESTOR
Copyright © Timothy F. McCarthy, 2014.

First published in 2014 by
PALGRAVE MACMILLAN®
in the United States—a division of St. Martin's Press LLC,
175 Fifth Avenue, New York, NY 10010.

Where this book is distributed in the UK, Europe and the rest of the world, this is by Palgrave Macmillan, a division of Macmillan Publishers Limited, registered in England, company number 785998, of Houndmills, Basingstoke, Hampshire RG21 6XS.

Palgrave Macmillan is the global academic imprint of the above companies and has companies and representatives throughout the world.

Palgrave® and Macmillan® are registered trademarks in the United States, the United Kingdom, Europe and other countries.

ISBN: 978–1–137–27910–1

Library of Congress Cataloging-in-Publication Data

McCarthy, Tim (Timothy F.)
    The safe investor : how to make your money grow in a volatile global economy / Tim McCarthy.
        pages cm
    ISBN 978–1–137–27910–1 (hardback)
        1. Investments. 2. McCarthy, Tim (Timothy F.) I. Title.

HG4521.M395 2014
332.6—dc23   2013033579

A catalogue record of the book is available from the British Library.

Design by Newgen Knowlegde Works (P) Ltd., Chennai, India.

First edition: February 2014

10 9 8 7 6 5 4 3 2 1

Printed in the United States of America.

CONTENTS

Acknowledgments   vii

Preface   ix

PART I
LESSONS FROM INVESTORS

1 The Day I Became an Adult: How Low Risk Became
   High Risk   3

2 Diagnoses for My Doctor: Diversifying Can Be Tricky   9

3 Dieting and Investing: A Broad Range of Ingredients
   Keeps Your Portfolio Healthy   15

4 Single Points of Failure (SPOF): How to Guard
   Against Financial Catastrophes   19

5 My Randy Old Great-Grandfather: What If You Live?   31

6 It's About Time: Understanding Financial Cycles
   So You Invest for the Long Haul   37

7 How Am I Doing? How to Evaluate Fund and
   Portfolio Data   49

8 Balancing Greed versus Fear: Understanding the
   Emotions of Investing   65

9 The Reversal of Nations: How Global Diversification
   Is the New Safe   77

PART II
INVESTING SOLUTIONS

10 Three Pockets: A Tool for Managing Money
and Emotions   101

11 The Risk Prism   113

12 What's Inside Your Pockets?   133

13 Beyond Borders: Understanding How to Invest in
International Markets   167

14 What About Your Personal Portfolio? How to Build
and Monitor Your Portfolio   197

PART III
FINDING THE ADVISOR YOU CAN TRUST

15 Who Is Most Dangerous? It's Who You Least Suspect   235

16 Where Do I Go For Advice? Brokers, Banks,
Independent Investment Advisors, Financial
Planners—Which One Is Right for Me?   245

17 The Naked Advisor: How Do I Select the Right Person?   263

PART IV
FINAL WORDS OF ADVICE

18 The Seven Critical Lessons   279

Information on Website: www.timmccarthy.com   283

Important Legal Information: Disclaimer   285

Notes   286

Index   295

This QR code will take you to timmccarthy.com, which directs you to a glossary of financial terms and the appendix covering the unabridged research.

ACKNOWLEDGMENTS

There are many important people that I owe a debt of gratitude to for helping me learn the keys to successful investing. Most important are the thousands of investors and hundreds of investment advisors who showed me the path.

Specifically, in building this story, I owe Prasoon Raghuwanshi for his hours of dedication over the past ten months in carefully building all the support documentation for the book as well as the website. In addition, there were several investment advisors who supplied important research to help define my approach to investing. In particular, Dr. Andrew Rudd, Dan Kern, and Gerard Cronin of Advisor Partners conducted joint research with me on fund survival rate and the review of fund analysis tools. In addition, Curt Brown and Sean Stannard-Stockton of Ensemble provided great insight into the focused investing strategy. Norman Boone of Mosaic Financial Partners lent me his deep expertise in structuring a proper portfolio for investors. Linda Rossi of LL Rossi and Co. and Ted Lucas of Lattice Strategies provided valuable input into behavioral investing, demographics, and country analysis. Bob Pozen, both personally as well as in his book *The Fund Industry*, were a great source of insights.

My colleagues at Nikko Asset Management, led by Takumi Shibata, were instrumental in providing much assistance over the past several years in the refinement of many of the book's ideas. Other companies providing me key insights include: Rongtong Fund Management, Tyndall Investments, Sumitomo Trust, Development Bank of Singapore, Ambit-India, Suncorp-Australia, Franklin Templeton, Janus Capital, Mathews Intl., and Janney Montgomery Scott.

Also, over the years, professional research companies such as: Cerulli Associates, Avi Nachmany's Strategic Insight and Chip Roame's Tiburon Advisors have been immensely helpful in keeping me abreast of the latest trends.

As to the illustrations, we all owe Rich Harrington and Joe Kulka so much for providing a friendly way to understand and even enjoy the otherwise tedious but important graphic information.

Regarding the editing of the book, Laurie Harting and the Palgrave Macmillan team did an outstanding job in polishing the final copy into an easily readable form. Additionally, this book would not exist were it not for my agent, Leah Spiro. She navigated me through the enigmatic waters of the publishing industry.

Lastly, I want to acknowledge all my friends and family who struggled through the dozens of Word documents and Excel spreadsheets in order to provide me with detailed critique and ideas, in particular:

Tom Abraham
Kathy Adams
The Bone Family
Bruce Batkin
Pete Briger
Dennis Clark
Jim Donatell
Hydorn Family
Chuck Johnson
Jeff and Susanne Lyons
James McMahon

Frank McAleer
McCarthy Family
John Murphy
Ryon Paton
Robert C. Pozen
Gwynne and Shauna Rose
Harold Rosen
Greg Ryan
Ben and Charlie Smith
Robert Waterman

PREFACE

During my college years, I taught karate. Part of learning karate requires competing in *kumite*, which are fighting bouts where the primary objective is to kick and punch the hell out of each other. At times, I had to warn certain students, "Watch your back ribs! You're forgetting to guard them!" Inevitably, despite the third or fourth warning, for some students their body language indicated impatience, as if to say, "Yeah, yeah, Tim. I hear you already." Still, they'd soon forget and leave their ribs vulnerable.

So, during the next match, I'd give them a quick, hard wheel kick to the back of the ribs, just as my sensei had done to me in my early years. After that, I never had to remind students again. The "tiny brains" in their back ribs would send up strong signals to the big brain every time the student got on the mat to fight: "Hey! Remember us? These are your ribs speaking. GUARD US!"

After just one strong kick. The ribs would do all the reminding for me, and for the students.

And so it goes with investing. The lessons we learn, and the lessons we rarely forget, come not from listening to long lectures, or thinking rationally about what we heard or read. The real valuable lessons come from either experiencing financial pain firsthand or witnessing other's mistakes. Those lessons never leave the cortex.

The emotional dimension in investing has been researched by experts in the field of finance and investing, but is generally discussed in a clinical, even dispassionate way. Even sophisticated investors can still fall into a variety of emotional traps. Even after learning about such traps, the reaction of many investors is, "Yeah, people should learn to control their emotions and just think rationally. But of course, I don't have that problem." The lesson is not internalized, as many people do not personally identify with the findings in behavioral finance. One of my goals is to sensitize readers to the issues in emotional investing and help them better keep it under control.

By way of background, I spent much of this past decade running an investment bank/brokerage firm as well as a fund company outside the United States. After previously managing similar companies for many years in the United States, I thought it would be rewarding to bring this knowledge overseas to countries and investors that were new to investing. In many ways, these investors reminded me of American investors back in the 1970s, when retail investing was just beginning to emerge. Most novice investors were extremely risk averse and stocks were considered only for gamblers. Most had no idea about how to construct a balanced portfolio.

When I returned to the United States last year, I expected to see even further advancement in the field of investor education. After all, the United States was at the vanguard in both product innovation and in refining the most effective approaches for people in building their investment portfolios. I knew from talking with advisors that much progress had been made in constructing better formulas for successful investing, and the US financial services industry had been able to reach large segments of investors. And with the onslaught of quality information being piped into people's homes on a 24-hour basis, the collective awareness had been raised. However, I was surprised to learn that despite all the efforts to educate the public, many people I talked to still felt uncomfortable with how they should actually grow their money. I heard many investors voice complaints like

"It *used* to be . . ."

- I thought I only needed to have enough money after I retire to last 15 to 20 years. I have life insurance in case I die. But now I am asking myself, "What if I live?" I see the reality that many people are now living to be 90 or even 100 years old. Especially considering health care costs, my money might not last that long. I need my money to grow.

- If I wanted to be safe and still grow my money over time, all I had to do was leave it in the bank. I could get 5 percent or 6 percent and not worry about what the Dow was doing. But now, interest rates after inflation remain at or near zero. I can't ignore that my money will not grow if I just leave it in the bank. And with some governments pushing for moderate inflation, even with a 2 percent a year inflation rate, if I do nothing, my money could be worth maybe 20 percent less in a decade.

- I never worried about the value and safety of the US Treasury or the US dollar. But now I see we have more debt than our annual GDP. China now owns over $3 trillion of our government debt. They are America's biggest bank! So, is it so safe anymore to only have investment exposure in the United States, especially over the next 30 years? Whom can I trust to help me? I've seen too many examples of people losing their money to complicated schemes and high fees. What can I do?

Unfortunately, many in the industry have not adapted their visions and their models to help people grow their money in light of the new reality of our global environment. While overseas, I was able to refine what I had learned in the United States and adjust my investing approach to incorporate both the ever-changing international environment as well as the demographic impact of the rapidly aging societies. After years of working with clients and reviewing the results of successful investors, it is clear to me there are ways to successfully invest in this brave new world and grow your money in a relatively safe manner over a period of years. My message to readers is that you can rest assured there are investing approaches that can be adapted to succeed in this very different twenty-first century, and you can learn them in the next few hundred pages.

Over the years, I have wrestled with how best to help more people learn and feel comfortable with the lessons of successful investing. I have seen what does not work, such as acting like a Wall Street guru throwing formulas and mathematical equations at investors and then leaving them to figure out how it fits into their lives. Rather, through stories and scenarios about real investors, I will communicate the simple lessons to growing your nest egg in a low risk manner.

In Part I of this book, I share the stories and key lessons that have most resonated with investors I have worked with around the world. These lessons serve as the foundation for any effective portfolio.

Part II applies these lessons to help investors structure an investment plan tailored to their particular personalities and helps them manage their emotions as they build and monitor their portfolios. Even if they don't want to personally bother to manage the investments themselves, at least they will understand what their advisor is saying and how the various parts fit together.

Part III recognizes that, as in sports, even professionals often seek advice, if only for validation of their views and decisions. Although it is fine for some to practice Do It Yourself, the majority of personal financial assets are still at least partly managed by advisors. Through my personal stories, I lay out a guide so the average investor can feel comfortable evaluating and managing various intermediaries and advisors. In particular, you will learn the key questions to ask an advisor, and how to interpret his answers.

I also share the results of my recent research with Advisor Partners in areas that the financial services industry has chosen to largely ignore. These topics are critical to investors, covering the true life of the average mutual fund, how to "evaluate the evaluators" of funds, and other not so little secrets of the financial services industry.

In Part IV, I sum up the seven key lessons for investment success and answer questions where I think some of you may still have doubt or concern. I address those nagging worries that may prevent someone from starting or continuing to build an investment portfolio.

At a conference in New York recently, I heard an intelligent, well-educated woman say, "I am a financial idiot." It is the fault of the industry that she feels this way. All too often, we see members of our industry use language and give arcane explanations that are meant to show off their expertise, to humble their clients into thinking that they, "the experts," are smarter than the average investor. This book is about making sure you feel comfortable with an investment process that doesn't require too much of your time to successfully grow your investment nest egg.

In the course of writing this book, I have asked for the help of all kinds of investors and advisors across the world. Their number one question to me was, "Who is this book for?"

The answer, I hope, is "your very selves!" Perhaps you are a young, novice investor who has only recently begun to build a small nest egg of money. Or an experienced, affluent investor who still has concerns about whether you are on the right track given how dramatically the world has changed. You may be a director of a large foundation, wondering if your organization is focused on the right investment issues for its own long-term objective. Alternatively, you may be a young investment advisor who still feels unsettled about how best to help clients become comfortable with an investing process.

If you prefer to actively trade your investments or are seeking maximum performance over a short period of time, there are many other books more suited to your needs. Rather, this book is for the "The Safe Investors," those that care most about not losing their hard-earned money and yet need to grow their nest egg in the most careful way possible.

By the end of the book, readers should be able to take comfort that they now have a blueprint that is easy to understand, flexible, and adjustable. Most important, they will know what is essential versus what just doesn't matter that much to growing a financial nest egg over a lifetime.

PART I
LESSONS FROM INVESTORS

CHAPTER 1

THE DAY I BECAME AN ADULT

How Low Risk Became High Risk

I awoke to my mother screaming, "Oh my God, oh my God!" as she ran down the hallway.

It took a moment for my brain to register her panic.

I had just returned from studying in the Soviet Union. And like many 18-year-olds, I was quite self-absorbed and unprepared to see a parent in such distress. In many ways, I just took my family for granted. That attitude was about to change.

She opened my door and said in almost a whisper, "Your father is dead!"

My father was killed in an auto accident on Sunday morning, October 12, 1969.

The house quickly filled with neighbors and family friends. He was quite a popular figure, and it seemed like everyone we knew came over to help, to console, to just be with us.

Helen, my mother, was in deep shock. I tried to comfort her and my brother as much as I could. I soon began to realize there might be things that needed to be attended to, some perhaps quickly.

The authorities required someone in the family to identify my father's body, so a few of us took the responsibility to go down to the San Jose coroner' office to make sure the body was properly identified. I also wanted to make sure there was nothing in the car that could be possibly used against him.

The weeks following my father's death were emotionally overwhelming for the family. When my mother could finally talk about her finances, we saw she would have just enough for her and my brother to live in modest comfort. I was already making enough money for myself teaching karate, but she was only 48 and having trouble finding a teaching job. And my brother, Danny, was only 13, so their financial nest egg would still have to last for a long time.

We didn't know many people who could give us advice. My uncle and aunt were San Francisco cops. Even the wealthier of my dad's friends did not have much understanding of long-term investing. Indeed, the entire investment industry was quite primitive in the United States, even as recently as the 1960s and early '70s. Most people looked at investing in areas like the stock market as dangerous. Fortunately, one dear old friend of my dad's, Bill O'Farrell, was a controller for the town of San Mateo and was in charge of investing reserves for the city, so he had some experience.

Bill was a good judge of a man's character and he introduced us to a reputable stockbroker. My mom was quite specific in our first meeting with the broker. She wanted conservative investments only, no stocks. She made it clear she could not afford to lose the money, as that was all she had and her new teaching job was not enough to support her and my brother.

After careful consideration and much discussion, the broker put all my mother's money into long-term, fixed-rate, high-quality bonds—mostly governments, utilities, and corporate bonds. It sounded to me like the prudent course of action, but what did I know?

Through the early seventies I was busy studying, teaching karate, and occasionally squeezing in a little time for fun. During this time, my mother and I watched with consternation as interest rates climbed. Later, at its height around 1980, the prime lending rate actually passed 20 percent! Long before then, my mother was panicking. Marked to market, her long-term fixed-rate bonds had fallen to nearly half their value. In general, when interest rates fall,

Fig. 1.1 My Mother Rides the Interest Rate Roller Coaster
(1-Year Treasury Rate [Yearly]: 1970 to 1990)

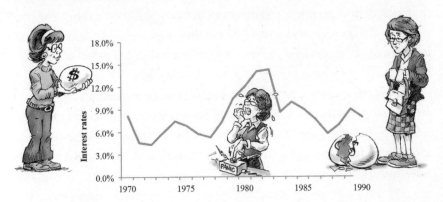

Source: Economic Research Division, Federal Reserve Bank of St. Louis

prices of bonds with higher rates rise; when interest rates rise, prices of outstanding bonds with lower rates fall. I shall never forget that look of fear on her face as she exclaimed, "I can't make this money back again. What am I going to do?"

As the seventies progressed many financial industry experts were saying interest rates were going to stay high, maybe go higher, which would mean that my poor mother would lose even more money. She became so emotionally distraught that one day she panicked and sold all her bonds and put the money in money market and bank accounts.

As the eighties wore on, interest rates began to drop. Ironically, had Helen kept the bonds and held them to maturity instead of sticking all the money in the bank, she would have recouped all her principal.

The result? My mother had lost nearly half her financial nest egg. It affected her attitude, how she managed most everything in her life. Helen would often exclaim to her friends, "But who could have told me what to do? Where could I have gone for sound advice?"

A MESSAGE TO THOSE THINKING OF
A CAREER ON WALL STREET

Watching my mother so needlessly suffer, and knowing that there were hundreds of thousands of individual investors that were vulnerable to financial markets without sound advice, convinced me that I should build a career in financial services. There had to be a better way for people to grow their money without taking on too much risk. Though today few think this way, I still believe helping people invest is a noble calling, a noble mission for advisors in our industry.

In recent years we have heard much about the greed in our industry—how all brokers, traders, Wall Street execs think about is how much money they can make, often at the expense of the customer. However, being an investment professional can and should be an honorable profession. It is critically important to so many families.

My message to young people coming into the industry is to always remember your number-one job is to help people grow their money more than savings, but with less risk than trading. If you keep that motto as a constant reminder, you can make a difference in this world, much like a doctor or a minister—but only if you genuinely care about your mission. Once you qualify as an advisor, you will have the opportunity over the decades to help at least a thousand families ensure financial comfort in their later years. Above all else, anyone who works on Wall Street has to ask himself each day, "Would I sell this product to my mother?"

THE LESSONS I LEARNED FROM MY MOTHER'S MISFORTUNE

1. **There is no such thing as a no-risk investment.** All investments, even cash, have elements of risk. An investor has to understand those risks, especially the subtle or indirect risks. In the case of the bonds my mother bought, the credit quality was fine. Indeed, all the bond issuers at maturity paid back the principal and interest. It was the interest rate fluctuation that contained the risk. As you shall see in other examples, like my mother's portfolio, one of the greatest ironies about investing is that a concentrated portfolio of only low-risk investments can be actually riskier than a broad, multifaceted package of investments.

2. **Don't put all your eggs in one basket.** If my mother had only broadened her investment instruments by investing in bonds with different maturities, and invested broadly in the stock market even a little, she never would have lost so much money. I know—many of the experienced investors and advisors are saying, "Of course, you have to diversify!" However, I tell this story first because lack of diversification remains among the biggest mistakes I still see being made by even the "sophisticated" investors. The idea of diversification may be easy to understand, but too many times I have observed it is not easy for people to follow, even when they have been properly instructed. And as you shall also see in subsequent chapters, getting the mix right in your portfolio can be more difficult than you think.

3. **Keep your emotions under control. Be patient.** If my mother had not panicked, and instead simply held those bonds until maturity, she would not have lost half her money. No one was there to tell her to wait it out and hold the bonds through maturity, so she followed her emotions. I still meet investors who have made the same mistake as she did. But what others can learn from my mother's experience, and what I learned, is that understanding one's true, long-term horizon and sticking to a basic plan are critical to growing your assets safely.

CHAPTER 2

DIAGNOSES FOR MY DOCTOR

Diversifying Can Be Tricky

One of my closest friends is a heart surgeon in Silicon Valley. And like many successful folks in 2000 to 2001, he often told anyone who would listen about his investing prowess. He had done so well with his investing over the past decade that he planned on retiring soon. I asked him if he was diversified, and he replied that his equity portfolio was quite diversified by industry, size of companies, and individual stocks and mutual funds. He had one-third of his portfolio in stocks he chose, with the balance divided among a variety of four highly rated stock funds and the Standard & Poor's index fund. He put most of his money in equities, as he was impressed by his own stock-picking ability over the previous five years.

Soon afterward, I moved back overseas, mainly to buy a brokerage firm in South Korea, and I didn't see him for a few years. Upon returning to the United States, we got together for dinner. He complained he would now have to work another five years due to his poor investment performance. After the dot.com bubble burst in 2001 and 2002, causing most of the technology and internet-oriented stock prices to collapse, he lost nearly half his money. He asked me to help him figure out what went so wrong with his portfolio. After all, the Dow had only declined around 15 percent in the same time frame. In the 2000–2002 price plunge, the technology-heavy NASDAQ lost a whopping 66 percent.

In studying the details of his portfolio, it became crystal clear that he had been lulled into a false sense of safe diversification. Indeed, he was correct that all his money was not in one investment portfolio, but instead was mixed up with other fund managers and some in indexing funds as well. So, what was his mistake? Why had his port-folio dropped so much more than the blue-chip market?

First off, his personal stock-picking portfolio was concentrated in large high-tech and internet stocks, many of which were natu-rally connected with Silicon Valley. During the OTC market crash, these stocks were crushed the most—many dropping as much as 90 percent. They were often valued in excess of 100 times annual earnings, so they had a lot of room to fall.

Second, the funds he chose were the top-rated performing funds of the previous five years. By definition, since the major high-tech stocks were the best performers in the late nineties, most of those funds were exposed to the very same stocks he bought in his own portfolio. Buying many of the highest-rated or multiple "stars" funds

Fig. 2.1   Performance of NASDAQ vs. Dow Jones Industrial Average (1997–2001)

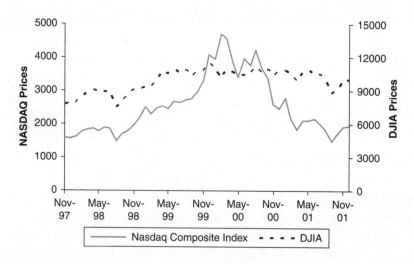

Source: Yahoo! Finance

Fig. 2.2 Performance of Top-Rated Technology Funds* (1998–2001)

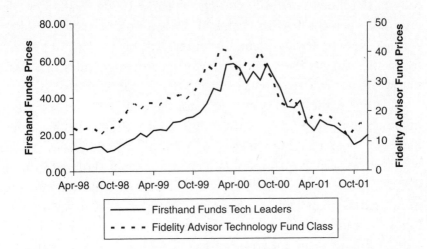

Source: Factset

* Firsthand Funds' assets rose to $8 billion from $1 billion, in a matter of months, in 1999 and 2000. "Mutual Funds Report; Technology Is Back, but Is It Here to Stay?," *The New York Times*, July 6, 2003.

doubled his concentration risk rather than helping him to diversify. I was able to see firsthand how fund ratings can be quite misleading[1] and should be evaluated very carefully to avoid overconcentration.

Third, the major index fund, the Standard and Poor's or S&P 500, like many index funds and ETFs (exchange traded funds), are "cap weighted," i.e., the amount of shares bought for each stock is determined by the value of the company relative to the total market. So during the late nineties, though many people thought an index fund does not follow an investment strategy, it turns out that if you bought most index funds, they would be weighted or concentrated in the blue-chip momentum growth stocks.[2] After all, it is this group of stocks that will have the highest market values. Naturally, during the late nineties the large or blue-chip high-tech and internet stocks were indeed large-cap momentum growth stocks. So, my poor doctor friend ended up being triple concentrated—the index fund also had large concentrations of the same stocks he was buying and his funds were buying.

Take Sun Microsystems. It was a great company in the nineties with a high market value versus other companies. It had a major position in the doctor's personal portfolio, as well as in most of his

funds due to its good performance, and had a large weighting naturally in the index portfolio. During the early 2000s crash, Sun fell
around 85 percent from its peak and, for the most part, did not fully
recover. No wonder my friend lost nearly half his money. All his different investments contained large portions of companies like Sun,
but he did not realize he was so inadvertently concentrated.

Of course, the good doctor was not the only one who lost a lot
of money at the beginning of this century. Over the years, I have met
many smart and capable doctors as well as business professionals
who were extremely successful in their careers, and yet lost fortunes
due to their investing decisions. Indeed, even many full-time investment professionals have made serious mistakes in their own portfolios. It is not so easy to beat the market, and often, in trying to
outperform, you can put your portfolio at risk.

Fig. 2.3   Rise and Fall of Sun Microsystems

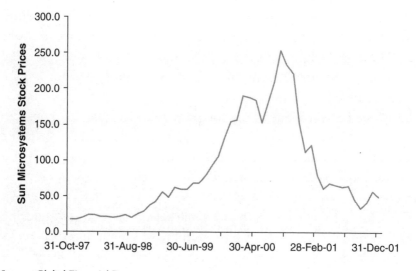

Source: Global Financial Data

Image 2.1 The Good Doctor's Patient Portfolio

THE LESSONS I LEARNED THROUGH MY DOCTOR FRIEND

1. **Diversifying can be much trickier than you think.** Just like the doctor, you may think you are diversified because the investments are with different managers, or in different parts of the world, or even in different asset classes. But unless you and/or your advisor are regularly checking the details about how similar the underlying investments are, or how an event can affect all the exposures you have in your overall portfolio, don't be surprised if you get surprised and are more concentrated than you think.

2. **Selecting a fund just by its rating doesn't ensure success.** Simply taking a rating on a fund, or looking at the last one-, three-, or even five-year performance of a fund or a manager often doesn't help you much in selecting the right fund. In

many cases the funds that had the highest ratings through-out the late nineties—had the best performance, were the highest in evaluations by experts—crashed the hardest by the end of 2002.[3]

If that's the case, how then does one make the right choices?

CHAPTER 3

DIETING AND INVESTING

A Broad Range of Ingredients Keeps Your Portfolio Healthy

There are a lot of people whose eyes glaze over every time they even think about investing. All those numbers and terms and graphs...they neither have an interest nor perhaps an ability to grasp abstract concepts easily. I recall learning from a colleague in education that something like 85 percent of people have difficulty thinking conceptually. After all, investments are not something you can smell or touch or kick. To many people using numbers to symbolize anything is like taking high school algebra all over again.

In the finance and investment industry, however, there is a concentration of people who relish thinking in numbers or thinking conceptually. When people in our industry explain financial terms and concepts, they don't realize many of their clients actually don't like being there, having to listen to something they think is boring. I remember once working at Tyndall, a major investments company in Sydney, Australia that takes a lot of care in investor education. One of the novice investors said to me, "When I walk into a broker or a bank, to me, it is like going to the dentist to get a tooth drilled, or worse, going to a proctologist!" But since we in the industry don't share that feeling, we often overlook the idea that our lectures don't help many people.

Perhaps it was best said to me by a great manager in a local Asian bank: "Just give me a product where none of the explanations have even as much as one detailed graph in it. My clients hate it and complicated graphs even scare a lot of my staff." It was a revelatory moment for me as I realized just how much more work we need to do in the area of communication with investors. Otherwise, no matter how brilliant our strategies, the average investor won't benefit from the basic tools of investing if they can't easily identify with them.

Fortunately, there are excellent examples outside of investing that can help people get more comfortable with our basic concepts. For instance, many of the principles of a good diet, surprisingly, turn out to be the same principles needed for a good investment portfolio.

Over the last decade, diet experts and food scientists have discovered much about what our bodies need. The human body and brain do much better when we have a very broad diet—much broader than was realized before. As many people now know, it turns out that a natural mixture of "old-fashioned" meals our grandmothers made often deliver the broad diet that is so good for our health. For instance, when one takes a vitamin E tablet once a day, it is too narrow or too focused in only one subtype of vitamin E.[1] A broad diet, however, inherently gives us a nearly infinite variety of vitamin E subtypes. It's the same story with chia, which is high in omega-3, notably valuable for our brain health. Yet we only need to eat a small amount of chia seeds throughout the year to capture this form of omega-3 without adding a lot of extra food to our diet.[2]

With investing, a very broadly diversified portfolio does much better for investors over their lifetimes and keeps the annual volatility lower. And just like the chia seeds, very small percentages of your portfolio in relatively discreet asset classes can be helpful to your long-term performance and to decreasing annual volatility.

Let's look at just such an example for your portfolio. Gold as an investment, from the early eighties until this past decade, was a terrible performer.

Fig. 3.1 Gold Price ($/oz) Since 1931

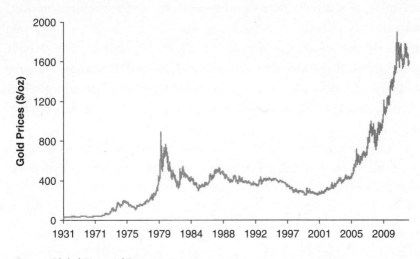

Source: Global Financial Data

Table 3.1 Gold Prices (1980–2012)

Year	1980s	1990s	2003–2004	2012
Gold price ($/oz) range	$300–$890	$250–$450	$320–$450	$1,530–$1,780

Source: Global Financial Data

However, gold stores value, and if a person only had 5 percent of his portfolio in gold, it would have substantially decreased the loss in his overall portfolio in recent years. In essence, gold had the "chia seeds effect."

Food, just like investing, can often be a very emotional topic. Since I was a child, I have lived and worked in over 40 countries. It has always amazed me how in one country people will love a dish that in another country would be considered wholly unappetizing. In countries around the world I have continually noticed that men often are not as interested in trying new foods when they have a choice. They would just as soon eat their local food, like noodles, the "comfort" foods their moms often served them when they were young. Women, on the other hand, are much more likely to be adventurous in exotic cuisine. When you see local men in a fancy Western restaurant in Asia, they are either on a date trying to please their partner or entertaining a Westerner for business purposes. Like investing, it is often hard to get people to try different things they are not used to. I recall laughing along with a Chinese business partner who said that whenever he hears his Chinese compatriots arguing in restaurants, he knows that it is likely about differing views of types of Chinese food. "China would be more advanced," he complained, "if we didn't argue and obsess so much about different styles of cooking."

As you will see in coming chapters, just like with food, one's prejudices are often buried deep into why one either likes or despises one asset class over another.

THE LESSONS I LEARNED FROM DIETS

1. **Invest for life.** A portfolio that contains a broad array of truly different types of investments and asset classes is often better for investors throughout their lives.[3]
2. **Even an asset class that has underperformed for years, just like gold, can still help in lessening the volatility of the total portfolio.**
3. **Broccoli is good for you.** Just like food, there are some types of investments you may not like, but still, having a little in your portfolio can be good for your long-term financial health.

CHAPTER 4

SINGLE POINTS OF FAILURE (SPOF)

How to Guard Against Financial Catastrophes

Back in the 1980s and '90s, I spent a lot of my time designing and building technology applications in financial services. Most of these applications focused directly on customer need, making it easier to execute cash management or trading, creating more access to more fund companies, online investing tools, and the like. I came to realize how dependent we had become in making sure the core processing system worked all the time. I don't mean most of the time; I mean *all* the time. We had become so dependent on these giant, complicated systems, that even if the system shut down only occasionally or merely for a brief time, it would be a financial catastrophe, for us *and* our clients. I began to work closely with technology operators, learning their language, which mostly consisted of a package of acronyms, such as BCP (Business Continuation Planning), DR (disaster recovery), and UPS (uninterrupted power supply). It's a wonder they didn't abbreviate "the" with simply "T." Of all the acronyms, I think my favorite and most meaningful for investors was SPOF: single point of failure.

This phrase in systems, especially for large systems, must always remain a mantra. The systems team has to do all that is possible to avoid a single point of failure. When a firm has millions of customer records and people need to access them with the click of a finger at any time, or on a stock exchange when thousands of investors want to buy and sell a myriad of stocks immediately at the price this second, the firm cannot afford to have the system take a coffee break, for any reason. The goal must be one of building a fault-tolerant system so even if some things don't work, the "hot," or active, backup system will always work.

In one famous East Coast investment firm I worked for, they took the responsibility of their system working all the time very seriously. Not only did they have full-power backup in their main building to run the computers uninterrupted, they also constructed the building that housed all their systems right between two power company grids; if one utility's power grid shut down, they could rely on the second power company. Additionally, the firm put the access points to the power supply on opposite sides of the building. It was such a large complex that even if a fire or other emergency happened on one side, the power coming from the other would not be affected. Furthermore, the firm built a separate battery supply building outside the structure so that if all the sources went out, there would be at least four hours of extra electricity available to finish the nightly tasks. Our firm's systems division had triple backup so there was no single point of failure to interrupt processing. The result: The firm's 6 million customers could be assured their accounts could be updated fully every night, even if lightning knocked out one of our two power companies.

However, they missed one SPOF: a tractor's backhoe.

Late one afternoon, the lights began to flutter. Upon investigation, it was quickly discovered that a backhoe was digging alongside the north end of our systems building per an order to upgrade the irrigation pipes. The underground electrical power pipe was two feet deep. However, the original plan for the building showed the electrical pipe to be three feet deep. So when the backhoe operator carefully dug only two and a half feet deep, he cut the electrical conduit in half, cutting off all power to the building.

Everyone inside remained at ease and assured each other: "Thank God we have a backup power source on the south side of the building." The power returned virtually immediately and all seemed okay—until an hour later. The backhoe operator's work order required ditches on both the north and the south sides of the building. After unknowingly breaking the north power connection, he moved his tractor to the south side of the building and proceeded to drive the backhoe bucket down through both the second electrical conduit *and* the battery triple backup connection. Power to the entire building and system was completely shut off for over 18 hours until rewiring and rebooting the system could occur.

Six million people did not get their data on all their brokerage accounts updated. The next morning was chaos across the United States. Hundreds of offices, thousands of advisors, and over 3 million customers trying to access the system could neither trade nor verify what was in their accounts. The costs of not having any pricing available due to the systems failure, especially for trading, quickly climbed into the millions of dollars.

Where was the SPOF missed? Who would have thought a single work order would be an SPOF for the entire company and its customers? That it would shut down an entire system for a day? What was missed is that the backhoe order, indeed, any work order, always needs to be divided into two separate orders, and even best done on two separate days. In that way, no matter what happened, there could be no SPOF.

What does this tragic story have to do with running your own portfolio?

I remember the look of fear and shock in the eyes of those systems managers when they had failed at their core task. It was like a deer in the headlights. That same look of absolute helplessness was in my mother's eyes when she realized she had lost so much money on her bonds. It dawned on me that what The Safe Investor wants most in their primary investment portfolio is no chance, not even a remote chance, that they will lose all or even half of their money. This experience taught me that when those of us in the investing field help people put together their investment plan, the first goal, even above performance targets, is to check the entire investing process for SPOFs, to eliminate any chance for a person or a family to lose all or a major portion of their money.

Most importantly, what SPOF-averse or Safe Investors must worry about isn't just decisions on investing, any more than the SPOF in the systems story had anything to do with the systems design itself, but rather an incorrect work order outside the building. After all, the above story shows how a seemingly unrelated ongoing building maintenance order can inadvertently screw up the core systems process. In investing, SPOFs come from all angles. A person has to worry about who is the custodian of the assets, can their broker or advisor somehow take their money, or what if the bank or the fund company goes under? Investors also have to ask themselves: What are my geographic, political, and weather risks? Even if the risk is quite remote, can I really afford to take it?

This kind of cautious attitude is so often simply taken for granted in our industry, or ignored. This was the case in the Madoff fraud, where a major company was controlled primarily by one man who had a great reputation and an exceptional performance record; yet people were wiped out because they did not think of the SPOFs. A person needs to say, always: I can't have all my money with just one man, one firm. In addition, each investor in the fund did not ask a very basic, simple question: Is the person managing the money also in charge of processing my account, and operating the custody company, and sending me the statements? Is one man or one group all the same? Are there true checks and balances?

In the case of Bernie Madoff, the SPOF was that the individual money manager, the broker, and the man overseeing the custodial process of the investment were all reporting to the same person. Normally, when you buy a mutual fund, the broker is different from the fund company and different from the bank custodian. You don't give your money directly to an individual. Instead, you transfer your money directly to the brokerage company. Importantly, the instructions specify your account in the institution, *not the name of the personal broker*. Furthermore, the mutual fund company is separate and not allowed to touch the money; they can only send selling and buying instructions and information to the custodian and brokers. That way, you as the investor always have independent verification of where your money is, how it is being invested, and how it is accounted for.

This means there will be tradeoffs in cost and return in order to eliminate SPOFs. For instance, it can be cheaper to put all your money with a single bank, broker, advisor, or fund company. But then you are disobeying the SPOF rule. Even if it costs you a little more, whenever possible, make sure to have at least some diversity in all of the above institutions that are involved in your transaction. It decreases that slight chance of losing it all, which is what is most important.

Even if someone says to you, "This manager has so much better performance! You are going to sacrifice too much in profit if you divide it all up"—don't listen to them. The wisest investors, those who have not lost most their money, are constantly on the watch for SPOFs. They don't often talk about it, but over the years I've observed their actions, and these smart investors allow no chance, no matter how remote, of losing it all.

In studying mathematics, I learned about the concept of certainty equivalent. In this case, a person doesn't care about what the probability of success is; he just wants no chance of failure. The best analogy is Russian roulette. Even though there is only a 1-in-6 chance of blasting our brains out, we would all turn down that bet, even if we had a chance to win a million dollars. In fact, if I lined up ten pistols on a table and only one of the pistols had just one bullet in its chamber, but you didn't know which pistol, you would still turn down that bet. That is the same lesson to practice when it comes to your primary investment portfolio. You don't want any chance that you will ever run out of money in your lifetime.

This goal is the key to how a person should set up a portfolio. However, worrying about eliminating SPOFs does not mean that a person should only leave his money in the bank with no growth. Indeed, a no-risk portfolio actually has risk for an investor long term because it will not keep up with purchasing power. As you will see in Part II, the way investors can get the growth they need without risking an SPOF is through broad diversification.

Here's another example of how broadly one has to think in order to eliminate SPOFs in your portfolio. I have a close friend who has worked for state government for the past 30 years. He needs to work for ten more years in order to collect his pension. His house is in an area surrounded by a major state university. My friend wants a "conservative" portfolio, so the natural inclination of any investment advisor is to put a majority of his money in bonds, and since the state's bonds are tax efficient and have a good yield, it would be a natural home for a lot of my friend's money. Yet this particular state is having financial difficulties. Even though it is a large state, and will likely be okay, my friend did not realize that he has a large SPOF. What if the state's finances deteriorate further? He could be retired earlier than he wants due to severe budget cuts, his pension could be at risk (as has already happened to several governmental entities), and there could be defaults or, even more common, multiyear delays of payments on his state bonds. Furthermore, the value of his house and the liquidity of the house is highly dependent on the state college continuing to operate at the same level of students and budget; if that college gets severely cut back, as also has happened recently, even my friend's house as an investment is severely hampered. When he now looks at his investment portfolio, he realizes he must get as much exposure as possible not connected with the future prospects of his state, even if it means some sacrifice in yield. If you think this risk is too remote, look at what people are now encountering in Detroit. It can happen anywhere.

Even if it has never happened before, an investor has to always assess: "If one area fails, will it affect another area I am investing in?" Could there be a domino effect even if experts say otherwise?

Over the decades, I have seen so many SPOF-related mistakes that I cannot emphasize enough the importance of this point. So often, when one watches different investment shows or reads various books and articles on investing, the focus is on getting the highest incremental performance. Yet, first and foremost, when it comes to investing, people want to eliminate any chance of losing money. Time and effort need to be dedicated to examining a portfolio and the rest of your financial picture to ensure you have minimized the SPOFs. The good news is that it doesn't take a PhD in physics or math to see many of these kinds of SPOFs. They are easy-to-understand concentrations of risk that simply get overlooked when constructing a portfolio.

Eliminating SPOFs requires a broader and more systematic approach in looking at your total risk, which we will cover in Part III. I learned the importance of such systematic review best one weekend 25 years ago when I was invited on a trip in a US nuclear attack submarine, the USS *Boston*. It was still during the Cold War, so such subs were always on a basic alert and carried "real ammo," so to speak. What impressed me most were all the procedures done daily, hourly, etc., which must have often been repetitive and boring for the crew. Yet the attention to making sure there were no accidents was impressive. The way the captain and crew looked at their jobs each day was that it is unnatural to be hurling a long metal cigar tube full of 130 men at 30 knots under 100 meters of black water. If anything goes even a little wrong, all 130 men could be dead within minutes. There is no room for error.

This same mentality is needed when you sit down with your advisor and look at your portfolio. No matter what strategy is decided, make sure there is no chance to lose most or all of your money.

WAYS TO SAFEGUARD AGAINST INVESTING SPOFS

In the developed world, we have been lulled into thinking we are safe with the process of dealing with financial institutions. It is just taken for granted. Indeed, before the Madoff fraud, most people assumed the structural industry protections, checks and balances, and so on had all been in place for a long time to protect them from just such a crime.

As we must remember about human nature, mistakes can and will be made once in a while. There are times when the structure is not fail-safe. Just ask anyone living near the Fukushima or Three Mile Island nuclear power plants.

In some ways, those who have grown up in developing nations are more aware of the basic problems of ensuring someone doesn't lose or steal your money. One valuable lesson for me was working in several countries before their basic safeguards for money were in place. When I was working with money managers in Mumbai just 20 years ago, there was no central custodian and all transfers of stock were physically traded and cleared—often hundreds of certificates of soiled paper wrapped together to represent just one trade of a security. In any given fund, perhaps as much as 30 percent of the existing stock positions were not readily saleable, due to forgery, still undelivered certificates, poor accounting, or all of the above. So investors and brokers took the close oversight of the process very seriously. They took nothing for granted. However, in the developed world, the process has been so systemized for so long that we no longer feel we have to look at the details of the operations of our accounts. We would be well advised to continue to take nothing for granted. You always should know where exactly and physically your money is, as well as the certificates representing your investments.

So, how does a novice investor get reasonably comfortable with the process? Two principles need to be followed, both of which we have touched upon already: independent verification and diversification.

The beauty of independent verification is that you need no formal financial education to make sure you are safe. What you need to do is always check that there is a truly independent entity at each stage of the process to verify that an action is indeed taking place. Let's walk through a sample transaction.

You work with an advisor, making sure the person is part of a legitimate organization, has sufficient capital according to outside experts, has been independently audited, and reports to a person who is regulated by a regulator that you also verify. The regulatorily defined category of a Registered Investment Advisor does have advantages that we will cover later. But it is important to note here that if the advisor is independent from any regulated financial institution, then you will have a little additional verification work to accomplish. First, check with references to see if he has operated his business in an ethical and legal manner. Also, ask to see and review his regulatory filings. As you will see in Part III, the regulators, via the internet, give easy access for investors to verify that the financial advisor is duly registered with them and operating properly. The reading will contain a bunch of legalese but do not be intimidated. What you are looking for is simply: What is the regulator giving him permission to do? And what is he obligated to tell you? Is he allowed to charge you a fee and also collect commission from product providers? It is not always bad; it is just that you want to know it in advance because it could mean he has a conflict of interest—he may be inclined to sell you certain assets for which he'll receive a commission. You also want to see if he has committed any violations of rules in the past.

Ask about the basis for all his recommendations. Is it based on his personal research, or the company's? What were the criteria for selecting them? Are the distributor and the representative both paid more for recommending one product over another? These are simple questions and you should expect straightforward answers.

Are you worried that you won't understand the answers? There are two ways to fix this fear. One, get very comfortable with saying two or three times, "I am sorry, but I still don't understand you." Don't agree if you don't understand. If you don't feel you can be so brave, no problem—bring a nice, rather obnoxious or pushy friend along. Your friend might enjoy asking the tough questions you may feel reluctant to ask. Two, talk to multiple advisors from multiple companies. Over the years, I have been amazed at how much I learned about fields that I have no prior knowledge of, just by asking a lot of questions of several different firms. Pretty quickly, I could separate who knew what they were talking about versus who was either not competent or not ethical or neither.

Find out where the money is physically going. Who exactly is the payee? This sounds obvious, but it is here that many an investor has lost his/her money. Don't be embarrassed to ask for details. You want to know where and how exactly your money will flow. You want to know, upfront and ongoing, where the actual money or evidence of your purchase resides. Is it in a custodian? Are they a bank, a broker? What is the financial position, and under what regulator are these institutions? What evidence will you receive that the money is there? When you receive the ongoing statements of value, how has this value been independently verified? Naturally you would prefer to receive it separately in the mail or via an email from another entity. Even in recent years and even in developed countries, with certain securities there have been many examples of the person or entity valuing or pricing your investment having a vested interest in setting the value much higher than you could actually sell it. You need to know the valuator has no vested interest other than ensuring it is an accurate valuation for you.

You don't have to make all investment decisions and actions at one time. In fact, it is highly recommended you break up the large transactions and do them over time. You may lose some volume discounts, but it is much better, from an SPOF standpoint, to do a small or modest investment amount first, just to make sure after a few months everything is working out as promised.

The second principle you need to follow is diversification. The most important lesson in eliminating SPOFs is to have backups.

Do not concentrate your investment in any one asset class, company, bank, or advisor. Whenever making a large transaction, it is best to divide up the trade and/or transfer into two or more transactions. Time is also a key dimension of diversification.

To many people in the West, diversification is obvious. However, I learned the hard way that in other nations and cultures, the concept of "don't put all your eggs in one basket" is not fully internalized in all societies.

This is especially true in Asia, where Confucian single-mindedness still affects many people's subconscious. As I worked with many investors around the world, at times I could see incomprehension when I brought up the word *portfolio.* Even some regulators have trouble understanding that diversifying a portfolio actually decreases risk. Some regulators inadvertently force investors to overconcentrate by setting high minimums for risky products, which actually makes the risk worse for even high-net-worth investors. Often, Asian investors want simply to know, "What is the best investment opportunity? I will put all or most of my money there." Spreading one's investments around does not feel right to them. After seeing so many looks of confusion about the value of diversifying, I asked one of my local staff in Asia to take the Western phrase of "don't put all your eggs in one basket" and find the equivalent popular expressions in Chinese, Korean, and Japanese. After an exhausting week, he walked into my office with an exasperated look. He exclaimed, "Not only did I not find any exact Asian expressions, I actually found multiple Confucian expressions for 'put all your eggs in one basket'!"

More than any other strategy, ensuring that you have a broad variety of asset classes in your portfolio helps eliminate investment SPOFs as all your eggs are not in one basket. This concept is not natural in many cultures, but if a person wants an optimal portfolio, it is a concept one needs to become very comfortable with.

THE LESSONS I LEARNED ABOUT SPOFS

1. **Don't put all your eggs in one basket.** Never allow all your money to be:
   - invested or even transferred at the same time
   - put in the same type of investment
   - all managed by only one person or one entity
   - reviewed only by a person who also has an ulterior motive
   - placed with a single custodian
2. **Have you invested too much in that investment?** Frequently step back and make sure that even if the unthinkable would happen, you would not lose all or most of your money.

CHAPTER 5

MY RANDY OLD GREAT-GRANDFATHER

What If You Live?

In the late 1880s, Richard Sinnott (my maternal great-grandfather) and his brother James graduated from college in Dublin, Ireland. Despite their education, they were unable to find decent jobs in Ireland, so like many people around the world today, they decided to leave their home country and fulfill their dreams overseas. Leaving your home country was even more traumatic a hundred years ago. The going away party was typically called an "American wake" as the friends and relatives who remained knew they would likely never see their departing ones again after they climbed onboard the ship bound for America.

Fortunately for these brothers, the queen of Hawaii was building a new palace in Oahu and went looking in Europe and the United States for trained architects and engineers. They jumped at the chance for the adventure and for employment. It must have been an arduous journey for them—being on a ship cramped with hundreds of other immigrants, then crossing the United States on an even more crowded train, always in third class, and then again on a slow-moving ship to Hawaii.

When I compare what my ancestors went through, it does not even hold a candle to the suffering of so many other immigrants—to the over 60,000 Irish who lost their lives building the canals in New Orleans and in Panama, to the tens of thousands of Chinese workers who died in the Sierra Nevada mountains in the 1870s building the transcontinental railroad. Today, when I look out the window of my air-conditioned hotel room in Dubai or Doha and see hundreds of guest workers from Sri Lanka, Pakistan, and the Philippines dangling from wooden scaffolds in temperatures over 40 degrees centigrade, I know the travails of immigrants have not dramatically improved. This scene is played over every day, across the world. I think of those who have worked the hardest to build up a nest egg for their families and how important it is for us in the industry to take seriously the mission of helping them grow their hard-earned money.

After the construction of the queen's palace was completed, the two brothers decided their honed skills could be best used in California. It was a growing state, and architecture and building talent were rare. They sailed back to San Francisco and started a construction company in the late 1890s.

In 1906, a massive earthquake and fire destroyed most of San Francisco. Out of such a horrific experience, as is often the case, came opportunity. The brothers already had a proven reputation and a strong crew. It was hard work, but the next six years were more prosperous than either brother ever imagined.

When "Old Dicko," as my great-grandfather was called, and James were talking one day, Old Dicko said to his brother, "Let's face it, we have each made more money these past few years than we ever thought we would both make in a lifetime. We don't need to work anymore. And when I look at my four spoiled daughters and my wild, horse-racing son [who was, of course, my grandfather], I don't see any reason to keep working. Any more money we make will just go to our least deserving relatives. I have made enough to take care of myself and my family until I die." So, he decided at the ripe old age of 50 to take it easy and retire.

His brother Jim was thinking the same, but he preferred to move back to his birthplace in Ireland and buy back the family's original farm.

Old Dicko then built a large, four-story Victorian house in the upper Mission District of San Francisco, including quarters for his maid and butler as well as a small bungalow nearby for his mistress. The decades rolled on and everyone lived as happy as anyone ever was on my mother's side of the family (a notorious group of complainers by nature). However, there was financial stress at the end of Old Dicko's life. As he had predicted, none of his children had figured out how to make as much money as he did. But what he didn't predict was how long he was going to live.

In 1912, when he and his brother decided to retire and live off the fruits of their labor, life expectancy in the United States was not even 70 years old. Since Old Dicko was around 50, he assumed he only needed to budget for the next 20 years, with maybe an extra cushion if he and/or his wife made it another five or even ten years. As it turned out, my great-grandmother died young when she was hit by a milk truck while crossing the street. But Old Dicko lived until he was 93. For the last five years of his life, he didn't have much money left. He had no idea he was going to live so long. He wasn't destitute, but in his later years he had to live much more modestly than he liked and it made him quite bitter.

WHAT IF YOU LIVE?

You must be very realistic about how many years your money must last. Without some kind of growth over multiple decades, the last years of your life could be quite miserable.

So what did Old Dicko miss in his financial planning? He didn't realize there was this mathematical phenomenon in statistics, even in the 1900s, called given or conditional probability. It means you personally don't care about the average life expectancy; you care most about your own life expectancy. If you make it to 50 or 60 years old, you are then likely to live a lot longer than the average life expectancy.[1]

Today, if you have made it to 60 and you're a woman, you have survived the dangerous childbearing years. As a man at 60, you have survived all those wild, carefree years of your teens and early 20s. Especially if you are thin, don't smoke, and have no major illnesses, guess what? Either you, or your spouse, or even both of you have a high chance of living over 90 years. So, at 60 you need your money to last more than 30 years, maybe more than the number of years you actually were working.

Why do so many people think they won't be around so long? Over the last decade, I conducted a series of focus groups in several countries. Specifically, groups of 50- and 60-year-olds were asked how long they thought they would live. Though there were exceptions, the typical answer for men was around 75 to 80 years; for women, around 80 to 84. We observed that many thought they were being conservative by stating even a little less than their national average. Thus, their natural instinct regarding investing was to keep a lot of their money in cash as they thought, with a little interest coming in, their savings would last as long as they lived.

Behind the one-way mirrors, I listened in on these focus groups and saw many were surprised when told that the national average is not nearly as relevant to them as is *their personal life expectancy*. Some got worried looks as they realized that they and/or their spouses are likely to live deep into their 90s—and like it or not, might well make it to 100.

In further discussions, people talked about making sure that they had a minimum amount of life insurance, a prudent step to make sure they take care of loved ones in case they died prematurely. The insurance industry has done a great job in their marketing to make sure we are aware of this risk. After all, insurance companies wisely did not name their policies "death insurance," even though that is when it is paid out. The problem is that many didn't recognize the risk *if they live*.

Even scarier, as my great-grandfather learned too late in life, the cost of *underage* is much more painful than the cost of *overage*, meaning you would rather have your money last a bit longer than you. You do not want to run out and be penniless a year *before* you die. That is why even when you are 50 or 60 or even 70, I still speak about your money continuing to grow over decades, not just years. Since you will take out only a small sum each year for living expenses in your retirement years, you don't need to worry about fluctuations in value within each year and even within each decade. Just make sure you leave your portfolio relatively stable and broadly diversified.

This means that taking what many consider a "no risk" tactic, such as leaving all your money in the bank, now can actually be a risky strategy if you live longer than you expect. Today, due to either zero or low effective interest rates, you won't get the growth of your money in bank savings accounts that you will need in your later years.

The good news is that 30 to 40 years of investing is a long time; with money compounding, you don't need your investments to grow a lot each year to ensure enough money to last throughout your life. I discuss managing a conservative portfolio in your later years in much greater detail in Part II, but for now, you will be amazed at how, even with a low rate of return of 3 percent or 4 percent above inflation over time, this slow growth can make a major difference later in a person's life. It can be the difference between running out of money and having to rely on your children or, heaven forbid, the state, versus having enough of a nest egg to cover your key expenses for life.

THE LESSONS I LEARNED FROM MY GREAT-GRANDFATHER

1. **Recognize your personal average life expectancy.** If you have made it to your 50s, and have no health issues, you will likely live a lot longer than the national average in your country.
2. **Make sure you plan for your money to outlast you.** You can't afford to run out of money if you happen to live longer.

CHAPTER 6

IT'S ABOUT TIME

Understanding Financial Cycles
So You Invest for the Long Haul

The trouble with our times is that
The Future is not what it used to be
—Paul Valery

The concept of time is one of the more important points of this book. When it comes to setting the proper units of time for evaluation, many of us think differently or don't think at all about the true impact of decades. It is also where people make one of their biggest mistakes in investing, so I thought it important to spend some time (pun intended) giving a different perspective.

A unit of time is a common denominator—a key method of how we measure and evaluate so much in our daily lives. As the technology and network age emerged, slicing units of time into smaller and smaller units (for example, megahertz improvement in computer processing and network protocols) became one of the key drivers of progress.

And in our day-to-day lives we have become faster at everything and are often able to do multiple things at once thanks to the smart phones most of us carry around. Even activities meant to be relaxing, like watching movies, now seem designed only for people with ADHD, given how fast they jump from scene to scene.

In the investment world, the drive to slice time almost into nano-seconds to be able to trade thousands of stocks at the blink of an eye is seen by some as innovative. However, when it comes to a person managing life investments, slicing time into smaller units is no help at all.

As with so much in life, a single year offers the ability to "anni-versary" a task; many consider it the most frequent time unit upon which we humans focus. There are few areas in our world that do not divide well into annual review, but they are looked upon as excep-tions. A great Bordeaux wine or single malt scotch is often not at its peak and cannot be truly evaluated until after 10 or even 15 years. Fruit and nut tree farmers look at cycles over 7- to 10-year periods. Many things that are truly exceptional take time. Extolling patience as a virtue has been replaced with "I need it ASAP!"

Perhaps among the most famous of quotes about the proper time period for evaluation came from Zhou En Lai in the early seventies; when asked what he thought about the 1789 French Revolution, he replied, "It is too soon to tell."

Although later some disputed that the question was lost in translation—as Zhou might have been referring to either the French protests of 1968 or the Chinese student riots of the same year—historians have long understood that it can take a much longer period of evaluation in order to gain a proper perspective. Sadly, the mindset of allowing sufficient time to elapse before making judg-ments is not often at the forefront of how most experts and investors evaluate their portfolios.

Generally speaking, we think in monthly, quarterly, or annual units of time, which is what most people do when they think of their investments. So it took me a long time, in fact over 20 years after I started my career, before I realized the investment industry inadver-tently does a disservice to investors by not helping them understand the correct timeframe in evaluating and managing a portfolio.

Unlike other discoveries, it was not a single story that cata-lyzed my thoughts or created an epiphany about time and invest-ing. Rather, it was simply stringing together a series of small events, seemingly unimportant conversations and stories over the years that finally resulted in an "aha!" for me.

It started with listening to many of the independent financial advisors (IFAs), or more appropriately, the Registered Investment Advisors (RIAs). These registered advisors, of which there are tens of thousands, emerged as a force to help people invest in the mid-to-late eighties. Some of them had grown up in the stock brokerage industry and had realized that helping their clients trade stocks for a major part of their portfolio, especially when based on their broker-age firm's recommendations, just was not getting the right results, even over a long period of time.

Unlike the traditional Wall Street broker model, where brokers were paid only when they did a trade, this new group of advisors was paid a fee based on assets only and had no incentive to turn over people's portfolios. They also had no incentive to sell their clients needlessly expensive investment products. So, these rather diverse and very independent-minded advisors helped in getting people to broaden their investment portfolios and also to do more index invest-ing[1] as they helped investors keep down their costs. Many of them also began to preach the value of a "buy and hold" and a longer term investing approach to assembling a portfolio, and even discouraged active trading. They became strongly independent of whatever Wall Street was preaching.

The advantage of the advisors that followed the "fee only" approach is that the advisors and the customers are on the same side of the table, as there is no incentive to trade more frequently than the customer should, nor buy needlessly expensive products.

With the advent of fee-based pricing on customer assets rather than charging for each trade, more brokers and investors could begin to think about longer term investing rather than daily trading as these advisors no longer had such an incentive to push trading.

In the late 1990s and early 2000s I saw thousands of customer portfolios that over 10- and 20-year periods actually ended up with pretty steady net growth, despite a big dot-com bubble. They were far from sexy, exciting returns, but the results showed that over time, people did not lose their money, and their money actually grew more than if it had been left in a bank savings account or even been actively traded on a daily basis. It was inspiring to me to see customer portfolios—especially those managed by IFAs and some of the "wrap" account brokers[2] in the United States that weathered the dot-com bubble of the late nineties through 2002, and again, the subprime crises of 2008 to 2010—relatively unscathed long term.

But at the same time, there were many investors and advisors in the United States and overseas that still did not understand the true meaning of "long-term investing." It was best said to me at a conference in Taipei when one Taiwanese investor exclaimed, "Don't worry, I get it. I am a long-term investor. I sometimes don't sell out of a stock or an asset class for a whole year!" Clearly, regarding investing as opposed to trading, he just didn't get it. He was saying what too many investors and even advisors in the United States and Europe actually still practiced by frequently making major adjustments to portfolios, even though they intellectually understood the value of buy and hold.

Why is there such a mismatch between how long people should be investing, and how long they *think* their investing period should be? The reasons are important to discuss if investors are to have any chance of breaking out of one of the biggest evils of growing their investments throughout their lives—i.e., breaking away from "short-termism." Clearly, despite all the evidence and communication, too many people still don't realize how long long-term is.

I have frequently seen five key causes for why investors and many in the industry don't get the "time thing" right. By understanding each of the reasons, investors may see themselves and their investment objectives in a different light. Only then, perhaps, can they begin to understand and execute under an investment clock that better fits their life financial plan.

1. UNDERSTANDING THE LENGTH OF
FINANCIAL CYCLES

We know with the majority of asset classes, as well as with countries' financial cycles, the ups and the downs can take decades to complete a full cycle, as we saw with gold in an earlier chapter. Viewing long term as merely one-, two-, or even five-year periods is simply too short to gain the true advantages of long-term investing, of smoothing out all the bad and good years. Investors often bail out of a sector or do not invest simply because the last few years have not been favorable. The result is a long-term underperformance in their portfolios as well as increased risk due to more volatility arising from trading too frequently in the portfolio.

By our nature, humans are impatient beasts. Although a sense of urgency can help us accomplish feats as soon as possible, in the case of investing, our impatience can get in the way. Often, our natural inclination when we buy something is to look up its value online the next day and mutter, "Why hasn't it gone up yet?" The reality is that sometimes markets move up quicker than expected and sometimes they get delayed longer than expected. It is typically crowd emotion that drives market values short term, and often we as individuals just lose patience with an asset class if it does not perform as quickly as we thought it should. If I have learned anything the past 40 years on Wall Street, it's that just because something has not yet risen in value, even though it is by all metrics undervalued, even though it has been delayed by years, it does not mean that it will not go up tomorrow. This understanding of time and asset class fluctuation cycles is simply not talked about enough in investing, but it is an extremely important concept.

Harry Markowitz formulated the modern portfolio theory problem as a choice of the return and risk of a portfolio of assets. The theory emphasized that assets need to be selected not only on characteristics that were unique to the security but also based on how each security correlated with all other securities in a portfolio. These correlations helped an investor construct a portfolio that had the same or higher expected return and less risk than a portfolio constructed by ignoring the interactions between securities.

In the 1970s many academics and practitioners had advocated the idea of a portfolio simply replicating the entire stock market that would provide better results than trying to beat the market by picking individual stocks. On August 31, 1976, Vanguard founder Jack Bogle launched the world's first index mutual fund despite wide criticism by much of the investing establishment, which termed it a formula for average results.

Despite criticism, index funds continue to gain market share over actively managed funds; index funds are cheaper to trade and also active investment managers have demonstrated a mixed record. At the end of June 2011 there were nearly 290 stock and bond index mutual funds in the United States and 990 US-based passive exchange-traded funds with nearly $2.3 trillion in assets, which represents less than a third of the $7.3 trillion in actively managed funds.

2. THE WINNING SPIRIT

As to why so many people still do not utilize passive or index investing, it seems that so many people just cannot accept that their investments will do no better than the average of the market, that so many people feel they have to find a way to beat the market. In learning about the neurotransmitters in our brain, how they interact with one another and how they create in us the drive to succeed, I came to understand that the very chemicals that helped make us so successful as a species can also get in the way of success in investing.

It has been clear, since the first articles broke in the late sixties about the "Random Walk Theory,"[3] that indexing is a logical form of investing for the average portfolio investor for at least part of one's money. In general, one can garner all the advantages of multi-asset class, broadly diversified investing at much lower costs by buying index funds and now, more popularly, index ETFs (exchange-traded funds). Yet although index investing has increased substantially in popularity, I could not figure out why so many people still only wanted to trade stocks and buy and sell actively managed funds, not just for their trading portfolio, but also for their larger investment portfolio. After all, the majority of investable money still remains actively managed, either in funds or individually. Humans just like to win—we love to beat the other guy—to beat the market. It is our nature. And when a person thinks in terms of beating the other guys, the clock, the unit of time they think in, is going to be shorter. The average competitive person does not want to wait until they are in their 90s to say to their friends that are still alive, "See, my strategy beat yours over the last 50 years!" It is just too far away.

There is nothing wrong with this spirit to win, but it has ruined as many portfolios as it has improved. Our goal is to create a safe and successful investment strategy. It is critical that we not delude ourselves into thinking we are actually focused on the long term when we *are not*. Just like the Taiwanese investor I mentioned, I saw an example of this predicament in my own family when one of my relatives said, "My money is invested for the long term. But I do buy and sell frequently as I actively try to time markets." Yet he was frustrated when he lost close to half his money over the last decade. There is another dimension in how we must manage our emotions. The stock market has been glamorized at different times during the past 50 years as the media profiled huge wins and dramatic, record-breaking highs. During bull markets, it is boring to simply buy and hold your assets for a long time and to only make minor changes every few years. It is the right thing to do, but terribly boring. I remember one cantankerous old client of mine who said, "My doctor won't let me drink anymore. I'm too old to chase women. I don't have any excitement in my life. Trading stocks is an old man's sex!" I understand the need for excitement, but you better make sure you first have enough safely invested elsewhere. It makes more sense to limit your trading to the amount of money that is over and above the amount you need to grow and live comfortably for the rest of your life.

3. MUTUAL FUNDS AND ETFS STRENGTHS CAN ALSO BE THEIR WEAKNESS

When I first started designing funds, the standard view was that we were creating a product category that would help people get away from active trading. Most funds were designed to take advantage of the buy and hold strategy. However, despite all the preaching about thinking long term, many investors still do not listen. Because investors can buy and sell their funds every day, and because each day the exact market value is published online and in newspapers, many people naturally are driven to panic if their funds drop for a day or week, and then they sell. It is almost comical that we in the industry thought we were helping customers invest for the long term by making it so easy for them to access the prices of their funds on a daily basis. Instead, for many customers, such ease has made them react in too short term of a manner and defeat the original purpose of the funds, which is to buy and hold.

An old friend from the life insurance industry once said to me, "I don't have to worry like you guys in the fund industry that people will bail out of my products so quickly. First off, our clients in many of their traditional insurance products still can't easily see what their underlying investments are doing each day, so as far as the client is concerned, what he doesn't know doesn't bother him. In addition, we have educated our customers that, 'You are now 50 and you need a plan all the way until your death.' So we have people thinking in the right time frame before we even bring up the product ideas."

My insurance friend's comment was an eye opener for me. Those of us in the fund and securities industries had created a relationship and a product set that mistakenly fed into many people thinking too short term, or at a minimum, not long enough irrespective of what we said. It was *our fault* for not focusing on a person's lifelong investment program from the very beginning, unlike the traditional life insurance industry professionals.

4. ADVISORS AND BROKERS HAVE TO FOLLOW THEIR CUSTOMERS' IMPATIENCE

Understandably, advisors normally do what their customers want them to do. The customers expect their advisors to work full time on the management of their accounts, and "working" means "doing something" and "doing something" means trading at least some of the positions periodically, at a minimum.

Sounds confusing? I knew an advisor in England who did a good job making sure his clients' wishes were followed. I asked why he virtually always bought all the individual country funds from our fund company, rather than simply buying an Asian or Latin American region fund. I wondered if his specialty was in country rotation. If he bought a regional fund, he would not have to trade in and out of each country so frequently. After all, it cost his clients more in transaction fees than if he simply left the money long term in a region-wide fund. His answer knocked me over! "Here's the problem," he lamented. "In the beginning, I simply bought for many clients Asia and Latin America regional funds. Then I could rely on you guys and all the work your analysts and portfolio managers do to properly manage the best allocation on an ongoing basis. But at each quarterly and annual review, when I met with clients and told them that I haven't made any changes the clients would say to me, 'Hey, you haven't done anything new. Hell, I can do this, just buy one fund and sit on it forever. Why should I pay you one percent just to put the portfolio together and then do nothing for the next five or ten years?' So, very quickly I realized that even though I was doing a lot of monitoring and checking out all the asset classes on a regular basis, if the clients saw little or no activity in the account, they just assumed I was sitting on the beach somewhere relaxing. So, I switched my strategy and began to buy single country funds. I would use your research to make allocation changes so there wasn't much difference in performance, but it made the customers feel like I was doing something. Then I could say in the meetings, 'Well, the Thai banking sector is scaring me and so I decreased 10 percent our weighting in Thailand and increased 10 percent our weighting in Brazil as stocks look undervalued there.' Then, customers were happy, as it looked like I was doing something."

It is sad that in many countries, even the regulators don't get it. They say "if you are leaving the portfolios alone, then you are collecting a fee for not doing anything, which is wrong."

Another interesting advisor I knew well was a former astrophysicist who liked trying to see if he could beat the market for his customers. (He told me he preferred the stock markets to building rockets.) One day he confided in me, "I know that I don't make much of a difference in long-term performance by constantly rotating all these sectors. Yeah, some years I do better, but then, I miss it one year and I am really not much better than if I had just left it alone and weighted the sectors by their cap weightings.[4] I don't lie to myself. After all, I am a scientist by training and taught to think deductively, not believe my own BS, and accept the reality of the numbers. But you have to understand: I just can't come into this office every day and do nothing. I don't want to be like the Maytag repairman in the old commercials where his product was so good he just sat there and watched TV. And besides, changing stuff, albeit in a minor way, gives me something to talk about with clients. They think, 'Oh my, our brilliant scientist is so smart. Thank God we have him.' It's part of my 'secret sauce,' I guess."

At the end of the day, if your clients don't think you are working, they switch to another advisor. And sadly, a portfolio that sits there and doesn't change much, year after year, with only minor adjustments each decade, looks to clients like they have a lazy advisor.

5. THE PRESS AND THE PUNDITS

When I entered the industry in 1973, business news was generally limited to a few minutes on the evening network news. Then the challenge was how to cram so many business and financial events into short, on-air segments. Any full-story reporting came a day later in the newspapers.

Today, we have multiple 24-hour business news channels on cable and network TV, along with all the blogs and news sources on the web bombarding us with real-time events, each being touted as "breaking news." Many reporters have told me off the air that their challenge is to come up with enough topical news to fill the airwaves all day long. So naturally, reporting on any news that can affect a stock or a market that day or the next is the obsession, which focuses investors into thinking very short term.

It is not intentional, but the collateral outcome is in direct conflict with assembling a portfolio and then leaving it alone for years, with only minor adjustments. Of course, the press and many financial experts pay lip service and say investing for the long term is best. But if the media spends most of its time on short-term changes, one can't help but empathize with consumers constantly thinking they have to change their portfolios in frequent and dramatic ways.

It is similar to many of the frenetic beer commercials that run during football games. For example, one shows a vignette of monkeys going crazy, acting like frat boys and drinking their favorite beer. But at the end of the commercial, the advertisers run a quick, "drink responsibly" tagline. We all know that a bunch of guys watching these commercials between plays are not saying to one another afterward, "Yes, indeed, we do need to drink responsibly."

The key issue for investors to focus on is to disconnect the state of fear or call to action that the press accidentally instills in their audience on a daily basis, from the precept of leaving their portfolios alone. After all, it is extremely rare that any news on any given day will really affect how your investment portfolio will do throughout the rest of your life.

It adds an additional element of risk when you actively trade your major nest egg, as we have all heard examples from our friends. Whereas by slowly building your portfolio over the decades and then leaving it alone, the range of outcomes is much tighter, and therefore, a lower risk.[5]

As I will show in subsequent chapters, even if you are unlucky and miss trends, even if you build your diversified portfolio through the peaks and valleys of the crazy global market, investors can still reasonably expect a return of anywhere from 3 percent to 6 percent per year above inflation, depending on their profile, by the time they have slowly drawn down their investment proceeds throughout their later years.

THE LESSONS I LEARNED ABOUT TIME

1. **Know the power of time.** Despite the information overload you receive each day, despite all the temptations, learn to use time to your advantage by leaving your portfolio alone for longer periods.
2. **Time is your positive leverage.** Portfolios left relatively stable even over decades will likely grow as much or more than portfolios that are in constant flux. Patience has never been more important than in investing.

CHAPTER 7

HOW AM I DOING?

How to Evaluate Fund and Portfolio Data

Naturally, investors want to know how their portfolio of funds is doing. Are the funds I purchased doing better than its peers? If so, should I buy more of a particular fund? Can I rely on the performance evaluation information I get from the industry?

In this chapter, I focus on what is important for investors and advisors in evaluating the performance of their portfolios over time. Some of the concepts can be a bit complicated. I give some additional descriptions on my website and also at the end of the chapter, and I provide some simple takeaways so readers can understand what really matters when evaluating portfolio performance.

Interestingly, little has been written for the average investor about the weaknesses of the industry's performance measurement methods for the masses—naturally, industries don't like to criticize themselves. It is important to start where many investors and even some industry professionals focus too much attention—on the performance of the specific fund managers.

TINY TRACKING ERRORS

The first time it hit me that we in the industry were being distracted by trivia was when I sat on the board of trustees meetings of Charles Schwab Investment Management. It is an important requirement that the independent trustees of all funds be frequently updated on the performance attributes of funds. As we had a myriad of index funds, the presentations centered on how each fund actually performed each quarter versus the index. We would be proud if the tracking error (the difference between the actual performance of the fund and the theoretical index) was small, e.g., only four basis points this year versus five basis points the year before. If the competitor's fund reported a terribly embarrassing six-basis-point tracking error, we were even more pleased: Our sales personnel could tell their advisors and customers of our tight tracking error and that they should buy more of our funds instead of our competitor's funds. I heard the exact same sales pitch from salesmen from other companies as it was a standard discussion within the industry. And sadly, such trivial discussions about basis-point tracking errors inadvertently focused the clients on minutia.

I asked myself, "Do I care, does anyone really care, about four- or six-basis-point differences in fund performance versus an index? Are we focusing so much on such minor performance differences that we may be missing out on more important issues such as the challenge of proper asset allocation?"

Just for perspective, a basis point represents one ten-thousandth of your fund position. How much time do you want to spend worrying about one ten-thousandth? What we should be doing is addressing the bigger issues, like how is one asset class over another doing over the past five and ten years? What are the big risks that we may encounter in the coming years? Factors that affect 2 or 3 percent of my portfolio are at least worth talking about, but does 0.0003 performance difference really matter?

For me, this obvious focus on differences in relative fund performance of often less than ten basis points tells me that we were not doing a good job helping people evaluate the important metrics of all the fund categories, not just index funds.

IT'S BETTER TO BE VAGUELY RIGHT
THAN EXACTLY WRONG

When I was at Nikko Asset Management, my partner in Japan, chief investment officer Bill Wilder, told me he had informed one of his portfolio managers (PMs) that if he gave Bill one more comparison number that went out three decimal points in the percentages, he was going to throw him out the window (a problem, as we were on the forty-second floor). The PM was literally writing statements in his analysis on individual stocks like: "The company's sales declined 1.659% which is smaller than the previous decline of 1.776%."

The more important question is, Why is the firm stagnating? Tell us those reasons. We don't need all these other numbers. Bill told the PM it is much more valuable to understand why a particular company's sales had slowed down overall; his inquiries into the company and educated guesses as to what he thinks in general is happening with a stock are much more important than to get mired in miniscule changes, however accurate. The PM responded that since he can't know for sure, he did not cover it.

I have seen this mistake dozens of times in other situations. People focus on what they can measure exactly, like past performance. Sadly, they ignore trying to figure out what might happen at least in a general direction, which is often what is most important to your long-term performance.

In analyzing the subprime crisis in 2008, one could easily see that there were many PhDs in math continuing to structure predictive models to determine the probability of loan loss for mortgage portfolios. Very bright people continued to work diligently to make sure they were exactly measuring the risk of each portfolio, given the history of past portfolios—again, things they could accurately measure, which was past data. However, they missed that since around 2004, the loan documentation and loan acceptance standards were getting too easy. In early 2007 with one package of loans, our due diligence team did a detailed, full review on each new loan. It turned out that individual loans were much lower in quality than what we had seen a decade before. One loan document said it all: The borrower claimed he was making over $100,000 a year. His job description? "Window man at McDonald's." Wow. If that is what a fast food window order taker makes, I think I want the job. There was no income verification done on the loan, as was the case with many loans made between 2004 and 2007. So, rather than many due diligence teams of financial institutions first simply trying to get a picture of the quality of the present loans, they were instead focusing exclusively on past portfolios' loan loss ratios, since they could quantify this loss rate accurately. No one at a senior level bothered to check to see if the new loan package was comparable to the old loan packages. And after all, many people thought that since the sophisticated models run by PhDs were used to crunch the numbers out to the thousands of decimal points. It must be right.

In my experience, experts tend to want to work on what is cool, trendy, and exciting. Clearly, it was boring each year for the experts to go back and do a spot check on each loan to make sure the prudent lending standards of the past were still being followed, which was why no one at a senior level paid attention on each deal to this important step. Yet that was important for investors. How do you guard against such lapses in annual due diligence by brokers, bankers, rating agencies? Sadly, you as an average person can't. That is why adhering to the principle of SPOF management is so important. Make sure you are spread across many asset classes and many investment managers in order to better ensure against a single asset category disaster. For the average investor, careful diversification is a safer and easier approach. You really can't rely on a single institution, no matter how large, to always do their proper homework—even though they may give you impressive reports that show lots of math.

TOO MANY COMPUTERS, NOT ENOUGH WINDOWS

One morning in the late 1980s in Manhattan, my colleague and I were getting ready to leave our offices on Broadway near Wall Street and walk uptown to a meeting. I asked him to listen to the radio before we left to hear the latest weather report as it was looking quite dark outside (the pre-internet days!). A few minutes later, he walked into my office and said, "The weatherman just announced that it will be clear all morning." I looked outside just as it started pouring rain. My colleague laughed and added, "This is an example of too many computers and not enough windows."

Since then I have seen many similar examples when it comes to fund performance measurement. Of course, you want to use all the quantitative skills you can muster to check results and make predictions. But in the final analysis, you have to step back and take a look at the whole picture and see it if makes sense. Just like the example of my doctor friend back in Chapter 2, if all your funds are up because the market has skipped all the old-fashioned value stocks and is just chasing momentum high growth stocks, driving valuations far beyond what even optimistic earnings projections of the companies can justify, maybe you don't care if most of the funds concentrated in these stock sectors have 3- and 4-star ratings. The bigger issue is, Will these extremely high valuations continue? Or perhaps it is wiser to at least spread your money around some other funds and asset classes that are focusing on more boring, even lower-performing areas, like value stocks in nontech sectors. In this way, at least you have focused on diversification, rather than simply looking at the mathematically best performing recent funds for all your investments.

Just so I don't scare away all beginning investors, if you don't understand all the work that goes into evaluating funds, or have no interest in the process, simply making sure you have a broad diversification of styles of funds does decrease your risk substantially. Making sure your advisor has given you broad diversification is probably the easiest way for you to know you are safe.

PAST PERFORMANCE DOES NOT PREDICT
FUTURE PERFORMANCE

In most developed countries, regulators require that the industry makes it clear in writing to clients that the past performance of a fund does not indicate that the fund will perform well in the future. It is sound advice, but here is the problem of how we practice communicating this message in the industry. When I listen to lecture after lecture from industry specialists, they of course know they have to make this statement or they will be in trouble with their compliance department and regulators. But after the disclaimer, the majority of the presentation is often focused on the past performance of the fund. It is like saying to your children, "Don't do as I do, do as I say."

Of course, the experts will often cover other issues, such as changing economic factors and the like. But all too often, especially if past performance is the only key positive point, it will be the presenter's primary focus despite the initial warning about the limitations of past performance.

SURVIVOR BIAS

Survivor bias in finance refers to a tendency for failed funds or companies to be excluded from performance measurement that is reported. Here is just one of many tricky little secrets about the investment management biz, especially regarding the more complex asset classes and fund structures, such as hedge funds and private equity funds.

When a firm shows the past history we see that a particular fund or group of funds across an asset class has performed reasonably well. Let's say a potential customer is looking at what he thinks are all the existing long-term funds in a particular category and their average return was 9 percent per year for the past three years. Naturally, anyone would say, "Fine, sounds like any one of these funds should be OK." And in fact, if the top fund on the list made, for instance, 20 percent last year, potential investors will get really excited. If the bottom fund made, let's say, 3 percent, it was still positive so the prospective customer doesn't worry too much.

What's wrong with this performance evaluation process? What's missing are all the company's other funds that did not perform well and were often then shut down. Let's take an example of a specific fund launched by a fund company that shall remain nameless. This fund over the last three years has made between 6 percent and 27 percent a year. Wow! You are ready to buy. "Honey, get me the checkbook!"

But just a minute . . . what you don't know is that the same fund company, and even many of their same fund managers, over the past five years have launched three other funds, of which two took in customer assets. All three of those funds bombed, lost a lot of money, and were shut down with the remaining money returned to their investors. The track records of those failed funds are no longer available because they no longer exist. It is nearly impossible to find out how one of the failed funds performed as it did not take in money from outside investors. So what is missing in your evaluation of the single fund that was successful? You don't really know if the surviving fund really has a decent chance of performing well in the future. After all, the fund company was only able one out of four times to show good performance long enough in a fund for a three-year track record. That's a bad success rate. Thus, an investor needs to have an investment evaluation process that does not rely too much on just the past performance charts of a single fund to ensure his or her portfolio of funds will grow over the rest of their lives.

How else can stated fund performance be misleading? Often, the first two years of a fund will have a small amount of money invested. Most fund managers will tell you if they only have to invest a small amount, they can often get much better performance. After all, they only need to use their best ideas. And they are buying and selling such a small amount of each stock their actions will not move the stock prices of the stocks they chose, especially in the stocks of smaller companies. However, later on, after they have established a great track record with a relatively small amount of money, the fund company can now spend a lot of marketing money to increase the size of the fund, often exponentially. How does an investor know that the following year, with such a big fund, the manager will be able to still keep such a good track record? The answer is, You don't know. You don't even have a clue. As often as not, it will not perform as well because fund managers have brought in so much new money that it will be hard for them to replicate their past track record.

It turns out that survivor bias, and being misled by a fund that performs well only when it is small, are just a couple of examples of the difficulty of evaluating the relative past performance of many funds, even the basic funds.

There is also another big issue: Many funds don't last more than 10 to 15 years! That means your investment portfolio will last a lot longer than many of the funds you buy! Out of 8,723 funds analyzed between 1995 and 2013, only 39 percent survived; the others were liquidated or merged (see Fig. 7.1 below).

Interestingly, the research in Fig. 7.2 does at least show that the Morningstar multiple star funds on average do last longer than no- or 1-star funds, which does give the rating agencies some value. Based on an analysis by Advisor Partners, 5-star funds are 27 percent more likely to survive in five years, compared to 1-star funds. After ten years, that advantage increases to 39 percent.

So predicting whether a fund will live longer can be more important than whether the fund is basis points ahead of a competing

Fig. 7.1 Survival of Funds (1995–2013)
Less Than Half of Your "Pie of Funds" Survives!

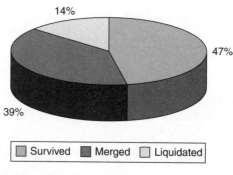

Source: Advisor Partners and Morningstar

Fig. 7.2 Survival of Funds Based on Stars

Ratings in 2002	Ratings in 2007 5-year survival	Ratings in 2007 10-year survival
★ ★ ★ ★ ★	90%	78%
★ ★ ★ ★	85%	69%
★ ★ ★	77%	57%
★ ★	66%	43%
★	63%	39%

Source: Advisor Partners and Morningstar

fund. In Part II, I will cover simple tools to help you predict the likelihood of fund longevity.

THE OBSESSION WITH COMPARABLES

Fund measurement agencies and in-house evaluation programs at distributors all want to compare funds from different companies in the same asset class and style. It makes a lot of sense. After all, how can you do a true comparison unless it is "apples to apples"? However, there is an unintended and very negative consequence to such focus on comparisons, which is best illustrated by sharing a remark my dad once said about a neighbor.

It was not a nice observation, so I am glad he is not here to hear me repeat it. This neighbor had eight children and we used to go to their house frequently. It was a blast for me because around our house there were not a lot of kids. However, one night when we were returning home, I overheard my dad say to my mother, "You know, George and Mary didn't have eight children. They had one child eight times over!" It was actually true; all the kids looked and acted exactly the same.

This story came back to me when I returned to the United States in 2012 and began to look at the variety of international funds available to Americans. There are hundreds of choices, which made me think there are many alternatives. But after I delved a bit deeper, I discovered the fund choice was not unlike the family my father so derisively commented on: There were hundreds of funds, but so many had the same fund charter and design, people would in reality not be getting a broad mix for their international exposure. What causes this lack of diversity? It is because the fund companies need to get their funds categorized and rated by the fund-rating companies, which often forces them to make their fund look just like the other fund companies' funds. After all, if a fund management company launches a unique fund that doesn't fit into a nice, neat, popular category, the fund can't be compared to other funds, so it gets left off many fund ratings lists, which means less marketing exposure for the unique fund. Because the focus of the industry and investors is on relative fund performance, the unintended consequence is to drive too many funds to all look like one another. Investors then lose the ability to get the broad diversity of style a portfolio needs to decrease risk and increase return.

An even bigger problem grows out of this obsession with relative fund performance. Naturally, no fund wants to be at the bottom of the list of performers in any given year. So what do many fund companies do to minimize their own performance and marketing risks? They simply try to mimic the index they are being compared to as closely as possible; they try to find a low risk or small bet on a stock or sector where they can pull a little ahead of competing funds to show why they are better than the index. In effect, the majority of funds often end up "hugging the index," i.e., their performance does not diverge too far from the index for fear of ending up at the bottom of the list.

Unfortunately, for investors this means it is difficult to find funds that diverge far from a single index to get the diversity they need without the assistance of a good advisor that does a thorough search through the breadth of funds available.

ACCIDENTAL INVESTING OFTEN "ACCIDENTALLY" WORKS

Around 2000, I noticed various clients were posing the same question to me: "What happens if I buy funds that end up performing in the bottom quartile versus other funds in the same category? On average, how much would I lose versus buying a top quartile, or better performing fund?" Fair question, so I did the homework. The results floored me.

Often the difference between lucking out and buying a fund that was at the bottom of the top quartile versus buying one that was at the top of the bottom quartile was only 60, maybe 70 basis points. As an industry we were doing all this analysis, charging customers, telling them we are doing a great job putting them in the right funds, when often, over the long haul, it only mattered less than 1 percent! Of course, after the fact, one can always find a fund that "lapped the field," i.e., beat all its peers by 3 or 4 percent or more per year even over a moderate period of time. However, one must ask, "How could I have known in advance this fund manager would truly continue to outperform?" This is especially true when a fund manager has a few good performance years and he attracts many new investors. However, if and when the next financial cycle comes along, as it invariably does over the years, this manager may lose his edge in picking the better stocks in the next investment environment. Hence, he ends up delivering no better performance than any other manager—or even worse, underperforms the average. Many in the industry know this reality; it is extremely difficult to know who in the future will consistently outperform.

I began to wonder if investors could do just as well putting the newspaper listing of funds up on the wall and throwing darts at a mixture of funds. Could they do any worse over the next decade or two than if they put extra money, time, and effort into trying to pick the best fund of the future? As you will see below, throwing darts can often be just as good as picking 4- and 5-star funds.

In recent years, I have been asked frequently to take a look at older people's portfolios. I love this exercise because I can see what other investors have actually done in the past 20- or 30-year period, as opposed to listening to a lot of marketing hype about expected future performance stories from industry pundits. One of the things that bothers me most about our industry is how often, after the fact, the fund manager or advisor finds some creative way to polish his performance to make his fund look better than other companies'.

Of course there are portfolios that have been poorly constructed, overconcentrated, and had terrible investment oversight. Typically, over time these portfolios have shrunk or not grown much at all. However, I was struck by how often many portfolios actually did OK. I remember when it finally dawned on me. My neighbor asked if I would take a look at her mother's portfolio. Her father had done all the investing for the family in his 50s and 60s, but later he developed dementia and the portfolio was simply forgotten. The statements on his long-term investment portfolio were gathered each month and put into a file, where they sat unopened for more than a decade. Since no one had paid any attention to what he bought, my neighbor's mother was understandably worried about her remaining nest egg after his death. In looking through 30 years of statements, it became clear that Papa, as he was called, had spread out his purchases of funds mostly through his 50s as he received good-size bonuses. He bought over a dozen different equity and bond funds—directly and via an account with Schwab—notably from major, respected fund companies: T. Rowe Price, Franklin Templeton, Fidelity, and Vanguard. These funds were sprinkled across many different asset classes, styles, etc., and once bought, he left them alone. The result was that the portfolio had grown just over 4 percent a year after I adjusted for annual inflation. Even when there were some mediocre or just average-performing funds, it didn't seem to matter much, especially if he did not pay too much in fund marketing expenses. Accidentally, my neighbor's parents, like so many other silent investors, had done adequately. It happened enough in other portfolios I examined that I decided to take a look at the data by replicating the timelines of building sample portfolios slowly over a long period, and by assembling broad groups of funds across multiple asset classes. I purposely picked funds that had only performed at or even below the mean of their peers.

It turns out that so long as a person does what some of these "accidental investors" did—i.e., spread their purchases out over a decade or more—and so long as they made sure to broadly diversify across reputable fund management firms, their investment portfolios did just fine.

True, there are certain asset classes where picking the right funds can matter 1 to 3 percent or more per year even over a long period. However, it is important to note that the funds that were highly rated ten years ago didn't necessarily perform much better than their peers over the subsequent ten years.

There has not been a lot of research done by the industry on how a package of mediocre-performing funds does over time; after all, it is not in the best interests of industry folks to reveal such information. So I decided to see what happens if a person purposely picked lower-ranking funds, again over many asset classes and many years.

Performance Ratings Often Don't Matter Much

Morningstar-rated funds in the fixed income category also show an inconsistent trend.

Fig. 7.3 Performance of US Equities Funds*

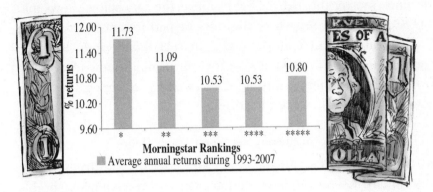

Source: Morningstar

* Includes performance of funds rated in 1993 and still in existence in 2007.

Fig. 7.4 Performance of US Fixed Income Funds*

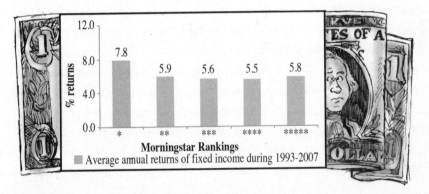

Source: Morningstar

* Includes performance of funds rated in 1993 and still in existence in 2007.

These results could be a bit embarrassing to some in our industry, because over multiple decades the relative performance was not much different and investors grew their portfolios irrespective of the number of stars the fund had.

In fact, the expense ratio or cost to the customer for operating the fund often mattered more to relative performance than the star rating. To Morningstar's credit, they published in their recent research that expense ratios can help an investor make a better decision. In every single time period and data point tested, low-cost funds outperformed high-cost funds.[1]

There are a few exceptions where relative fund performance in the past does seem to matter. For instance, the data below shows that the only asset classes where the stars or performance rankings do matter is in high-yield and emerging-markets bond funds. But even there you don't have to pick the top performing funds to do well. You just have to stay away from the worst-performing funds and pure index funds in these categories.

In High Yield, Just Not Picking the Worst Funds Helps

The good news is that all you have to do is select funds from the top three quartiles and you have a good chance of receiving a favorable return relative to the bottom quartile. It's like running a race where all you have to do is just not finish in back of the pack.

Still, it is understandable that any person will want to know they actually have selected the right fund. In reality, you can't know; in fact, it is probably the most honest thing you can tell yourself or your advisor can say. Still, so long as the investing is broadly spread out over a lot of funds and a lot of asset classes, and spread out over a number of years, picking just "OK" funds does not matter much. In particular, if you and your advisor focus on staying away from consistently weak performers, which is a much more realistic objective, you should do fine. It is also more valuable for you and your advisor to focus on the specific investment styles of each manager to ensure you are getting proper diversity within each asset class across your portfolio.

Fig. 7.5   Performance of High Yield Fixed Income Funds*

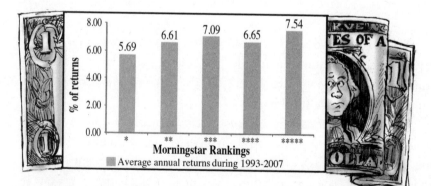

Source: Morningstar

* Includes performance of funds rated in 1993 and still in existence in 2007.

Many in the industry will disagree with this statement or this research, as many experts justify themselves, and their fees, based on picking the best funds. To tell them that it just does not matter that much, beyond a simple basic screen and a broad array of selected funds over a long period of time, challenges their raison d'etre. But there it is.

In Part II, I will cover some basic work that an investor can do to decrease the probability of owning a lot of bad funds. But at this point let's just say that the above-mentioned experience of real investors coupled with the referenced unbiased research means that you don't have to drive yourself crazy spending a lot of extra money and time and worrying about trying to always get the best possible fund. Indeed, if you spend extra money in your overall expense ratio, i.e., your cost of each fund, then the data shows that you will more than likely underperform. As said above, expense ratios are strong predictors of performance. In every asset class over every time period, the funds with the lowest expense ratios produced higher total returns than the funds with higher expenses. For example, the cheapest funds from 2005 in domestic equity returned an annualized 3.35 percent compared to 2.02 percent through 2012 for the most expensive group of funds. The gap was similar in other asset classes such as international equities, taxable bond, balanced funds, taxable bonds, and municipal bonds.[2]

THE LESSONS I LEARNED FROM EXISTING PERFORMANCE ANALYSIS

Bad News: Trying to use primarily past performance to pick funds that will perform well in the future just does not work. Although the various tools available—for instance, Morningstar, Lipper, and Marketwatch—can shed light on the relative effectiveness of various funds, they often do not give you the full answer.

The industry, often inadvertently, misleads us by:

- diving into the minutia of differences measured by basis points and decimal points taken out to the thousands in order to give us a false sense of precision and analysis;

- focusing on quantitative fund ratings that do little in helping investors predict future performance;
- using relative performance measurement tricks such as survivor bias to make it harder for even professional advisors to figure out what funds will be good in the future.

Good News: You don't need to spend a lot of money on sophisticated tools and detailed analysis.

- By buying a broad group of reputable funds covering most all asset classes slowly over a period of time and then leaving them alone, investors will be able to successfully grow their money even if their fund choices are not above average. And an experienced, trustworthy advisor can help you ensure you have a good package of funds for the future.

Remember, making sure you have enough money in your 80s and 90s is not a contest. Don't worry if someone else in the neighborhood tells you he is doing better. All you care about is growing your money safely and not risking your nest egg.

You can relax. The diversification approach means you can make a lot of mistakes and still grow your money and be okay. It turns out to be far less risky than simply leaving all your money in the bank.

CHAPTER 8

BALANCING GREED VERSUS FEAR

Understanding the Emotions of Investing

I have covered the general mistakes people make in investing across all types of investments as well as what has actually worked well for investors, even if it happened accidentally. Now, let's devote some special time to equities. Many people still think stocks are so risky and speculative that a prudent person, particularly over 60 years of age, should not expose themselves to investing in equities.

In talking to investors for the past 43 years, starting with my mother, one fear is consistent throughout most conversations—people hate that the markets go bouncing all around. None scares them more than the stock market. One man said to me, "Do I really have to buy the risky stocks as well? Can't I just buy the ones that only go up?"

To understand why equities are so important in a portfolio, it's probably best to start with the fixed income or debt securities. After all, if you buy a bond, you will get your interest and also your principal back, so long as either the government or the company doesn't go broke. It is much safer, right? So, why do I need to buy anything else?

When you look into the math (most of you don't want to, but please, humor me if you can), it turns out you sacrifice a lot in exchange for low volatility. In effect, you pay an insurance policy to the issuers of the bonds, either the government or the company, as they only have to pay you back what they promised. If they make more money, they then can keep it. After inflation, this insurance "penalty" you pay via a lower return, for instance, when you buy just US Treasuries, costs you around 1 percent to 3 percent per year after inflation. It is fine to have a portion of your money in low risk bonds. After all, you need the liquidity, but to have all your money in fixed income means that you are giving up a major opportunity for long-term growth, and needlessly so. You likely won't make your lifelong financial goals unless you put in substantially more money to make up for not investing in any equities.

Allow me to illustrate over a sample lifetime for you and your children, just how much you lose.

Let's say I took three major asset classes—gold, government bonds, and the entire stock market—and I invested one dollar in each class, and simply left it there for a century—how much would I make in each asset class?

Let's look at the characteristics of each asset. Gold, in and of itself, intrinsically does not increase in value (although you may not realize it based on the past decade). In fact, if you have a lot of it, it can cost you money: You have to pay to store it, guard it, etc. Over time, it barely grows above inflation. It is good to have a little in a portfolio, as it does help smooth out fluctuations, especially in dangerous times, like when governments are printing too much paper money. But over your lifetime, you can't expect much of a return for it. *Gold is simply a good storer of value,* but no more.

With bonds, as with any fixed income instrument, the lender has committed to giving you your money back, so they don't have to pay you so much. In fact, if they are a low risk lender, they generally

Table 8.1   Returns on Investment of $1 Across Major Asset Classes*

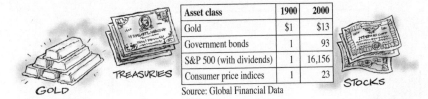

Asset class	1900	2000
Gold	$1	$13
Government bonds	1	93
S&P 500 (with dividends)	1	16,156
Consumer price indices	1	23

Source: Global Financial Data

GOLD   TREASURIES   STOCKS

* Results based on S&P composite price data and dividend information. The equity appreciation figure includes dividend reinvestment. See website for detailed assumptions.

don't have to pay you but a little bit over the expected inflation rate, normally less that 1 percent more. That is why in a hundred years of growth one dollar invested in Treasuries didn't even make it to a hundred dollars when inflation is considered. *In bonds, you end up paying, in effect, an implicit risk fee to the lender,* so you don't make much income over the rate of inflation.

What happened when you invested in the stock market over a century? One dollar grew to over $16,000. You had to wait a century, but wow! You not only received capital gains on your investment but also gained immense returns from reinvesting the dividends you received throughout the year to increase the value of your nest egg. To explain it best, Chuck Schwab said to me in 1997, "Stocks are organically designed to increase in value." He meant that when a company is created, its purpose is to grow, and its investors are supposed to make all the excess net profits so long as the venture works. Of course, some ventures don't make it, and markets will fluctuate throughout various cycles. But at the end of the day, stock markets in their entirety will rise. Their returns are not super sexy—only about 3 to 5 percent or so each year on average above inflation. However, taken over a number of decades, it is a very powerful push to your overall portfolio.

You may say, "Yeah, but a century is a long time." In Chapter 5, I told you about my great-grandfather and how long he lived. If you are in your 40s and 50s, you have to plan for your money to keep growing for the next half century. And if you are thinking of leaving anything to your children and grandchildren, bingo! The investment horizon including your children's lifetimes can be up to 75 to 100 years.

Fig. 8.1   Investing in Fixed Income

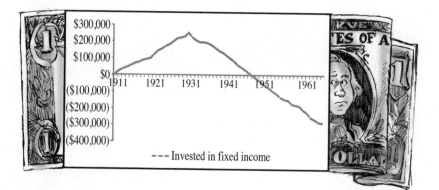

Source: Global Financial Data

The true power of long-term investing is that over enough time, and making sure to invest in a variety of stock markets, volatility doesn't matter. You will get the kind of growth you need so you have excess money in the end to cover your final years and to give to your heirs.

What is especially illuminating is that after as little as two decades, even if many stock markets during that time were terrible, you still recouped all your money. Over enough time, *your downside risk with stocks is no worse than bonds and gold*, yet your upside is substantial.

Figure 8.1 above assumes you invested a little amount each year for 20 years, but only into AAA-rated corporate bonds at little or no interest rate gain above inflation. Then, at 65, you began to take out the same amount of money you put in on a monthly basis. In the worst-case scenario, which is to be fully invested in 1930, you can expect to run out of money when you are around 77.

However, when you do the same exercise but instead invested in a diversified portfolio that includes a portion of your exposure to stock markets, then even if you reached your maximum investment time at the worst possible time last century (1930, the beginning of the Great Depression years), you still never run out of money (see Fig. 8.2). That is how powerful equities are, so long as the portfolio is diversified and left to grow for enough time. *Even if you are unlucky in your timing in investing, your portfolio will still increase.*

Fig. 8.2 Investing in a Diversified Portfolio

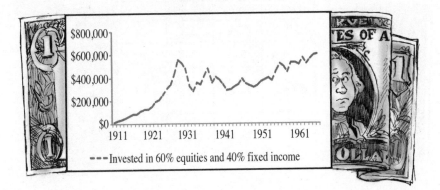

Source: Global Financial Data

A mixture gets you growth at lower risk.

Still, so many people have said to me over the years, "Oh, but I want to wait until it is the right time in the market. It's a little too scary right now." I have so frequently heard this the past 43 years; in response, I'll tell you about my arrival on Wall Street to start my career in late summer 1973. Just out of college, I cut my long, San Francisco–hippie hair, shaved off my beard, and bought my first pinstripe suit and red and blue striped tie. I was fortunate enough to meet an experienced senior executive near retirement who had spent his entire career accumulating a fortune on Wall Street. We talked about the stock market, and I asked him the most important lessons he had learned over the decades. He stopped dead in his tracks and shook his finger at me: "The bulls surprise you. Always remember, young man, *the bulls surprise you.*" Meaning that since markets run so much on crowd emotion, it is nearly impossible to figure out when the markets are going to move up, until they actually do.

Over the years, I observed just how often he was right. Several times I went back and reviewed the financial papers' headlines just before a bull market had started, and almost never was anyone predicting that "tomorrow, the markets are going to start a bull market." It became clear to me that Wall Street runs not on today's news, but on what a critical mass of people are guessing tomorrow's news will be.

Table 8.2   "Market Timers" Often Miss the Best Months

Decade	2000-2009	1990-1999	1980-1989	1970-1979
Day count	2515	2528	2528	2525
Actual return	-2.6%	15.1%	12.8%	1.5%
Less: 10 best months	-9.3%	8.0%	2.2%	-5.8%
Less: 10 worst months	8.5%	23.3%	22.2%	11.2%

Source: Global Financial Data

You can see in Table 8.2 above that, if over a decade you just took out the ten top performing months, i.e., the surprise months, your stock return falls to around zero.

Just waiting until you are sure will cost you plenty. Chuck Johnson, one of the key men instrumental in building the fund giant Templeton, told me an oft used expression of Sir John Templeton: "If you can see light at the end of the tunnel, it is probably too late."

Indeed, when analyzing tactical asset allocation funds, those funds that try to time markets and go into and out of stocks and bonds tactically, do not consistently outperform the markets. Many of these tactical allocation funds are often out of the market and into cash at the right time before markets correct. It is just that they are more often than not, too late investing back into the stock market at the right times and the markets have already risen again.

What causes this inability to judge when stock markets in the near term will go up or down? Crowd emotion. Among the best examples of how crowd emotion works in the stock market happened to me around 2000 when I was working with Hambrecht and Quist (H&Q) investment bank to raise capital to buy a troubled Korean broker. It was just after the South Korean financial markets had crashed; it was hard to find courageous institutional investors to venture into that market, let alone to buy a near bankrupt stockbroker. However, we were able to persuade a reputable private equity firm to join the syndicate to buy the broker based on the low price and profit potential with me bringing in new management. When I informed Dan Case, the CEO of H&Q, he replied, "If they are in, the value of this company has just jumped up 25 percent." He knew that once the investment community saw that a highly reputable buyer was in, others would join in overnight, which turned out to be true. It reminded me of popularity contests in high school. Valuations of stock in the short term operate by a similar code of conduct. Even though Wall Street analysts claim to do thorough research without emotion, when some people hear a rumor that a well-known, successful investor likes a particular company, they can't stop themselves buying the stock at almost any price.

In the stock market, price movement comes from a constant tug-of-war between fear and greed. One angel is whispering into your ear, "I gotta get into this stock before it's too late." That is the greedy or "pig" side of our emotions. Then, a minute later, another angel is whispering into your other ear, "Uh oh. Somebody smart may have just sold this stock? I'm scared, I better get out fast." Ah, the fear or "sheep" side of your personality, is speaking. Short term, it is more helpful for investors to think of the prices on the stock market driven by pigs and sheep rather than bulls and bears.

If you ever wondered why many experts are so inconsistent in accurately timing various financial markets every day, it is because the crowd—buyers and sellers—are driven each day by emotion and short-term momentum rather than rationally evaluating the long-term valuation parameters within each stock and the market as a whole.

However, the good news is that over time, fundamental and more rational valuations invariably come into play. Sometimes, a market can stay mistakenly valued due to sentiment for multiple years. But eventually markets do get fairly valued. One just can't tell when it will change.

WHAT'S THE KEY LESSON?

1. Recognize just how powerful short-term sentiment can also whipsaw the prices in all markets, stocks, bonds, currencies, and commodities.

2. **Invest broadly.** As long as you are broadly invested across many of the stock markets, and you remain invested in the stock market long enough, you will reap the extra returns of the stock markets and not suffer the disadvantages of short-term volatility.

THE STORY OF THE ALLIGATOR FLEA:
THE MASTER OF EMOTIONAL MANAGEMENT

In 1994, I was the chief executive of Jardine Fleming Unit Trust Company in Hong Kong. Unit trusts are the British version of mutual funds. It was an exciting time for me, having local subsidiaries, investments, and clients throughout East Asia, India, the Middle East, and Europe. I worked closely and learned much from a host of characters during my time in Hong Kong. One of the more interesting Hong Kong tycoons was a man known by many as "the Alligator Flea."

The Alligator Flea invested via one of his many entities and kept his financial activities as discreet as he could. As I have often observed over the years, the wealthier a man is, the less he lets others know exactly how much he really has. Not standing out was not too difficult in Hong Kong, as there were lots of eccentric and quite visible billionaires who perennially made the headlines in the *South China Morning Post*.

I asked the Alligator Flea what his mythical nickname signified, but he ignored my question until after he got to know me. One day he finally replied, "Alligator fleas can jump around with no one noticing them, as they appear so small and unimportant. But when an opportunity arises, they can take a big bite in an instant."

The Alligator Flea frequently called on my investment team for ideas. If he liked what we said, he would send money to invest in one of our strategies. Over the next year, as he came to trust me more, he added a considerable sum of money into our funds and would frequently invite me to lunch to pick my brain for investment ideas. One of his talents was that he was a great listener, and he listened to everyone regardless of rank or age; he felt that great insights did not necessarily come from people with fancy and important titles.

During my time in Hong Kong, I learned more from observing how the Alligator Flea conducted himself rather than what he said. For instance, it was quite clear to us that he spread his money around a variety of accounts across many brokers, banks, and investment companies, and made sure to operate in several countries and regions globally. He balanced his investments quite broadly across all of his accounts and entities. Clearly, the Alligator Flea followed the SPOF rule. For example, he would take considerable risk in a transaction over a brief period, watching it even by the hour, while at the same time he balanced this risk by having an ultraconservative portfolio of investments that had nothing to do with his high risk bets.

I once sat in on a small lunch with a handful of tycoons who all expressed the same sentiment: Because half or more of their money was concentrated in very high risk trading investments and business ventures, where they could lose it all, they balanced their portfolios on the other side by having virtually no risk in their other disconnected portfolios. They sometimes referred to this type of investing as the "Asian barbell," i.e., keeping few investments in the moderate risk category (especially as at that time, most local bonds were quite risky) but a lot of investments in extreme high risk and extreme low risk areas. Thus, on a continuum, their portfolio mimicked a barbell.

Image 8.1 The "Tycoon Barbell"

Although it is certainly not an approach I would recommend to most investors, the strategy had some logic for them. After all, if you are a billionaire, you don't need growth in your low risk portfolio as much as middle and affluent class people do. Nonetheless, I was continually impressed with how careful these high risk takers were with their "other pockets" of money. The lesson, even for modest investors, is clear. Even if most of your money is concentrated in a risky venture, like a business start-up, it is important to make sure that at least some of your nest egg is invested in a cautious manner not connected with your primary business or investment.

One weekend, the Alligator Flea invited me to a party at his house. He was introducing his architects to his mainland tycoon business associates.

I arrived at his mansion on Victoria Peak and was confronted with his fleet of Ferraris, Rolls, and Bentleys. As I entered through the main door, there were 20 black-and-white-starched-uniformed butlers and maids creating a tunnel directing me to his living room. I had to walk under two giant ivory elephant tusks and cross over a white lion skin. This was not an "eco-conscious" group.

After serving us all champagne, he took us on a tour of his mansion including through the refrigerated closets containing his wife's furs. He also went out of his way to show us each toilet throughout the house.

The dinner was quite exotic, consisting of a variety of endangered species. After dinner, he gave us a tour of his servants' quarters. Just as he had done in the tour of the main house, he came up to the toilet in his female servants' bathroom, and proudly flushed the toilet with great élan.

Although my job was to give him investment ideas and to manage his money, the Alligator Flea taught me more than I ever taught him. He was among the best I had ever seen in not falling in love with any investment. He could work for weeks analyzing a particular opportunity, and get quite excited about it when he was ready to buy. But the next day, or year, as soon as he thought it was the right time to sell, he sold without compunction. For example, he once built a brokerage virtually from scratch with a few other partners, but when it became clear the brokerage firm had reached maximum value, he sold it without hesitation. Consistently, he was able to separate his politics and his emotions from his investments. He used to say, "I don't mix my money with my political views or prejudices. I may hate someone, but that doesn't mean I won't invest in him."

Later that night, I figured out why he beamed the most when he flushed the servants' toilet. Decades earlier, during the Chinese Cultural Revolution, the then 18-year-old Alligator Flea had escaped from mainland China, naturally with no money in his pockets. He began working in restaurant kitchens and then, moved on to be a runner on the Hong Kong Stock Exchange, which set him on the road to riches. He was probably 25 or older before he ever sat on a toilet that flushed. And so, to him, being so rich that his female servants could flush their own toilets was the personal signal to him that he had made it.

Throughout my decades on Wall Street, I often saw that when it comes to money and investing, people, either rich or poor, strove to earn enough to reach a particular life goal, to finally do something that signified "they had made it." This goal gave them the ambition to achieve. But alas, there were so many times when a person put their investment nest egg at risk as they strove for something even bigger. For some, the only "signal" they needed was a good pair of shoes, or a nice car, which could be quite practical. For others who became rich, it could be buying a sports team or a vineyard, which could later prove quite financially painful for them, especially if they used too much leverage to fund their hobbies.

Flushing toilets were not costly to the Alligator Flea. He kept his wealth signal relatively modest. Unfortunately there are many others whose wealth signals buried them, particularly when they mixed up their hobbies with making money. The damage to their long-term financial plan could be irreparable. By watching so many successes and mistakes, I learned how important it is to make sure to keep the wealth signal goal in proper perspective, so it doesn't distract you from your lifelong financial plan. It dawned on me the morning after my weekend with the Alligator Flea: It can be motivating for a person to have an aggressive goal, to strive to own something that could be your signal that you have made it. But don't let that goal own you.

Image 8.2 Alligator Flea

With the Alligator Flea, he had his mansion and cars, but he looked at them as merely a part of his business or his personal brand which he needed in such an ostentatious market. In fact, privately he spent most of his time in a modest apartment nearby. The only wealth signal he personally needed was his servants having flushing toilets. He was in control of his money and he didn't let his money control him.

**THE LESSONS I LEARNED FROM
THE ALLIGATOR FLEA**

1. **Emotions and investing don't mix.** Don't confuse your emotions, your ego, your politics, and especially your hobbies with your long-term investment decisions.
2. **Balance is key.** Even billionaires keep their investments broadly invested in both low risk and high risk asset classes across multiple countries and currencies.

CHAPTER 9
THE REVERSAL OF NATIONS

How Global Diversification Is the New Safe

Once you realize managing your money is a lifetime proposition (even if you are in your 60s) rather than a three- to five-year process, your attitude toward investment better shift.

It is best to pay less attention to the latest fads or most topics in the daily news and think about what really is going to impact your investment opportunities over the next 10, 20, 30 years. This focus will guide you away from the onslaught of daily news and ups and downs of the markets and toward ensuring that your portfolio is properly positioned to take advantage of long term growth opportunities as well as not be hurt by emerging negative trends. History has shown that even if an area or asset class has been safe for the last 10 or 20 years, that does not mean it will remain attractive in the coming decades.

There are two powerful world phenomena that are dramatically affecting the first half of this century: the massive shift in global demographics, and the reversal of risk levels of countries.

DEMOGRAPHICS ARE KEY TO UNDERSTANDING GROWTH POTENTIAL

In the case of demographics, such a seismic shift has never occurred in human history. It requires considerable analysis to guess at the outcomes and how it affects a long-term investment portfolio. Most financial predictive models by design use the past as a predictor; these don't work in the case of this demographic change since we have never had populations as a whole so old.

In the case of the second phenomenon—nations changing their relative status—such shifts have occurred throughout civilization; history can help more in looking at the present fortunes of countries. But because often these changes do not occur overnight, we can miss the opportunities and risks to our portfolios as we are lulled into thinking such a fundamental shift cannot happen in our lifetimes.

In both cases the identification and analysis of these formidable changes has come late and has been often inadequate. Living abroad for so many years, I was able to see these shifts up close.

Let us start with demographics. I first noticed how powerful demographics impact our lives on a very personal basis. For my mother, her friends, and many of my investor clients around the world, once they retired, they stopped spending as much money as they did when they were younger. On average, a 65- or 75-year-old man or woman simply does not consume as much as they did when they were in their 30s and 40s. The research is lacking on this topic; in fact, what few studies that have been done can be misleading. Part of the reason is that older people do not think they are consuming less. In fact, many will deny it vehemently. They will say, "I just bought a brand-new car. And we're taking a long vacation overseas!"

However, after personally reviewing the savings and spending habits of hundreds of older generation investors over the last 20 years in multiple countries, it became clear to me that on average, older people spend less. I reviewed this hypothesis with dozens of financial advisors and they generally see the same phenomenon. Of course, more research needs to done, but at the micro level, this decrease in spending is what many advisors see in the spending habits of people once they get into their 60s. After all, financial planners and advisors are paid to look dispassionately at the annual spend rates of their clients. They will have a different but more accurate view on what clients are actually spending over a period of time versus what clients think they will spend.

For instance, take a look in the garage of the person who claimed he just bought a new car. This car may have been new when he bought it when he was 65. However, now he is 75 and still has the same car, and the odometer shows he has only driven 18,000 miles. When he was 40, he likely bought a new car, perhaps every four or five years. And the "new" suit in his closet was actually purchased 15 years earlier. And as to the trips overseas, typically people in their 60s and 70s will make one or two trips the first few years of retirement, have a fun but exhausting trip, come home, display the bottle of foreign whiskey on the shelf, and swear off any more long trips abroad.

The same phenomenon of relating to time differently as we age is affecting me. My brother noticed that I will say, "The other day . . ." and he will reply, "Tim, that was 15 years ago!" Time has a way of passing more quickly as we age.

Although some would argue there is an increase in entrepreneurship in people in their 60s, it is coming off of a very low base, as in the past, the over-60 crowd almost never started businesses. Accordingly, they do not borrow as much as they did when they were younger. And naturally, they all want to save money. Even for those who continue working into their 60s and beyond, it is often because they are concerned about running out of money in their later years and they know they can't make it again.

Of course, everyone spends money differently, but after retirement the majority of people often decrease their spending especially as health concerns bother them. So, they save rather than spend.

When an entire country begins to age, guess what? The entire country begins to consume less, and save more than it borrows. The unintended national consequences are that economic growth stagnates and risk-free interest rates go to near zero. There are more savers than borrowers, in effect, "more savers than builders."

It is true that in the near term, a few countries will see increasing portions of their populations emerging from youth to middle age; in these cases, there will be an increase in consumer expenditure. However, over the coming decades, we will have more developed countries moving from middle age to retirement age.

This reality first hit Japan starting in the late 1990s. They have among the oldest populations in the world, which explains several of the reasons why the economy has stagnated over recent decades. The aging impact has been lessoned in the United States, where immigration has delayed such a negative demographic impact. Foreign workers coming into the United States are on average much younger than the existing population. But it is only a matter of time before the United States begins to feel the same negative economic effect of an aging society as Japan. In fact, several countries in Europe are now beginning to feel such impact. As my driver in Milan told me last year, "You have an American novel called *No Country for Old Men*. We laugh here in Italy and say, 'We are a country of old men.'"

As you can see from Table 9.1, it is no coincidence that what I discussed above at a micro level is beginning to show up at the country level. The office of the Director of National Intelligence categorizes nations based on demographic window of opportunity.

Table 9.1   The Demographic Window of Opportunity*

Country	Window status	Median age, 2010	Median age, 2030	Demographic window of opportunity
Brazil	Window wide open	29	35	2000 to 2030
India		26	32	2015 to 2050
China		35	43	1990 to 2025
Russia		39	44	1950 to 2015
Iran		26	37	2005 to 2040
Japan	Window closed	45	52	1965 to 1995
Germany		44	49	before 1950 to 1990
United Kingdom		40	42	before 1950 to 1980
United States	Window closing	37	39	1970 to 2015

Source: Office of the Director of National Intelligence

* United Nations defines the demographic window of opportunity in terms of the dependency ratio as "the number of children (0-14 years old) and older persons (65 years or over) to the working-age population (15-64 years old)." The period when the dependency ratio declines is known as the "window of opportunity" leading to a "demographic dividend" as the society has a larger number of working people relative to the number of dependents. In quantitative terms, the window can be identified as years when the proportion of children in total population is less than 30 percent and the proportion of older persons is less than 15 percent.

The table shows a sample list of countries who are set to grow on demographic mileage and who are past the date for taking advantage of younger demographics. The research has shown that a large proportion of retirees in population structure is found to have a negative or relatively smaller positive effect on GDP.[1] Hence, you want to make sure you are getting more exposure to the younger demographic countries and not investing solely in the older demographic countries.

Table 9.2 shows how the top five countries with a high proportion of population with 65 years and older have faced a decline in GDP growth rate. The only exception being Germany as uniquely they were able to experience higher GDP growth due to wise government fiscal and monetary policy changes in recent times. However, such prudent and rare adjustments along with immigration promotion can lessen the sting and delay demographic related declines in GDP, inevitably, even the better run countries, such as Germany, will face similar pressures as the average age of its population continues to rise.

Another phenomenon dramatically exacerbates the negative demographic impact: Governments continuing to borrow heavily. Even if individuals are wise and pay down their debt in their elder years, societies have been electing governments that do not follow the same rules. As citizens of a country become a lot older, which is inevitable, the country's government should decrease borrowing. Most of its citizens are no longer earning wages that can be taxed

Table 9.2 Top Five Countries with High Proportion of Population Ages 65 and Above

	GDP growth annual (%)		% change in GDP growth	Population ages 65 and above (% of total)		% change in 65 and above population
Country	2011	2002		2011	2002	
Japan	-0.6	0.3	-0.9	23.7	18.2	5.4
Germany	3.0	0.0	3.0	21.0	17.3	3.7
Italy	0.4	0.5	-0.1	20.5	18.9	1.7
Greece	-7.1	3.4	-10.5	19.2	17.6	1.6
Bulgaria	1.8	4.7	-2.9	18.6	17.0	1.6

Source: World Bank: World Development Indicators (Growth rates of GDP are calculated using the constant price data in the local currency.)

so the government debt can be paid off. Most of Europe, the United States, and Japan have done the opposite and borrowed beyond the ability of their aging populations to service and pay back the public debt.

I read recently that an 83-year-old celebrity declared personal bankruptcy with millions in debt, even though he had made millions in his younger years. I first thought, "How stupid of him to be borrowing so much money in his 70s and 80s!" He clearly did not follow the typical path of wiser retirees. But then I wondered, "What stupid banks were lending an old guy so much money?"

The majority of the developed Western nations have been following the same path as this bankrupt celebrity. The gross government debt as percentage of GDP is set to reach 107 percent by 2015, as predicted by the World Bank. Some developed countries are in the worst shape; for example, Japan (238 percent), Greece (158 percent), Italy (127 percent), and Portugal (123 percent) had much higher debt as percentage of GDP in 2012 than the average of developed countries.[2]

This overwhelming debt problem will burden the developed world for decades. Many such countries now have a negative balance of payments, negative trade balance, and often weakening currencies.

What does this mean for your investment portfolio? The historically strong countries, those countries that you have depended on, taken for granted throughout your life to be low risk, have now become higher risk. You cannot depend on them to grow; the purchasing power of their currencies cannot help but deteriorate over time. Their ability to pay back their debt is questionable, as we have already seen in Europe, and their stock markets will naturally suffer.

This fundamental deterioration means that being safe, conservative, and only investing in the developed world is no longer a "safe" strategy.

Over the next decade, I suspect the implications of an aging society will garner much more media coverage. I think the reason this has not been broadly analyzed is that such a demographic shift has never happened before in human history. Indeed, it wasn't so long ago that we were all worried about the population explosion drowning the planet. We have no reference to understand all the implications of the increasing age of societies. For instance, if you think about the economic principles we learned in college from Adam Smith, Malthus, and Carlyle, unintentionally implicit in most of these principles is an average age of a population. Long held beliefs like people will typically operate in an insatiable consumption manner does not reflect what happens when the average age of the population reaches a point where they are, indeed, satiated.

Many economic predictive models will not necessarily work when they are based on data derived from past younger generations. For instance, when an entire society is saving more than they are investing, the supply of money to lend is naturally greater than the productive investments that create for young people and companies the need to borrow. All those that have predicted this past decade that inflation is soon coming and risk-free interest rates will soon rise have not had models that would have taken into consideration the aging society saving more money and not needing to borrow as much. Governments' excess borrowing can cause extreme volatility in such areas as risk adjusted interest rates and purposeful weakening of currencies to pay back debt with a cheaper currency, which also can result in higher inflation. However, the long-term trend of aging societies will undoubtedly continue to weigh down developed nations' economies, at least for the next 30 to 40 years.

I also saw how powerful this impact is in studying Japanese banks. I mention Japanese banks as they are an interesting indicator of where other banks in the developed world are headed. Over the past decade, the Japanese banks have consistently taken in 20 to 25 percent more in savings than they have been able to find loans for. Naturally, the interest rates have been effectively zero. Alarmingly, as the society ages, they can no longer keep renewing their purchases of Japanese government debt, and the banks have been compelled to buy upward of half of this government debt at near zero interest rates. Eventually it will result in a major problem for the country, but as we know from experience, governments can be quite short-term clever in finding ways to delay the inevitable, such as printing more money, which naturally creates more headaches for the country in the long run.

A bit of history sheds some light on the evolution of thinking about population growth. When I was in college in the early seventies, demographers were then preaching that the world's population explosion was our biggest problem. They taught us in school that until a society becomes wealthy, the population of a country continues to explode. The results of the past 20 years have proven that conclusion wrong. Even before the citizens become wealthy, all a society has to do is educate their women beyond about 15 years old, and the birthrate irretrievably collapses. Research[3] has consistently shown that in general, once a woman acquires even a basic education, she often comes to two conclusions: "I am not going to suffer the misery my mother did by having six or more kids. And I am going to wait until I am older before having my first child." Those two phenomena rapidly collapse a nation's birthrate. In the greater Shanghai area of China, where there has been no "one child" policy for some time, birthrates are actually now as low as Japan's due to rising female education and affluence. Governments around the world are waking up to the negative economic implications of aging population and lower birthrates. But does anyone really think such measures will actually stop the declining birthrate? The developed world may be able to delay the inevitable, but these mature countries will continue to shrink and get older, and their overall economies will have trouble maintaining any growth.

In some countries, what can delay the declining birthrate is when extreme poverty and illiteracy remain and/or extreme fundamentalist religions are present. In both cases, it hinders the ability of women to become more broadly educated. Many of those countries will likely remain extremely volatile economically or stagnant in growth; thus, certain countries may remain poor targets for core investing. Especially in emerging and frontier markets, greater investments in women's education are resulting in a higher GDP growth, as predicted by Goldman Sachs. Higher participation of women in the work force as a potential consequence of expanded women's education could push income per capita in emerging markets as much as 14 percent higher by 2020, and as much as 20 percent higher by 2030.[4]

GROWTH COUNTRIES EMERGE

Since 2000, there have been equally powerful forces at work in what I call the newly emerged "growth countries." Over the past decade a new group of formidable economies have begun to materialize. Within the so-called "emerging markets countries," a large subset of nations has already emerged and is in a sustainable long-term higher growth state. These countries now have a critical mass of political and economic structures in place to allow for such growth. They have an already emerged, commercially minded segment in each society that knows how to grow the companies successfully. These nations now have globally competitive products and services, so their currencies

Table 9.3 Emerging vs. Developed Markets: A Study in Contrast (Data as of Q1 2013)

	Developed markets	Emerging markets	Difference	Emerging vs. Developed market contrast
Next 5-year GDP growth forecast (IMF at PPP)	21.1%	46.5%	120.4%	*2.2X the next 5-year forecast GDP growth*
Deficit/GDP	-5.0%	-1.3%	-74.0%	*Three-quarters lower deficit/GDP*
Debt/GDP	85.2%	39.8%	-53.3%	*Half the debt*
FX reserves/Debt	34.5%	62.6%	81.4%	*Almost twice the currency reserves/GDP*
Government spending/GDP	38.4%	26.8%	-30.2%	*A third lower government spending/GDP*
Tax burden/GDP	27.9%	18.5%	-33.7%	*A third lower tax burden/GDP*
Current account balance/GDP	-0.6%	0.8%	1.4%	*Positive vs. negative current account balance/GDP*
Trade balance/GDP	-3.5%	1.2%	4.7%	*Positive vs. negative trade balance/GDP*
Median age	39.8%	32.7%	-17.8%	*A fifth lower median age*
Population over 65	16.6%	9.1%	-45.2%	*Half the amount of population over 65*
NTM P/E ratio	12.8	11.4	-10.9%	*A tenth lower P/E ratio for next twelve months*
Price/Book ratio	1.90	1.90	0.0%	*Similar price/book ratio*
Dividend yield	2.8%	3.2%	14.3%	*Higher dividend yield*
Last 12-month equity return	12.7%	5.0%	-7.7%	*Lagging trailing 12 months return*
Last 10-year equity return	176.7%	581.6%	404.9%	*3.3X the trailing 10-year return*

Source: IMF, World Bank, Bloomberg, and Lattice Strategies

are strong and their balance of payments is stable, and many of them even have a debt rating, which means they can now grow even faster. Most important, they have a younger demographic, often 10 to 20 years younger than the developed countries.[5]

The enduring opportunity for your investment portfolio is that investing in a basket or group of *these identified growth countries will result in a higher growth rate and potentially have lower risk than the developed world*. Although there are various classification guides for country groups in advanced, emerging, and frontier markets, I created my own classification guide to create a better representation of countries with high growth trajectory. For further details on the specific countries, please refer to Chapter 12, Beyond Borders, as well as my website.

To those who may be scared of less developed countries, I emphasize that we are not talking about all emerging countries; we are primarily talking about the subset of some 20 countries depending on the criteria covered below that have already achieved minimum acceptable levels of economic development.

One way to look at these countries today is to go back 30 years and examine the various countries of Asia. You may have observed that there were many countries that were too risky, too underdeveloped to warrant acceptance by cautious investors. However, if you just invested in the four countries that had already emerged, and were already in a high growth stage—Hong Kong, Singapore, Taiwan, and South Korea—your long term return was far more than

Table 9.4   Performance of Asian Tigers vs. Developed Countries during 2001–2013

2001–2013	Annual return
Portfolio: Asian Tigers	10.9%
Taiwan	5.0%
Hong Kong	9.7%
Singapore	9.8%
South Korea	16.3%
Portfolio: Developed Countries Ex-Asia	2.2%
North America	3.7%
Developed Europe	0.6%

Source: Country performance is based on FTSE indexes for various countries and groups

double what you would have made in even the most developed of countries.

Today, we now have not just four growth countries, but over 20 countries around the world to choose from. As a package, these countries are already slated to grow at double the rate of the developed, or now "old," countries. With some notable exceptions, their debt to GDP is much lower and safer than the old countries (refer to my website for debt to GDP ratio of growth countries).

I first ventured into China in 1979, just after Deng Xiaoping boldly announced "Black cat, white cat, I don't care so long as it catches mice!" He meant we have to give responsibility and even reward to those that do a better job of building the economy. I was in a restaurant in Guangzhou sitting next to a table of six men. It was a holiday lunch and they decided after much discussion to buy a foreign beer—one can of beer for all of them. They carefully poured the single can's contents into six tiny glasses as if they were pouring a bottle of Dom Perignon and ceremoniously shouted "Kam Bei!," meaning "dry cup." (Like "bottoms up!" in English.) It was only a single can of Pabst Blue Ribbon American beer, hardly a premium label, but they all exclaimed, "Se ge Pijo hun hao!"—What a great beer. It was their first taste of anything foreign. They decided to splurge and buy a second can. Sadly, only four had enough money and it was embarrassing for the two gentlemen with no coins left in their pockets. I called the waiter over and bought the six men two cans of beer. You would have thought I had given them the keys to Shangri La. I tell this story so we remember how poor China was not so long ago. Today, it is a safe bet the children of at least some of those men are now driving new BMWs or Jeeps. Such an economic revolution on this massive scale across the growth countries has never happened before.

By 2002, I could travel from the northeast corner of China to the southwest and often not see anyone starving. In the nineties, I was on a large junk in the South China Sea with a group of successful businessmen and officials. I asked the group why they thought China became so successful so quickly. One foreign-educated Chinese executive, clearly the accepted leader of the group, laughed and began his story.

"Until about 500 years ago," he said in a loud voice, "China ruled the world—at least most of the world that mattered. We had ruled for about 5,000 years. In fact, we always took our power as the Middle Kingdom for granted. But then, even though we had given the world so much in discoveries and inventions, through a series of political mishaps, we missed the new technology revolution born in the West by the Renaissance. Over the recent two centuries, we always claimed the West was successful only because of imperialism and exploitation of China and other poor countries. But in the 1970s, we saw that Hong Kong, Taiwan, Singapore began to emerge as wealthy states. This shocked us; after all, historically they had simply been considered our poor vassals. How could they organize and actually be much richer than China? It made many of us embarrassed and jealous, and it gave us ambition. Despite our size, a critical mass of leaders, both in government and in industry, we decided we can and should modernize and borrow some of the concepts that had made our 'vassal' states like Taiwan and Hong Kong rich. What has also driven each of us is knowing that west of us, in the hinterland of China, there is always another mother forcing her child to study even harder than we did. And this child as he grows up is willing to work harder and for less money than we make. So, this fear of being replaced is our daily motivator."

Soon after hearing this speech, I flew to India, where I had also worked since the early nineties. There, the attitude of many people was still, "But it is our fate as we are so poor and since India has over a billion people, we can't agree on anything anyway." Whenever children would come begging as I walked along streets all over India, my Indian colleagues would often say, "But that is their place in the world. They are exploited. It is the fate of India. And see they are happy."

But India was on the cusp of change.

As the years rolled on, I began to hear a new and different story coming out of the business leaders of India. Consistently, their message became, "If China can organize itself to grow economically so quickly, and they are bigger than us, we have no excuse for not doing the same."

Over the last five years, I have heard a very different message throughout India, even from my local colleagues. They now say, "Don't give the beggars any money. They and their parents can now get a job. They don't need to beg anymore; they are just lazy." I was seeing firsthand a major shift in the zeitgeist of this giant country. In the nineties, most of the people knocking on my window were simply begging for money. By the late nineties, many were trying to sell me something. The goods were not so desirable—unappealing fruit, crudely carved figurines—but at least some had moved away from begging. Now, in my latest business trips throughout India, the young men and women approaching my car at stop lights are selling *Harvard Business Review* and *Economist* magazines in clean plastic. Almost overnight, I saw one poor country after another emerge. People in other emerging countries were encouraged, even shamed, into saying, "If they can do it, then we can and must, too."

Of course, some may say both China and India still do not operate under the same standards and beliefs as America or Europe. Perhaps this is best answered by a colorful and articulate Indian friend who had worked throughout the world and once joked to me: "In China and most East Asian countries, it is difficult for a Western style democracy to work because everyone is, by culture and history, afraid to speak up. Whereas, in India, democracy often does not work well because everyone won't stop talking!"

We all laughed along with him, but knew there may be some truth to his declaration. After all, democracy is a Greco-Roman, Western invention that Asia, the Middle East, Africa, even Latin America all continue to wrestle with. We have observed that *a country doesn't need to follow the Western view of democracy to have long-term economic growth and even relative stability*. But the modern economic revolution is clearly ensconced in these growth countries, although each country has found different roads to success.

There are many other reasons this economic revolution has occurred so quickly. During the late nineties, I visited factories and call centers in Mexico and Costa Rica. I constantly came into contact with executives educated in the United States and trained in US companies. After working a number of years in the United States, many moved back to their home countries and brought their skills into local firms. I heard similar stories from our analysts as they visited firm after firm in Brazil. Starting in the early 2000s, we were finding many public companies whose stocks were attractive because they were so professionally run. A new "Corporate Brazil" has been emerging, quite different than in earlier years. I remember one example in the 1970s, when I was a young banker, where the primary owners of a major firm in Latin America were named Rodriguez—as was the management of the firm, the outside auditor, and the local state regulator. They were all the same Rodriguez family, all closely controlled by their octogenarian patriarch. In contrast, recently, one of the main reasons our analysts saw such improvement in how firms operate is that in many of the major public Brazilian firms, half or more of their top management had worked in companies in either Europe or the United States and brought back home their skills. The old days of only locally trained patriarchs running the business and few knowing how to run a globally competitive firm were changing.

I saw this same pattern across the globe, from Turkey to Taiwan, Mexico to India, and, more recently, from the Philippines and Indonesia to Morocco. This knowledge transfer is not just in business. Routinely, when I meet with officials in several of the growth countries' governments, even midlevel officials have studied at American business and government universities, and/or interned, for instance, at a Goldman Sachs or Deutsche Bank. These officials are often in constant contact with officials in both developed and other growth countries. Thus, the velocity of knowledge in the network age has resulted in countries amassing a critical mass of skills sets necessary to fuel rapid growth.

When you examine the investment opportunities in these growth countries, they cover a variety of asset classes and other dimensions. The major asset classes are similar to developed countries, such as equities, fixed income, and real assets, including commodities and real estate (refer to detailed asset class definitions on my website). However, growth countries also offer some unique asset classes, such as external sovereign bonds, local currency denominated corporate bonds, and currencies. Their stocks are now listed on more liquid bona fide exchanges, even dual listed in London or New York, and many operate closer to the global corporate governance standard. Accounting procedures, control systems, and regulations are converging, similar to US and European firms. When they are lacking or mistakes are made, the news quickly gets out and changes are made accordingly. It is more difficult now for countries to hide poorly operating companies. There are now hundreds of quality public companies available from these growth countries. In addition, many of the currencies are now allowed to operate at least closer to their fair market values, and their central banks often have excess reserves derived from net exports. Such currencies are ideal for investors to diversify their currency risk outside of the over-indebted, weaker "old" countries. No longer does an investor have to leave all their money in just dollars, yen, sterling, or euros. In fact, many of these growth countries' currencies are stronger than the old countries' currencies.

Regarding fixed income asset classes, many of these growth countries and their top companies now have improved credit ratings. This success has allowed them to tap into global debt markets, which in turn allows them to better finance their growth in such important areas as infrastructure and capital goods.

With the enhanced credit ratings of several growth countries, investors have access to higher quality bonds, at times even safer than US or European debt instruments, and with higher paying interest rates. After all, these countries are growing faster than the old countries and must pay attractive rates to ensure sufficient capital inflows to fund their growth. In the last five years, emerging and frontier markets had more positive changes in risk ratings while their developed counterparts went through more negative changes (refer to my website for detailed information on changes in foreign currency risks ratings for emerging and developed markets).

It may sound funny to novice investors, but one critical area to examine when looking at a country's borrowing is the ratio of borrowing for good reasons versus borrowing for bad reasons. "Good" reasons mean that a country is financing productive growth, such as infrastructure projects that are truly needed for the economy to grow and make good economic sense, like better roads in key areas and container terminals. Conversely, "bad" reasons include borrowing to fund the unnecessary purchase of yet more consumer goods, or borrowing because a country cannot pay back either the interest or the principle the government owes, similar to Southern Europe and Japan. When a country uses debt to invest in itself, to facilitate growth, the country has a much better chance of paying back the debt. This is the case with much of the borrowing by several of the more attractive growth countries and why purchasing debt instruments from a package of growth countries may have actually less risk than many OECD countries that are borrowing for riskier purposes.

Equally promising about growth countries is the recent access to real estate investing via Global Real Estate Investment Trusts (REITs).[6] Particularly over the past five to seven years, several major fund companies have created Global REITs with low minimum investment limits to attract small investors. Except for specific areas such as funding developers in China and most all real estate investing in Russia, there are a variety of attractive yield opportunities in real estate, especially as the more conservative REIT funds are focusing their acquisitions more on buildings already built with existing rent rolls. Fortunately, there has been a growth of global REIT fund companies that have local research teams around the world. These funds are quite diversified; they have put together a broad package of high-quality investment trusts, each investing in dozens of high-grade properties around the globe. The result for investors is that they can obtain further diversification for the real estate exposure of their portfolios yet have more liquidity than was available even ten years prior.

It is also important to recognize the indirect investment opportunities derived from the emergence of these 20-plus growth countries. Over a 20 year period starting around 2000, nearly half the world's population are moving from extreme poverty into becoming consumers. They are moving from having no shoes, or only sandals, to having two pairs of shoes, from no transportation to a bicycle, a motorcycle, and in the case of as much as 100 million people in the growth countries, the chance for their family to have a car. The result is a massive increase in the demand for virtually all commodities. When you are dirt poor, you do not consume a lot of resources; once you can get a job, however, even a low-paying job, and you can buy basic items, you create demand for goods, and thus, for commodities. If you wonder why oil, gold, lumber, and several food items have all gone up over the decade, it's because the world now has a lot more new consumers, new demand for goods. Thus, although commodities can be quite volatile and even under performing for periods of time, it is important to have at least some exposure in your portfolio to a variety of commodities, even as the world becomes more energy and resource efficient. And in case you haven't noticed, the reason so many luxury goods companies have done so well the past ten years is due to the new demand coming from Mumbai, Shanghai, Dubai, and others around the world. Thus, in global portfolios, it has become increasingly important to know what companies in developed countries are benefiting most from the growth countries' emergence.

Last year, while visiting companies in Sri Lanka via India, I checked into a hotel for the weekend to relax. Historically, when I traveled around the subcontinent, I was used to seeing Western tourists at breakfast with ashen faces. Clearly, they had eaten unsanitary food and were paying for it. It was hard *not* to get stomach ailments in many places. But during this weekend in India, I noticed a large group of Westerners enjoying a meal that contained raw vegetables. I thought for sure they would be in trouble tomorrow. Yet, I noticed they were all tanned, so had been there for at least a few days. I went into the back door of the kitchen and spied cartons of lettuce from Salinas Valley in California. Then, I remembered touring containers yards around several of the major ports in the subcontinent. It seems that once a country can plug into the global food network, where refrigerated containers can be delivered to the port almost daily, these growth countries have access to virtually all the world's foods. The quality of life, even for locals, improves often within a decade.

CONSIDERING FOREIGN SHORES AS PART OF YOUR CORE INVESTMENT

In the 1870s, a Scottish firm founded by a man named Robert Fleming invented the concept of a fund. The primary purpose of creating such "unit trusts"[7] was to diversify the investing risk of a large young country far to the west of England. This emerging and younger country needed massive amounts of capital to build a nationwide railroad system. The name of this wild often lawless young growing country was (drum roll) the United States.

So, in this sense, we are merely seeing a repeat of what happened in the late nineteenth century. Except this time, we are not just talking about affecting 50 or 100 million people, but rather closer to 3 billion people.

After such success in these growth countries, and given the lower yields and increased risks of the OECD or old countries, why do so many investors, especially in the United States, continue to put so little of their long-term money into growth nations?

First off, there is a natural Euro-American skepticism about the manner in which many of these countries run, what their cultural philosophies are, the amount of corruption prevalent, the political unattractiveness of dictatorships, communism and other one party systems—all these factors add up to a concern that many Western investors have about looking at growth countries as an area that should be a part of their core long-term investing.

There is this attitude in the West that a country must first look like us before we can take it seriously in terms of investing. Yet the success, and the amount of profit that has been made and will continue to be made in the coming decades means *that if you only invest in countries that look like yours, you will leave too much profit on the table.* In fact, it will leave more risk in your portfolio than you should have, as several of the formerly "safe" Western countries have now entered a much riskier phase of having too much debt and populations too old to pay it all back.

Corruption Isn't Just Somewhere Else

Many a Western investor has shunned investing in markets because of the level of corruption they read about. It is true; corruption is a problem for the commercial soul of any country. And there are many countries where corruption is so rampant that one almost can't do business there. However, at present, many of the accepted growth countries have made considerable improvements in this regard. It is still a major problem, but at least there are movements in many of these countries to genuinely weed out corruption as much as they can. I should add that from my direct observations, it is a constant battle for the powers that be in each country to keep corruption from pulling down their economies, and it seems like for every two steps forward in progress in fighting corruption, one step is taken back. But in the countries that are improving, the problems with corruption should not necessarily be used as an excuse to still wait until it is perfectly sterile before investing.

To eliminate all but the least corrupt countries in the world from your palate of investment opportunities results in an overconcentration of your portfolio into too narrow of a country selection. Remember, if investors had followed that strict of a guideline in the past, they would have never invested in the US railroads in the late nineteenth century, and all that opportunity profit would have been lost.

I have yet to work in a country where corruption has been eliminated. Let's start with the United States. One need only look at the headlines the past five years to see that almost daily, we have supposedly high integrity gentlemen being convicted of a whole host of crimes, including insider trading, fraud, bribery, accounting manipulation, etc.

Some may still be saying, "But these people in those countries are corrupt by nature." When I hear such comments, I recall an incident just after my father's death. As I mentioned in Chapter 1, I wanted to quickly get down to the coroner's office to claim my father's possessions. I was concerned that he may have contents in his wallet that he would not want others to find. Specifically, he helped out his friends and business associates by getting their speeding tickets "fixed," meaning he would give the tickets to his friend in the highway patrol so they would magically disappear. Sure enough, his wallet was fat with a half-dozen speeding tickets to be fixed. I immediately took them to his patrolman friend to see that they were handled. When he opened the door and I handed him the tickets in an envelope, he put up his hand and said, "I don't know anything about these. I can't take them." I replied, "And I don't know anything about the package of meat that I delivered every Friday to your house." Reluctantly, he took the envelope and said, "I don't want to ever see you again." The point is that corruption has been (and sometimes is still) quite prevalent in America and every other country. And although I suspect that fixing tickets today occurs much less frequently than in the past, we all know how difficult it is get rid of corruption completely. But we should remember that during much of the nineteenth and twentieth centuries, the United States was likely not materially less corrupt than many of the growth countries are today.

This story is not comfortable for me to talk about, but I tell it so none of us should ever forget, many people do whatever they can to feed their family. I also remembered learning in Delhi, India, that if I did not carefully dry the stamp on an envelope before mailing, some postal employees might remove the stamp for resale and pocket the money. As Eric Severeid, the famous CBS commentator once said, "No man was ever more than about nine meals away from crime or suicide."

These stories are not told to justify corruption, and it is critical that we strongly encourage laws to be followed, even by withholding investment in many cases. But we should never think that just because there is corruption in any given country, it means that these people are not improving, cannot come out of their subsistence level of survival. Especially over the last decade, there are many new examples of cultures and countries improving their lot and entering the more acceptable world of doing business properly and thriving in a legitimate manner. For many countries, such improvement may be a long way off. But it is important to recognize that there is now a large group of countries that are thriving and warrant serious investment. To ignore them will be very painful for your long-term portfolio.

To those who do not feel comfortable investing in cultures that are foreign to them or that are new countries struggling to enter the global society: So long as the investment management company you are dealing with has done their local homework, all their local advance work, you should be able to broaden your investment geography, increase your returns, and actually lesson your risks of overconcentration in any one country. Of course, any one country might inevitably get into trouble—and that country may not recover for decades. But so long as you have a true globally diversified portfolio, that package of investments will likely grow much more than if you just confined the investing to the present developed world.

Over the years, I have heard many excuses for why people shy away from investing in any emerging market country. Even some educated people will say, "You can't make any money in these untrustworthy foreign markets. I am going to wait and see what happens. I can't invest where it is so dangerous." Yet in many of those countries, over this past decade, I have seen high returns made by investors who recognized that developed nations were no different when they were in their high growth stages, and invested across many of these same countries via fund companies that had strong local due diligence teams. To ignore growth countries and consider them highly speculative, as many American analysts still do, may actually put more risk into your overall portfolio than you may realize and likely decrease your long-term returns.

THE LESSONS I LEARNED FROM AROUND THE WORLD

1. **Global investing is key to safe portfolio management.** To put all your investments in only one country, even if it is a great country, puts too much concentration of risk into your portfolio.
2. **Selected emerging markets are worth the risk.** Investing only in Europe, the United States, and Japan likewise puts dangerous risk into your portfolio. The basket of growth countries will continue to grow over the next few decades, at times, twice as fast as developed nations. Some will also have stronger currencies and debt service ability.
3. **Don't judge emerging markets too harshly.** It is critical to overcome your negative emotions about the cultures of growth countries. There is a greater risk to your long-term portfolio if you *don't* invest in these markets.

PART ONE WRAP-UP

In this first section of the book, I laid out the key principles of smart long-term investing that I have learned from working with investors over the past 40 years. I especially emphasized views that are often not covered by the traditional press and Wall Street. Now, we are ready to move on to how to actually execute the key success principles we have learned.

PART II
INVESTING SOLUTIONS

CHAPTER 10
THREE POCKETS

A Tool for Managing Money and Emotions

Over the decades, I have had the good fortune to observe thousands of presentations and discussions with investors about what to do with the money they had worked so hard to save. Naturally, I had many conversations with investors myself, but I seemed to learn much more from watching my colleagues make such presentations. I guess it was because all I had to do was listen.

Irrespective of the country or the market conditions, there were two things I heard repeatedly that indicated the financial services industry was not often helping their clients understand the investing process. First, investors, especially beginners, would get this exasperated look and say, "All these acronyms and complex charts and so much legalese, I really am lost." We in financial services have focused on our own internal terminology, not understanding that our clients were not following. Second, some of the more experienced but disgruntled investors would say, "I've heard this before, so no need to repeat it." However, all too often, this response begs the question, "Then, why have you not followed a sound long-term investment plan, and instead, switched in and out of so many investments?" It was like talking with someone who is regularly trying to lose 20 pounds following dozens of different diets, yet, in the end, they haven't lost a pound.

In both these cases, we were not being helpful; we were not communicating to clients in a way that helped them understand our advice and our strategies. More of the same types of presentations were not going to get these investors to stick with a plan to fulfill their financial goals.

Starting about 12 years ago, and working closely with dozens of advisors and hundreds of clients, I developed a process and a tool that could help all investors, whether new to investing or actively engaged in managing their own portfolios. The objective was to ensure investors actually internalized what a proper investment approach for them looked like, as opposed to merely understanding our words. I ended up calling it "Three Pockets," as people often thought of their money as being in different pockets. Plus, this way, investors didn't need to view so many graphs.

Rather than a presentation, which to many investors felt like a lecture, Three Pockets was more of a *customer conversation guide-line*, where advisor and investor could interact. Since many people had not followed what they were being told, the Three Pockets process incorporated directly what people were actually doing or wanted to do into their overall plan. It also served as a guide to help investors stay on track and fulfill their long-term goals.

The most important discussion that has to happen first between an investor and an advisor concerns how much money needs to be set aside for the **Savings Pocket**. It is critical to start here, as naturally anyone would first need to be reassured that the advisor genuinely

Image 10.1   The Three Pockets

 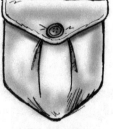 

SAVINGS   INVESTING   TRADING

realizes there is a large portion of your savings that cannot fluctuate short term. This is your "just can't afford to lose" pocket. Then, from the outset, you can judge if your advisor can be trusted with helping you make decisions that is in your best interests.

This Savings Pocket has just two objectives for an investor: Do not lose any of my principle, and the money must be kept liquid, i.e., easy to access in case of emergencies. The question is not whether you need a Savings Pocket or not. Everyone needs one. Rather, after you have decided how much money to keep in the risk-free pocket, how can you get some growth out of the remaining funds? Nowadays, there is nearly zero real return when inflation is considered in most all risk-free investments; you will never get the growth you need in the Savings Pocket.

The conversation can then move to the next challenge, which is how to get growth on the additional money you don't have to leave in your Savings Pocket. The problem is that many people think their only choice is to go into risky investments, to take a chance. They think their only option is to have a pocket for their trading money. And when people think of their **Trading Pocket**, they think the only way to grow their money is to make bets of one or two particular markets, or asset classes, or even stocks; or to make a bet as to the best time to get into or out of a market.

However, what many still miss is that there is a pocket between the Savings and Trading Pockets. People often ask, "Well, what else can I do? Is there any way I can get a better return than savings, yet without the risk of trading?" The answer is yes: the **Investing Pocket**. How does it accomplish this challenging goal? There are just two things that you have to do in the Investing Pocket to be successful in minimizing risk: Stay broadly diversified in as many different types of investment as possible, and leave the money alone. Don't move it around too much. Later on, take out only what you need.

In this way, two powerful risk-decreasing weapons are maximized:

1. **Diversification:** This means you win by not losing, as your money is spread across so many asset classes and countries that volatility is substantially reduced while still affording you

the opportunity to reap the inevitable growth of the majority of these different asset classes.

2. **Time:** This means utilizing the power of time. Letting time work its magic is maximized. Take a broad and diverse group of asset classes, leave them alone for a long enough period, and your money will eventually grow at a greater rate than Savings Pocket money, but with substantially less risk than in the Trading Pocket.

Easy to understand, but why hasn't it been followed more often? It was best answered by a close investment advisor friend of mine in Nevada, Jim Laughton. "Lots of people understand the concept of keeping diversified and staying invested for the long term—that is, until something bad happens in the market. The first time their portfolio value drops, they say, 'Look. I can't make this money over again. I just can't afford to keep losing any money.' So, customers want to pull their money out."

Jim's point is a good one. All of us can understand that fear if you see the market turn south in crisis times and your portfolio declines suddenly. This is where the lessons we learned in Part I on how to win in investing really need to be internalized. To execute on the lessons we learned, simply:

- Put in a small portion of your money into your Investing Pocket quarterly or annually over several years, decades even.
- Make sure it is very broadly diversified and leave it alone. In time, your Investing Pocket will grow more than your Savings Pocket irrespective of how many financial crises you live through.

Let's take a good hard look at why I say this with such conviction. Let's say you followed the above advice in the worst possible times over the past century. In other words, you were big-time unlucky. Let's say you were fully invested just as the 1929 market stock crash hit, or during the oil shock of the early 1970s. As I pointed out in Chapter 8 (see Fig. 8.2), even if you invested over time such that you had maximum exposure to the markets at the worst possible time last century, which was 1929 and 1930, so long as you had followed the plan of consistently investing a little each year, say from 1914, you were still able to reach your financial goals. In this worst scenario case, you retired and were at your maximum investment level, the highest point of exposure to the markets in 1929—and then, you began to slowly redeem your investment pockets only for your annual living expenses each year. Notice that not only did you make a lot more money than if you had just left it in the risk-free savings account, but you also never ran out of money, even if you lived to be a hundred years old.

It is hard to believe with such bad timing and luck in the market that any portfolio would come back. But here is where the combination of the diversity of asset investing along with the power of using time as your weapon against risk really kicks in. Even though in each crisis it always seems like the sky is falling and all asset classes are dropping, the reality is that some classes and even some countries don't fall nearly as much as others; in fact, some actually go up. Even more important, some classes recover much quicker than others.

Likely, you wouldn't have noticed this phenomenon if you just followed the daily news; they report only what happened recently, or what everyone thinks will happen tomorrow or even next month—in other words, very short term. It is only when you look at how assets recover over a period of years that you see how helpful diversification is in lowering volatility in your portfolio over time. Even when you look at another of the worst crises of the past 100 years—the 2008 subprime crisis and its aftershocks—see how it took just a few years before many of the world's stock markets were right back to where they were pre-2008. The S&P 500 was at all-time high of 1,576.09 on October 11, 2007, before the subprime crisis. Then the bubble imploded. The index crossed the previous all-time high mark on April 23, 2013.

Also, in almost all the great crashes, not only last century but throughout history,[1] in the years just prior to a crash, the market and pricing had run up considerably in just a few years prior to the crash.

Even the years of Great Depression, an extremely unlucky timing of investing, do not affect your life financial plan because you

Fig. 10.1   S&P 500 Prices (October 2007–August 2013)

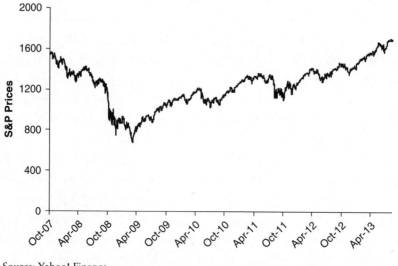

Source: Yahoo! Finance

invested small amounts regularly into the markets over more than a decade in a disciplined way. So, *your average purchase price when buying into the markets each year turned out to be a lot lower than the peak price.* The secret of investing just a little each year becomes a major risk ameliorator for your portfolio.

TRICKLE IN, TRICKLE OUT

This concept is easy to understand and to do, yet surprisingly many investors dismiss it or ignore it. Since it is such an integral part of how the Investing Pocket achieves its objectives, I should spend a bit more time on "trickling."

Some people will know at least the "trickle in" part of this formula by its traditional name, "Dollar Cost Averaging." I used to use that phrase until an evening meeting years ago when a well-dressed woman in her mid-60s said, "Please forgive me for being so up front, but none of my friends understood what in God's name you meant by this 'dollar cost averaging' thing." I went with her to the back of the room and spoke with her and her friends. As I recall, they were just starting an investment club so they could better share ideas. After showing them on a sheet of paper how just putting a little in every year really decreases your risk over time, one gentleman exclaimed, "Oh, you just tinkle in a little money at a time!" His wife interrupted and said, "George, I think you mean 'trickle,' not tinkle. It's a bit more genteel." He laughed and said, "The wine is already affecting me. But now I won't ever forget, 'trickle in and trickle out.'"

Why does trickling in and out work so well to decreasing your risk? Many of the examples used in the industry are quite detailed, but the oversimplified illustration below makes the point just as well.

Let's say you decide to buy three shares of a particular stock, and rather than buy all at once, you chose to divide your purchase and buy only one share each year for three years. Naturally over the three-year period, the price would be fluctuating and different each year. Then, let's say, the market declined in year 4 and fell back to $120. Because you had spread your purchases out over three years, you actually ended up losing no money. Of course, it was scary seeing it drop so much, but because you just "trickled in" your money over time, your average price was already lower before the market crashed.

And very importantly, trickling out is just as important during the period when you begin to redeem your investments. You don't take it all out at once; you only take out what you need. In any year the market goes down, since you leave most of the money in the Investing Pocket, the only amount you actually lose is on that very small amount you withdrew.

Again, let's use the example above. You decide to retire in year 4, and you plan to take out only one-thirtieth of your Investing Pocket each year, ensuring your money lasts at least 30 more years after retirement. But then, the market crashes down in year 4 back to $120 a share, or down $20.

Table 10.1 Purchase Price Averaging

Trickle investing works!	
	Purchase price
Year 1	$100
Year 2	$120
Year 3	$140
Your average purchase price	$120

Image 10.2   Trickle-In Trickle-Out

Year 4: Amount of sale $120 divided by 30 = $4

Only portion of realized loss: $20 divided by 30 or 67 cents.

As long as you leave the money in and only sell what you need to, you don't actually experience most of the loss in any of the crisis years. As we said above, over enough time, even though an individual stock could fall to zero and never return, if you are buying an entire asset class, there is less risk, because even when the majority of asset classes decline or are volatile, they typically return to equal or higher values. So, you don't lose on what you don't sell.

What do I mean by *asset class*? It means a class of assets is a group of common individual instruments that have common characteristics: stocks would be one asset class, bonds would be another. Often we speak of subclasses, for instance, small company stocks or corporate bonds. (On the website, you can look at a large variety of asset classes and see how, over a lifetime of investing, on average, the asset classes as a package end up higher than when they started.)

By buying in slowly into a broad variety of asset classes, and equally important, by only selling slowly over decades out of these classes, you ensure that any annual volatility doesn't matter. Over time, you are able to experience growth out of the various asset classes. Some skeptics might rightly say, "Some markets seem to stay down for decades. And they may not come back, ever." That is why broad international diversification is so important.

Sometimes I am asked, "Why would I even need a Trading Pocket? What purpose does it serve?" The answer is that most people don't *need* a Trading Pocket. However, it serves multiple valuable purposes for many types of personalities and needs.

Why Have a Trading Pocket?

As I mentioned in Part I, the human brain is a natural driver for us to want to win—or at least to beat the market. It is not a bad thing, in and of itself. But we want to make sure it does not get in the way of having enough money to last throughout your later years. So, rather than saying you shouldn't trade, it is much better for an advisor to say to certain more aggressive clients, "Active trading is a way that could possibly grow your portfolio dramatically; just make sure you are first putting enough money each year into your Investing Pocket." *Only when you have set aside enough new money each year in the Investing Pocket can you then fund a Trading Pocket.* Here you can show your prowess in picking stocks or any other market you please. If you win and bet right in the Trading Pocket, you will be vacationing in Hawaii; if you lose, you can spend your vacation barbecuing in the backyard. The important thing is that if you lose in this pocket, it won't risk your financial survival when you get older.

The Trading Pocket is also helpful for people that want to make much more money than possible in the Investing Pocket. They may not be satisfied unless they have focused their investments and are going for a 10 percent plus return after inflation. In and of itself, there is nothing wrong with this approach. After all, it is your money. My only recommendation is that once you concentrate your bets in one particular investment or class, and/or want to trade it frequently, it should be classified in your Trading Pocket. At a minimum, you would still want to have some portion of your money in the separate Investing Pocket that is broadly diversified and that you leave alone, just in case you don't become a millionaire in your Trading Pocket.

There is another purpose for the Trading Pocket. Many people get frightened when markets come tumbling down. When you wake up one morning and think the sky is falling, simply sell out your Trading Pocket and put it all in cash. Don't touch your Investing Pocket. We recommend for certain "trigger finger" investors to invest some money into the Trading Pocket, just so when they panic, they have something to sell. In this case, think of the Trading Pocket as a pressure-release valve that can give you an outlet. By having some "play" money in the Trading Pocket, you have a way to control your emotions; you can feel that you are doing something. In fact, you can do anything you want in this pocket. The Trading Pocket offers comfort as a way to channel your fears. Remember, on average, the majority of even smart people normally sell at the wrong time.[2] But that's OK, if it is restricted to the Trading Pocket, just like the Alligator Flea always separated his savings and conservative investing from his trading investments.

THE POCKET FOR YOUR ENTREPRENEURIAL SPIRIT

The entrepreneurial drive of human beings has greatly improved the world. We applaud those who have the initiative, the courage to go for it and try to build something great, a business they can call their own. This desire can be alone, in a partnership with others, or in a family taking a chance together. It can also take the form of concentrated investing or developing real estate. This entrepreneurial effort can take many forms. Often in the beginning, you have no choice other than to "bet the ranch," or put most all your money into an active venture. There is nothing wrong with following your dream; it is important, though, to keep in mind that concentration of your wealth into a single endeavor, an often illiquid endeavor is in reality a Trading Pocket decision. Your money here has concentration risk and thus, cannot be considered to be a part of your Investing Pocket. If you are young, you may not need to worry just yet about your Investing Pocket. But starting no later than 45 years old or so, you need to at least *set aside some money every quarter or year that is going into your Investing Pocket, completely independent and not potentially encumbered by your entrepreneurial venture.* You are simply making sure to follow the SPOF rule. You don't want to leave any chance that you and your family won't have any money when you are older. The sooner you start building this separate Investing Pocket, the better.

THE SLOTH AND TAI CHI

Back in the nineties, inbound call centers were becoming a central element to serving investors. In order to make sure I was focusing these call centers to most optimally meet investor needs, I visited customer call centers in different industries and in other countries. After visiting technical support call centers in Costa Rica, I took a break and went to the Caribbean side of the country to spend some fun time in the jungle and the swamps. The flora and fauna were breathtaking, but I found one animal that especially fascinated me—the sloth. This animal moves so slowly I wondered how it had survived. The many predators in the jungle should have long rendered the species extinct. Instead, I discovered why the sloth may be the best investment advisor in the animal kingdom.

As a boy growing up in California, my father's close friend was an American Indian, and he taught my brother and me how to hunt deer and bear. He always used to say, "Look for movement." Often, you can't spot an animal until it moves, as its shape is otherwise lost in the background. Once you see it move even a little, your eyes can grab that change, that motion. The sloth however, has a unique advantage. Everything it does is in unbelievably slow and smooth motion. It makes no sudden moves of any part of its body. It moves at such a deliberately slow pace that you cannot detect any motion. Predators have difficulty seeing them. What is normally in nature considered a disadvantage—not being able to move quickly—is actually the very strength and advantage of the sloth.

Observing the sloth move along a branch reminded me of my karate years performing tai chi forms. The beauty of these disciplined routines is in the steady, continuous motion. Ironically, there is a concept in tai chi called "Investing in Loss," which means to go with the movement of your attacker and use the movement to ultimately defeat him.

Tai chi is a great idea to keep in mind while managing your Investing Pocket. You will survive, even thrive, in your Investing

Pocket, so long as you think of it as your "Tai Chi Pocket." Make no sudden jerking movements of your investments in this pocket, and focus your mind away from whatever some expert is saying on CNBC. If you must do something quickly, do it only in the Trading Pocket. The Investing Pocket is only for gradual movements, buying or selling a small portion of each asset class or investment, and only over a period of time.

THE LESSONS OF THREE POCKETS

Creating your own customized Three Pockets and sticking to them for the rest of your life ensures you will get more growth than just leaving money in the bank. Three Pockets is easy to understand, but also easy to forget. The challenge remains in using this tool to channel your emotions throughout your life.

1. **The Savings Pocket** is your "rainy day" pocket for emergency money and short-term money you are using for short-term expenses and parking of money.
2. **The Investing Pocket** grows more than savings but with less risk than trading. It works because you diversify along three dimensions:
   • Broadly across a large variety of asset classes
   • Across many country types and geographies
   • Uses time via trickling as a powerful form of diversification across many investment seasons
3. **The Trading Pocket** is your ultimate manager of fear versus greed. This pocket fluctuates depending on whether you are greedy or panicking and have to convert your holdings to cash. Thus, the not-so-hidden agenda here is to make sure you leave the Investing Pocket alone. You only actively move money in the Trading Pocket.

CHAPTER 11
THE RISK PRISM

Virtually every time the topic of what to invest in comes up, the first question is, "But is this investment too risky?"

Before we discuss the specifics of each asset class, it is important that you develop a proper perspective about risk. Risk assessment is quite personal and subjective. What one person perceives as a risky pursuit, another is quite comfortable with. Recent studies have shown that even someone who considers themselves very risk averse in investing can at the same time feel quite comfortable in skydiving.[1] In order to structure a person's portfolio, it is best to look at risk as objectively as we humanly can.

In terms of risk in investing, there are two factors that should determine the degree of risk in each asset class, and how much risk an investor can afford to take. First, how much volatility is in each asset class? If there is considerable up and down movement in the value of an asset class, especially short term, then naturally it involves higher risk. You should be looking not only at the past data of the asset class to see how much volatility there has been, but also the expectation that there could be more volatility in the future. Within an asset class, high risk can also be present if there are chances that one particular investment may go down in value to zero and never return to its original price.

Second, how soon will you need to take the money out of the investment? If you are in your 40s and won't be tapping into this money for 30-plus years, volatility should not bother you as much;

you have time for asset class cycles to go full circle and recoup any loss. After all, the market typically pays you a premium in the pricing of volatile assets, so you can take advantage of this increased return given sufficient time. On the other hand, if you are going to need to liquidate a specific earmarked investment—for instance, to pay your child's college tuition starting in just five years—you cannot afford to take on too much volatility in this investment and should look to lower volatility asset classes. Another related factor in assessing how much risk or volatility you can stomach is how certain you are about your future income. If you think you could lose your job and worry about not being able to find another good-paying job, you would likely want to keep more of your investments in lower volatility assets. Likely, you should also be curbing your spending level in order to better ensure that if your income level drops, you still will have at least some money available for long-term investing. The longer you don't have to tap into that money, the more volatility or risk you can absorb.

It is through a solid diversification of the different dimensions of risk that we can grow your money over time with less risk. As we will discuss, by mixing the various risk types, your overall risk will be substantially mitigated.

As you and your advisor assess the risks in each asset class and the individual products you are considering, identify the specific areas of risk and estimated volatility in advance. You want to make sure you are being paid in anticipated additional return for this risk, and make sure your advisor knows to investigate the key risk areas for you.

Unfortunately, due to an abundance of regulations and lawyers needing to protect their companies, prospectus information[2] and marketing literature covering the risks of each product have evolved into this "leprechaun's green ribbons" approach. (See sidebar.) Most prospectuses now list virtually all possible risks, with dozens of unlikely risks buried within the few likely risks. The lists of risks are amazingly the same across many different product types; because they name all possible and even improbable risks, it is hard to know where the specific likely risks are in each individual product. It is advantageous for the fund and brokerage companies in covering

THE STORY OF THE LEPRECHAUN: GREEN RIBBONS AND POT OF GOLD

One of the most valuable lessons I've learned comes from an ancient Celtic story. One day, a leprechaun was captured by a giant man right at sunset. The man held the leprechaun down and said, "Tell me where your pot of gold is, or you shall perish now!" Quickly the leprechaun replied, "Come tomorrow morning into the forest and bring a shovel. Look for the tree with the green ribbon tied around it; at the base of the tree dig down six feet and you will find the buried gold." The next morning, the man entered the forest with his shovel—and found hundreds of trees with green ribbons tied around their trunks.

their behinds in case of lawsuits; they can always claim they mentioned this risk in their disclosures. However, it does not always help the customer understand the degree of his risk, nor where he should be looking. (Also, because what an investor is really trying to do is to mix his risks, diversify his risks by type, he needs information on the unique risks of each product, not the "leprechaun name everything" approach. If all products simply list all risks, how can you balance out one product's risks with another's risks?)

It is here that an advisor or a representative can and should help you out. It is their job to simply and briefly tell you what the likely big risks really are.

THE MANY COLORS OF RISK AND HOW TO UTILIZE THEM

My mother learned that low risk can turn into high risk when you concentrate your portfolio into only one asset class. There are many dimensions of risk that can sneak up on a person. Frequently, these individual risks can either cause other risks or be a part of multiple risks. Since risks are in constant flux, also recognize that the types of risk are always growing and morphing rather than static.

How can you parse out the problem of risk assessment and strike a balance with each type of risk so you can feel comfortable you know what you are getting into? Rather than worrying yourself silly, simply divide the risk assessment process into three key risk categories:

1. Risks you expect to be handled by the underlying fund managers
2. Risks your advisor should be catching
3. Risks you personally have to make sure are covered

Category I: Risks Handled by the Underlying Funds[3]

Credit: What is the probability the company or entity you invest in will not pay you back? Here the managers of your bond funds, for instance, are looking for a nice cushion between the debt servicing[4] and the amount of net cash available to pay you back. The bond fund manager is also checking to see how dependable the future earnings of the firms or government entities are. How much can you count on the earnings to be there to pay back your interest and principle on time?

Corporate/country ratings: If one or more public ratings agencies decrease their quality rating of a company, the value of your bond may likely decrease. And it may even be more difficult to sell your bond. Thus, your fund manager in particular must be anticipating what potential factors may cause the entities' credit to suffer a downgrade in their ratings.

Political—Federal, state, local governments and agencies—here and abroad: There are myriad political risk elements in every financial investment the bond and equity managers of your funds make, and you want your advisor to consider them. Even the value of your house depends on the local politics of your community, such as whether they will continue to support good schools and stick to sound fiscal management. Your investment is also dependent on other governments. Just look at the damage done to stocks and bonds of companies where a foreign government nationalized their local subsidiary. During my time as president of Schwab, I found I had to fly more times to Washington, DC, than to New York, just to make sure our company was being correctly reported to politicians and regulators. There are many instances where the value of a company is determined more by political risk assessment rather than economic factors. A capable fund manager is always checking his overall portfolio of stocks or bonds to make sure it does not contain too much exposure to any one political issue or category.

Company stock risk factors: Fund managers of fundamental stock and bond funds[5] are evaluated and paid based on their ability to correctly analyze myriad issues with each company they choose. I am frequently approached by investors who wonder how fund managers can evaluate the management of the individual companies they are considering.

I probably learned the most about what separates world-class fund managers from the rest of the world's stock pickers when I was a corporate officer of various public companies. In that position, I was on the receiving end of fund managers' questions and could see the rare star fund managers' progression in their analysis. Methodically, competent fund managers do a complete financial statement analysis to judge the firm's earnings power, expense management, cash flow analysis, debt burden, and revenue and profit growth; they review all the external factors that could affect the company, notably any regulatory issues.

What separates weak fund managers from the strong ones often comes down to their ability to gain great insights into two areas. They need a deep understanding of the products and the markets in which the target firm is competing, and they need a deep appreciation of the strengths and weaknesses of present management. They recognize that the corporate leadership team can often become prisoners of their group experience. The fund manager must judge if present company management is accurately anticipating future game-changing events that could either help or jeopardize their future earnings.

Other Individual company or stock risks: The better active equity fund managers are quite adept at identifying a variety of key areas of potential risk in each of their target stocks. They pay particular attention to:

- The corporation's management's depth and breadth, viability of their succession plans. Is the company too dependent on just one man?
- The management's ethics profile. Does the corporation operate to sound governance standards?

- Other key dependencies that could put the firm at risk, like a destructive labor union environment or particular vulnerability to one system or product.
- Risks due to capital markets dynamics. Are there potential mergers/acquisitions, or excessive debt service requirements that could negatively impact a company's stock quite suddenly?
- The degree of difficulty regarding the implementation of a company's strategy. Surprisingly, this risk is often overlooked. A good fund manager looks at each company's strategy and execution plan and asks, "What is the probability that they will actually be able to deliver successfully on time?" If the firm scores high in the "degree of difficulty test—due to risks such as "bleeding edge" technology rather than leading edge technology—or high market share gains are required to break even, the firm's stock could get hammered suddenly, and your fund manager should be making sure his/her fund did not pay too much for the stock.

Past performance: Just as you and your advisor should not solely focus on the past three years of fund performance numbers, you expect the managers of your funds to look closely at whether their target companies are also looking beyond a company's recent earnings and are optimally investing in their future. Are the target companies investing sufficiently in the right areas for their future growth and long-term viability? Professor Robert Hayes said it best to my class at Harvard: "A company makes its most profit between the time it stops investing, and it goes broke." So, even if earnings are strong with a company, a fund manager has to look further into the details to make sure earnings are sustainable.

In their final analysis, fund managers can make their own independent judgments on what earnings are really going to be in the future, and what they think the stock price should be. They don't fall in love with a stock. For instance, if they decide to buy a stock because it is undervalued, and then the price rises to a point even beyond their expectations, a disciplined fund manager has no problem selling it. Indeed, some fund managers have the ability to anticipate various markets' competitive dynamics and competing management groups and consistently do a better job buying and selling the stocks of these companies. It is a rare skill, but the best long-term fund managers have shown persistence in picking the right firms at the right times.

Category II: Risks You Expect Your Advisor to Handle

Assuming you decide to select an investment advisor to help you put together your portfolio and recommend what funds to buy, you can then rely on the advisor to perform a variety of risk assessment tasks for you. Below are the areas you should talk to your advisors about, just to make sure they are doing their jobs. Then, you won't have to do the work. Here is where you are expecting your advisors to look at far more than merely past performance.

Review of the fund companies and fund managers: In analyzing various funds and fund managers, your advisor will naturally be looking for funds that have solid reputations as fund managers. Good, thorough advisors also look beyond past performance. They will have a checklist of criteria to review on each actively managed fund manager. *From a risk standpoint, it is more important that your advisor is looking at the downside risk of a manager, rather than only the upside performance potential.* This sounds like the opposite of what you normally hear, but since the evidence[6] shows just how difficult it is to judge who will actually be a long-term outperformer, you have a greater interest in your advisor focusing in on the signals that a particular manager will not crater a fund. Such "at risk" signals you expect your advisor to be looking for are:

Scope creep: This is probably the biggest risk you want your advisor to look out for. In essence, this is when the fund manager goes outside of his fund charter as defined in the prospectus or, without notice, radically changes how he is managing his fund. It is a problem for you for two reasons: One, it may mean that the fund manager is grabbing for straws and doesn't really have a process anymore for finding good companies and is looking any and everywhere for other ideas. Two, your advisor cannot count on this fund manager to stick in one particular area or class of exposure. So inadvertently, you may end up doubling your bet on a particular asset class that you didn't even know about because the fund manager disobeyed his charter and drifted elsewhere in his strategy. Thus, one of your advisor's most important risk jobs in analyzing your fund managers is to stay away from managers known for "scope creep." This may sound like a rare problem, but it has often amazed me how frequently a fund manager thinks he is investing one way, and yet independent fund performance attribution analysis shows he is investing quite differently. I recall a most egregious example years ago in Southeast Asia when I was reviewing quarterly fund results with the fund managers that reported to me. One manager spoke at length of his particular strategy of buying only the largest, safest companies in the country fund he was assigned to manage. I asked my performance attribution specialist to show me the analysis. What had come out of the fund manager's mouth was entirely different than the fund composition of stocks I was looking at. Many fund managers can't evaluate objectively their own fund any more than a mother or father can tell if their baby is cute or not. Your advisor can't rely just on what the fund company is saying but must review independent analysis.

Overconcentration: These are big bets on one or two companies or in one sector. This is a tough one to gauge, as there are examples where you purposely pick a manager that makes certain concentrations of investment in order to give you broader diversity from the standard indices. (See Chapter 13). However, from a downside risk view, your advisor should be checking to make sure the concentration isn't such a major bet that there is a risk the fund could drop substantially in a short period of time, e.g., 30 percent or more.

High volatility: If a fund manager has much broader and more sudden value swings than other managers in his peer group, this may be a danger signal.

Fund company and fund manager changes: I have seen, countless times, a fund management firm that has been dependable for decades, and then a CEO or CIO (Chief Investment Officer) retires or the firm goes up for sale, and suddenly their funds' performance starts to suffer. As to individual fund managers, your advisor should always be looking for signs that the manager may not be spending as much time as he has in the past.

"At risk" funds for closing or merging: Our research described in Part I shows that after ten years, on average at least half of your funds will be shut down. As Dan Kern, the senior advisor at Advisor Partners, says, "Funds seldom if ever shut down for positive reasons for investors." You want your advisor to be looking for the early warning signals. He may recommend that you sell a fund in your portfolio if it is a "likely candidate" for the fund to close in the near future. Such signals for funds at risk include:

- Fund performance is extremely negative and/or substantially worse than their peers.
- The asset class is no longer sexy, and in fact in negative performance territory for a period of years and does not appear to recover.
- The fund company is in reorganization and looking to merge either themselves or their funds.
- The fund manager or team retires, or leaves the firm suddenly.
- The fund size is small, e.g., depending on the asset class, under $60 million could be a concern for your advisor.

I think you can see the value of mixing up your funds across a variety of funds and even fund companies as it decreases your overall risks. That way, if any one fund or fund company's performance deteriorates, it won't have a material effect on your overall portfolio.

Location or geographic risks: The one key risk one has to remember with physical location is that you can't move it. Over the centuries, many people have lost everything because they could not transfer most of their wealth out of an area of rising danger. Normally, these investors could not conceive of such a risk until it was too late. Even if you think it is highly unlikely, it is still best not to have an overconcentration in assets in one governmental jurisdiction that you can't move. Your advisor should step back and look across all your investments to get a rough gauge for how much geographic exposure is contained in your entire portfolio, including your own house. Note that risks like this do not have to be exactly calculated. For instance, it is OK to have 10 percent or 20 percent of your geographic exposure to be in one area, such as a state or city where you live. You just don't want to find out you have an 80 percent investment concentration after an earthquake levels the area, and on top of it, you lose your job.

Interest rate fluctuations: When rates go up, your existing fixed-rate bonds go down. In this case, your advisor should ensure the majority of your funds are not so long in fixed-rate bond maturities that a small interest rate rise could hammer significantly the value of your entire portfolio.

Currency: Historically this was not a major risk to Americans, but with increased globalization and the rising number of products countries buy and sell across borders, and with the high debt of developed countries, all investors now have to consider currency risk—even you are going to stay in the same country through retirement and only spend in your local currency. Dr. Andrew Rudd (chairman and CEO of Advisor Software) said it best: "If your currency is deteriorating, then the cost to you or your future 'Consumption Basket,' all the items you will need to buy, will likely become more expensive." Just think of all the items we buy today that contain a large element of foreign manufacturing: food, building materials, clothes. You will want your advisor to be broadly measuring the magnitude of your overall foreign exchange exposure in your short- and long-term fixed income and equity funds. As you will see in the next chapter, you will want at least some inherent exposure to a broad group of currencies.

How do you judge currency fluctuations, and how they affect your foreign stock and bond holdings? Ned Johnson, the head of Fidelity Investments when I worked there, once said to me about currency exposure, "In the long run, it is all net," meaning that currencies are a zero sum game—one goes up and another goes down, and it is often a waste of your money when your long-term investing funds pay for hedging. If you are investing for decades rather than for months and years, and if your funds paid for currency hedges throughout the decades, the additional cost of those hedges will hammer your returns. Many fund managers like to hedge in order to decrease this short term volatility due to currency movements. But for you, since you are investing for such a long period of time anyway, where possible, you do not want too many funds that absorb the costs of all those short-term hedges. Yet you want your advisor to make sure the currency risk in your overall funds portfolio is spread across a variety of currencies, including a large exposure to your own home currency, or the currency of the location where you will likely retire.

Inflation: This risk can be related to currency deterioration and/or government policies, but it does need to be in a separate category. Given that governments have so much debt, it is in their interest to encourage at least some inflation, but history has shown us it is not always so easy to control. If your investments are so conservative that they aren't keeping up with inflation, you are losing money. Over the decades, I have found it concerning that if people have not experienced in their own lives inflation for 10 or 20 years, they often no longer think it is a risk. However, when inflation rears its ugly head, it can be devastating to a portfolio. Even if you think there will be no inflation in the future, it is still best to build into your portfolio products and asset classes that can be a hedge against inflation. For instance, even though equities and real estate exposure have their own inherent risks, they can act as a means to ameliorate inflation risks.

Deflation: Historically, many countries have not had to worry about deflation. However, Japan could be a precursor to what we may experience in other parts of the world, particularly where the populations are aging rapidly and the productive economy is stagnating or shrinking. Deflation can be even scarier than inflation. Just think if the value of everything you buy decreases. The only item that retains or increases in value is cash. It is another reason why it is prudent to have at least some minority portion of your long-term money remaining in cash and resting in your Savings Pocket, even if you are making no return. It balances out your overall risk profile.

Note that I list inflation and deflation risks contiguously. This is because it illustrates just how positive the risk amelioration is when your advisor makes sure to use such offsetting risks to decrease your overall risk. By buying some funds that have risk exposure to inflation while buying other funds that have risk exposure to deflation, you have balanced them out and thus decreased each risk in total so you will be partially covered in case either event occurs.

Liquidity: Can you sell it quickly? Liquidity is often a risk that is misunderstood, such as when you look at present price levels of a particular asset; you may feel OK as the levels may not have changed much. The real risk here is, What if the number of buyers has been dramatically shrinking and you don't see it in the pricing because sellers are also staying in the wings waiting for movement in the price? Perhaps the biggest risk in owning real estate or low volume trading stocks or bonds is liquidity. When the real estate markets are growing, as they have for most periods the last 25 years, all is well. But when we take a broader perspective on history, there can be severe down-market times in real estate, which can stretch out for years. Even in the postwar US time frame, there were multiple times when people could not sell their house for four to five years, at any price, and in areas where people previously thought prices could never go down. Wise investors and their advisors keep a close eye on liquidity by looking at how broad the spectrum of buyers are for each type of asset they are considering to buy and how easy does the asset trade in various up and down markets. Regarding your financial assets, you also want your advisor periodically checking to see how well each fund manager does in short-term difficult markets when liquidity has dried up. That may be an indicator of how much liquidity risk is inherent in the fund in the event of a severe, long-term downturn.

Demographic: New risks arise from aging populations. Often this risk is ignored; the human race has never experienced the negative effect of a rapidly aging population. In some countries, where the high-consuming 20- to 50-year-old age group is growing, you can expect increasing economic growth. However, you want to talk to your advisor to ensure you don't have most of your money invested in countries where the proportion of the population entering retirement age is increasing.

Commodities: Energy, minerals, precious and semiprecious metals, agriculture—these are all assets that you touch or feel. An airline executive told me a few years ago that when oil goes over $85 a barrel, it is hard for his firm to make any money. This is just one example of why you want your advisor to be looking at the summation of your concentration of commodities risks across all your funds. Are you over concentrated in stocks that are negatively affected by the price of oil, or other commodities? In looking at the details of exposure by each fund's semiannual performance results, an advisor can quickly give you a rough picture of these types of high concentrations. Yes, you want some exposure to commodities, just to decrease the risk in case commodities shoot up in value. But you expect your advisor to keep the overall commodities exposure a minority of your total portfolio exposure. Again, it is about *the balancing of risks to decrease your risk and increase your return.*

Industry or sector deterioration: This covers specific parts of our economy, like financial services, auto manufacturing, and retail. In the above examples, we have covered many risks that can be relevant to an entire industry category, not just one company. As mentioned, you want your advisor to tell you roughly what are the major industries or sector bets you are exposed to across all your funds. You and your advisor don't have to know exactly how much, but simply have a general idea. For instance, are you too exposed to the tech sector, or financials, in your investment portfolio? This is especially dangerous if your profession and all your stock options from your employer are in the same sector. This sector risk can affect more than just your equity funds. For instance, in my money market funds, I noticed that some of the better-performing funds had a heavy exposure to the financial services industry. It makes sense; this industry needs a lot of short-term capital. However, as we learned in 2007 and 2008, this large industry faced collapse. As a result of that crisis, I have chosen funds that do not yield as much, but had lower exposure to the financial services industry. It may be overly cautious, but I wanted to decrease this type of SPOF.

You can work with your advisor to make sure he is looking at these risks and periodically reporting them to you, so you don't have to do the all the risk monitoring work and worry yourself. For many of these risks, you only need to know a general approximation of what portion of your total exposure is in any given risk, and where some of these risks balance or offset one another.

Category III: Risks You Have To Oversee Personally

Your financial institutions: including Banks, Brokerage firms, the fund companies managing the underlying funds, title company, insurance companies, registered investment advisors, and bank custodians. Verifying the safety of all the financial institutions with whom you deal is the one key risk that you cannot afford to delegate. Although you will likely ask your advisor for help, you have to personally oversee the review of the institutions you count on to make sure your money is safe.

When talking about financial products for your Savings Pocket, especially those positioned as "safe" products, it is critical to have the right perspective about the viability of financial institutions in general and brokerage firms specifically. Often, major companies in the financial industry will emphasize their longevity by advertising with phrases like "In business since 1825." What it really can mean is they may have bought a little firm with an old history, but the reality is that the present group is substantially a newer firm. A similar example of how firms try to show their establishment credentials is told about Charles Merrill and Eddie Lynch.[7] In the 1920s they only had a one-room office, but in order to make customers think they were larger and more substantial, they put a sign on the coat-closet door that read "Bookkeeping Department," knowing no one would want to bother to go into such a boring department—and preventing anyone from seeing how small they really were.

It first struck me how tenuous so much of our industry is when I was remodeling my old Victorian house in Wellesley, Massachusetts, during my tenure at Fidelity Investments in the early nineties. During the remodel we discovered a beautiful pocket door plastered over. As I pried open the doors, a newspaper fell out; it was dated 1935. I carefully turned the brittle pages to the business section. On that day in 1935, there was a lot of activity on Wall Street as evidenced by over a dozen 'tombstones" (notices of public offerings for raising capital for specific corporations). As is still done today, brokerage houses and banks were listed prominently in each tombstone. What struck me was how many of those banks and brokers were no longer in existence—and these were the ones that had already survived the 1929 crash. I only knew half the firms because I had started in the industry in 1973. Several names had disappeared due to mergers, and in many of the cases, customers did not lose their money.

Still, the lesson was important for me. Even though you may think an institution has been here for a long time and will be here forever, it may not necessarily be so. It is certainly okay to have your custody done by an institution and even okay to have a large portion of your money left with that firm. But just remember the SPOF rule: In just a year or a decade from now, that institution may not be around, so make sure not to have too much of your money exposed in a product guaranteed by any one financial institution. More recently, I was reminded of this lesson when I pulled a charity-sponsored T-shirt out of my drawer. The Fun Run was in 2007, and many of the biggest global names in financial services were listed on the back of the T-shirt as sponsors. Within a few years, due to the latest financial crisis, one-third of the names were no longer in existence.

In the 40 years since I started working on Wall Street, there have been three notable crisis times: 1974–75, 1987, and 2007–2008. Each time, one or more major institutions disappeared, and a dozen smaller institutions along with them. So it is always worthwhile to talk with your advisor about not being too dependent on the financial health of any one institution. Dig a little deeper than you otherwise would think necessary. For instance, even if the financial institution you trust has billions in capital, how much debt does it have? And in relation to its capital, does it have a lot more debt than other similar institutions? Does your bank or broker make more of its money in riskier businesses, like trading, than its counterparts? It is wise to at least look at an independent broker's stock research on your primary bank and broker for an opinion as to the risk profile of your institution. In financial markets, does this institution have to pay more in interest expense than other similar institutions for its borrowing?

This last point is a key indicator. For instance, if the CDS spread (the cost of insuring against the firm's default) of an institution's debt is widening, this may be a warning for you not to have too much of your money in this institution. Don't let the topic of trading or its acronyms scare you; it is relatively easy for your advisor to let you know key risk signals about the institutions with which you are dealing. Although you can have your advisor make sure the institutions are remaining credit worthy, this is a risk you must inquire about directly with your advisor as it is so critical to the safety of your assets.

An investor visited my office at Nikko AM in Tokyo and saw I had a second door that opened directly into the trading room if needed. "But Tim," he said, "I don't have a trading room next to my office at home! How can I possibly monitor my financial institutions?" I told him there was no need; he could simply ask his advisor to periodically keep an eye on the trading spreads of the debt of the primary institutions he dealt with. By *trading spreads*, I mean the gap between the buying price and the selling price of a financial institution's stocks, bonds, and derivatives. What it means is that if few people want to buy and many people want to sell, then, the gap widens, which is often a bad signal about the health of the institution. Even if you don't fully understand the implications of the spreads, it is still worth asking your advisor to check it out when you are looking at the quality of your financial institution. If it looks to the advisor like the trading markets are acting like the institution may be having financial difficulties, it is likely time for you to act quickly and at least remove a large chunk of your money to another institution.

"But Tim," you may be saying, "I thought you said 'sloth investing' is the way to think—'Don't panic and move your money around too fast in the Investing Pocket.'" There is an exception in the case of watching your primary financial institutions. Given how fast markets can change, how fast the health of even the giant institutions can deteriorate, and how dependent you are on a safe place to conduct your investment activities and keep your account, periodic monitoring and your speed of action can matter.

I did not first mention the ratings agencies' downgrade on your financial institution as a key negative early warning sign—because when an agency lowers the credit rating on a particular institution, it would be better to call it a late warning sign. All too often, these warnings come long after the market has already known of the institution's troubles. Most all published research and ratings, if it has to be put in writing, has to go through a lot of compliance and editing screenings, so the information has been so sanitized by the time it is released that it is old news. It may be worth reading just for further background information, but you can't count on most printed research or ratings to have much value in helping you discover in sufficient time that your institution is in financial trouble.

Frequently, the most out of date news of all is the audited accounting statement. In May 1998, one of the four biggest global auditing firms released the annual statements of a particular major broker/investment bank in Asia, which stated that its net positive capital exceeded approximately $180 million. Within five weeks, the regulator determined that financial situation had deteriorated to such an extent that the net capital had fallen to *minus* $188 million.

What happened? How could a firm's net capital swing from plus to minus, nearly a $400 million swing, in just a matter of weeks? How could the accounting firm make such a blunder? The answer has less to do with the fault of any one accounting firm and more to do with the flawed nature of how the accounting industry applies all its generally accepted accounting principles and decides on a company's value. Don't count on it improving any time soon. The profession does at times help in at least flushing out some problems and in getting most firms to follow accounting standards. But as an early warning signal of any future troubles, it has been my experience that you can't depend solely on a clean audit telling you everything is ok, given how many of the accounting rules are so archaic and backward. I remember one colorful old trader telling me, "There are so many different ways that a bank or a brokerage firm can disguise its true financial health that the audited year end statement can't often give you what's really going on. It's like trying to audit an Old West saloon where there is gambling in the back and the bartenders are pouring the bad booze into expensive booze bottles." And remember the obvious, if your advisor is working for that institution, it will be hard for him to opine on his own company. You will need another third party with no vested interest to help you evaluate what is happening in your advisor's firm. Who could this third party be? Your accountant or another advisor at a separate institution, or your banker at another bank are both great places to inquire. Analysts' reports available from brokers or independent stock research houses cover most of the major institutions. Also, the internet now can be quite helpful in checking out what the experts are saying about a particular financial institution.

But what if you don't have a lot of money to spread around many institutions? I still recommend not having all your money in one broker, or one bank. Even if you only have $50,000 to 100,000 in total to invest, you can still direct at least part of it to a second institution.

In sum, one of the great ironies of managing your risk is that individual risk can be good. After all, it is how you make more money than leaving it in the bank. You get paid in additional return for taking the risk. However, you do want to *make sure that your overall portfolio has spread around its individual risks, many of which will offset one another.* Just like in nature, certain bugs are good for us, and sharks help keep the oceans clean. As we discussed with pairing your deflation and inflation risks and mixing your exposure to currencies, it allows you to decrease your overall risk. It can be advantageous to purchase some riskier products, especially if you are younger than 49, as they have higher long-term growth potential. But you have to work with your advisor to make sure you are receiving additional return for your additional risk. Keep in mind that great southern expression: "The juice ain't worth the squeeze," meaning in this case if you aren't being paid additionally in potential appreciation and current dividend or interest income, the additional risk may not be worth it.

THE LESSONS OF RISK

1. **Risks can come at you from all directions.** Thus, it is critical that you take a methodical approach to reviewing each type of risk covered in your portfolio.
2. **Get help analyzing risk.** Don't worry, you have much help in analyzing your risks, but only if you work closely with your advisors. You can quiz them on the above topics just to see if they are looking at the specific risks outlined above.
3. **Risk is a balancing act.** Risks can balance each other out, so work with your advisor to see, at the level of your whole portfolio, how the risks offset each other or are kept to an acceptable level.

CHAPTER 12

WHAT'S INSIDE YOUR POCKETS?

There are hundreds of asset classes and subclasses, as well as thousands of products that can go into one or more of your Three Pockets. As you can imagine, this section could quickly grow into volumes. There is also a wide range of readers' experience, from those already knowing all the asset class details to those who may not know much at all or have little time or interest. So what do all investors need to remember to make sure their pockets don't end up full of high risk/low return garbage? And from the perspective of advisors, what are the key messages they need to communicate to clients about the major asset categories and products?

CHARACTERISTICS OF THE BASIC ASSET CLASSES

Let me clarify the meaning of *asset classes*. Classes of investible assets can be broad, as in "equities" or "fixed income." Within these broad asset classes, you can also add more specific classes of assets, like "US small company stocks" or "municipal bonds." Sometimes, it is best to call very specific asset classes *subclasses*, e.g., US small company value stocks are a subset of US small company stocks. In this chapter, we will primarily focus in on major asset classes; however, within each major class, be sure you do not over concentrate in just one asset subclass. For instance, if your entire equities asset class worldwide consisted entirely of just US small company stocks, you assuredly would have too much concentration.

Since many people perceive debt or fixed income instruments to be lower risk, let us start with the short-term debt product categories. Often, a product is marketed as "lower risk" when in fact there are hidden risks you should know about. Asset classes and products are constantly being reinvented or renamed by the industry as investment managers look for new ways to find better value for their investors. However, it is important to have a model in your head about the basic asset classes and how they are the core building blocks for your portfolio. (My website, timmccarthy.com, provides investors with the latest details and sequence of asset subclasses by level of perceived risk, maturity, and liquidity.)

Cash and equivalents: Cash is cash, and easy to understand. In a bank it is your current account (often referred to as your checking account) and savings account and often earns either a smidgen or no interest. "Equivalents," though, can be a dangerous word. Above all else, you want to know who is standing behind it. How strong is the institution that is responsible for giving you back your money, and what are their terms? And what specifically happens if they fail?

There are truly low risk liquid products, and then not-so-low-risk and not-so-liquid products. You need to know the true risk level of each product in your portfolio. A good advisor can be especially helpful in this process.

Money market funds (MMFs), certificates of deposit (CDs) from insured banks: An MMF is an open-ended mutual fund that invests in short-term debt securities such as treasury bills and commercial paper (corporations' short term debt). A CD is also a time deposit commonly sold by banks, thrift institutions, and credit unions. Money market funds and CDs are two of the more universal investing options, yet there are pros and cons to each. One of the failures in the modern global financial services industry has been the poor structure of MMFs. They have a fundamental weakness because they do not have any reserve to take the occasional and inevitable losses. When a bank lends money, they can pay back what you have deposited even when someone or some company defaults on a loan because the bank is required to have a reserve built up. And even if the bank eats up that reserve through lending losses, the FDIC, funded by the banking industry, ensures that you are paid back your investment.[1] With an MMF, sadly, the industry never put in a formal structure to build up such reserves, and there is no insurance behind them.[2] This sounds so silly, given that MMFs are supposed to be such a safe instrument. However, there remains an interesting dimension that can make an MMF actually as safe as a bank deposit, especially for more wealthy individuals, as your bank deposits and CDs are only insured up to $ 250,000 per person per bank (the FDIC limit),[3] and you are not technically covered over that limit if the bank fails. Of course, this is an extremely remote risk, but recognize it is an SPOF.

Conversely, by regulation an MMF is secured typically by hundreds of underlying, highly rated (A1-P1)[4] corporations' short-term debt from the highest-rated companies and governmental entities available. So, even if a money market fund loses a small portion of its principal due to the failure of one or some of the short-term paper[5] of those highly rated companies, in almost all cases, it is even more unlikely that most of the other companies and institutions represented in the portfolio would be in trouble as well. Whereas with a bank checking account or CD, after $250,000, technically you are exposed to a single bank's ability to pay you back. So nothing, not even your CDs over $250,000, are ever truly safe. As part of SPOF management, you and your advisor should periodically look at the contents of your MMFs to make sure there is not too much single industry concentration. Ironically, one warning sign, or at least yellow flag, about the quality of your money fund contents is if the yield in your fund is much higher than competing funds. MMFs are all pretty much buying the same paper, so if the yields in one fund are much higher, the fund management company may be taking more risk in your MMF than you would like.

One final comment on your bank and MMF money: It is best to have your "safest" money in a few institutions rather than just one. The risk is not so much that you will lose the money, but rather in a time of an extreme crisis, your institution could be temporarily frozen, and you may have to wait awhile before you can get at it. So, given this issue of liquidity, you have a better chance of getting some cash when you most need it by having a few institutions and money management firms rather than just one.

Other short-term accounts in brokerage companies: This form of short-term parking for your money is popular among clients of large brokers because it often can pay a little more than a money fund. This is because the brokerage firms often wisely use this source of cash to lend on the other side of their balance sheet for margin loans.[6] However, you should recognize that if the brokerage firm gets into trouble, the money you think is so safe is exposed to a single institution and thus riskier than either a bank deposit or a diversified MMF.

Short, Medium, and Long-term Bonds: Short term bond funds are normally less than 2–3 years in duration and hence, do not have significant interest rate risk. Medium-term bonds come with a maturity of 3 to 10 years; while long-term have a maturity of 10 or more years. (Visit my website to learn more about subtypes of the fixed income asset classes on a risk continuum.) Bonds issued by corporations are generally a safer form of investment since you are paid back your interest due and your principal before the equity holders of the corporation. So, although your upside is typically limited (with the exception of convertible bonds and warrants where you have a chance to gain some upside of the underlying stock) as you only get what is obligated to be paid, if the underlying corporation gets into trouble, you, as a debt holder, are paid first. Of course, others will still be in front of you—for example, if something is owed to the IRS or the state payroll tax boards. But at least you will normally be paid in full ahead of equity holders.

Regarding corporate and government bonds, governments are often considered safer, but with less yield for you than corporate bonds. However, given the over borrowing of many government entities, this is no longer automatically true. Indeed, we have seen sovereign debt securities that have to yield higher than quality corporate debt because these companies may have an even better chance of repaying you than the specific government entity. Since state and local bonds frequently have tax advantages if you live in that state, they can get away with paying less interest. Review your tax situation with your tax advisor as well as your financial advisor, as depending on your marginal tax rate, there are times where it does not make economic sense for investors to invest in municipal bonds. Municipalities have failed, so if you buy municipal bonds directly, make sure you or your advisor has reviewed an independent credit analysis.

In the case of corporate debt, high-rated corporate debt is generally safer, but you do want to know who, on your behalf, has looked at each bond to ensure they are high quality. Given how poor the ratings agencies responded in the 2007–2008 meltdown, you should have someone else with no vested interest review the quality of each security, or at least each fund. In the case of an actively managed bond fund, there are teams of corporate credit analysts that have performed this function on behalf of bond fund holders. In particular, in the case of the higher risk bonds, for instance, unrated or low rated bonds and subordinated debt instruments, this category is normally not for the average investor given the complexity of analyzing and understanding the true risk level.

Mortgaged-backed, asset-backed, and other short/long-term secured instruments packaged into funds: Mortgage- or asset-backed securities are investments secured, or collateralized, by the value of an underlying bundle of mortgages or assets. When you buy a secured or asset-backed instrument, you often aren't buying the actual underlying assets. Instead, you are buying a promise by the institution that has structured the investment to be paid the return the asset is expected to receive. Thus, you not only have the risk of the underlying assets to worry about, but also the institution that is standing behind the package of mortgages as well as the third-party servicer. You and your advisor, therefore, have these additional risks to consider.

In addition—in response to investors demanding more current income return while not wanting more equities exposure—the industry has also created a variety of new products packaged under a variety of headings: e.g., exchange traded notes (ETNs), leveraged exchange traded funds (ETFs), special purpose vehicles, and other derivative packages. These are normally only for sophisticated investors. Although some may be okay to invest in, I caution against many of them for the average investor due to the difficulty of ensuring you understand all the risks, and due to the short track record of many of these concepts.

One of the sad facts of the investment industry is that far too often, some products are positioned as safe and liquid and they turn out to be otherwise. This is especially true in low-interest-rate environments where people are anxious to get more yield and don't realize how much more risk is in the product. Here are just a few of the tricks you have to watch out for and ask your advisor about. There have been instances where the industry—both product manufacturers (meaning the investment bankers, traders, investment firms) as well as distributors—do not always communicate the true risk of some of the underlying investments under the umbrella of lower risk asset classes or instruments. Their motivation is to increase profit more by selling simple low risk products with a higher yield than standard low risk MMFs. Other similar examples of products that can contain more risk than you have bargained are numerous.

- *Asset-backed securities funds* have been sold as low risk, yet there is no active secondary market to buy back this product. There may be one broker, the same one that sold you the product, who says they make a market in the securities that you bought. However, if a crisis hits, you cannot count on that broker alone to buy back your product at an acceptable price. Thus, if there is not a broad base of market makers,[7] or an established exchange that makes a market in the underlying securities in this fund, the fund itself is not as low risk or as highly liquid as it is labeled.
- There are *short-term funds*, but in order to give you higher yields, some fund companies also purchase higher credit risk instruments to sweeten the yield of their funds. These products can contain even more risk than buying speculative stocks, yet you may not be receiving enough return for your risk.
- Recently, we have seen products that combine the bonds from one country and, via derivatives, do what is called a *currency overlay* from another currency to get you a higher interest rate.

This tactic is at times used to charge you a higher commission; the combination of the various exposures can mean you could be taking on more dimensions of risk than you had envisioned. A more conservative advisor may wisely recommend that you stay away from investing large portion of your money into such products.

In sum, some of these products and funds may be okay after you complete the analysis with your advisor, but you would be wise not to classify them as Savings Pocket products, even if they are popular. Rather, they are at best Investing Pocket products, and may even belong in your Trading Pocket only.

In your due diligence research, as with anything you buy, you simply want to know, the true risk and liquidity profiles, the total cost of each product, and how much you can realistically expect to earn. For the average retail investor's Savings Pocket, you are much better off sticking to simple-to-understand and highly regulated products, such as a mixture of insured bank deposits and publicly registered MMFs.

Packaging Issues with Bond Products

"Special" high minimum products: For more affluent investors with over a $ 1 million to invest, don't fall into the "you are so special now that you are rich" or "I have a special product that only people like you can buy" traps. These products have high minimum investment requirements in order to qualify. The problem is, you don't want too high of a proportion of your money concentrated in such higher yielding products when you are not sure they are actually low risk. Rich people can get ripped off the most. Buying the justification that it is "elite—for wealthy investors only" can actually be costlier and hide just how risky the products are.

One of the biggest mistakes regulators around the world make is in thinking that requiring a high minimum on riskier products means that only sophisticated people will qualify. Admittedly, there are also minimum total financial net worth requirements and minimum "experience levels" required. But this does not mean that you would be ok to be overly concentrated in such products. There may be nothing wrong with the product, but given its risk profile, maybe you only ought to have 1 percent of your portfolio in this "Product Only for the Rich"; yet the high minimums force you to buy too high of a percentage for your total Investing Pocket. If these "special" products individually represent no more than 1 to 3 percent of your total financial portfolio, fine, but if it is much higher than that, you are better off in a lower minimum product in a more standard asset class, one that doesn't need so much explanation. This tactic of marketing "special" products is also used to flog products in other asset classes as well, so keep such flattery in proper perspective. After all, they may not be so "special" for you.

Sometimes, products sold to you as short term in duration, are not always so "short term." A loan or fund positioned to you as safe because it will be paid back in a day or a week can devolve into you never getting paid back. Even if it is positioned as a very short-term product, it may not be so in a financial crisis. Don't count any product that has daily liquidity as automatically safe. You or your advisor still have to go through all the same analysis steps described in the previous chapter to make sure you understand the risk characteristics of the investment. Unfortunately, just because it is only a short-term investment, it can turn into a permanent loss that is never paid back if you or your advisor decides to skip the due diligence.

Liquidity in times of trouble is more critical than price. Your questions to your advisor should center on the liquidity backups in place for a fund. With each underlying instrument in the fund, who are the liquidity providers or market makers? Is there just one broker that makes a market in buying back this particular investment product? If so, that is likely too much of a risk for you. Conversely, if there are multiple brokers making a market in this type of investment security, or even better, if this investment instrument actually sells on an exchange and you can independently check the price, then the liquidity is likely better and you can sell more easily when you want. You might also want your advisor to check how broad the market volume is in the majority of securities or instruments inside the fund. In times of crisis, what has happened? Was there still an active market where you could sell, even if you didn't like the price?

Or do you not know because it hasn't happened yet with this type of new security? This would likely mean it is a riskier security and may not be worth it even if it does promise a higher return.

If you don't understand any of your advisor's answers, bring in your accountant and see if he understands. If he doesn't feel comfortable, especially for products that are to be placed in your Savings Pocket, then perhaps this product does not really belong there. If it is too complicated, it is not a good sign that you are in a safe product category. As Warren Buffet said, "I don't need to invest in things I don't understand."

When you are buying any product, even a registered public fund, and especially when you are buying privately registered funds, limited partnerships, or direct obligation instruments, you or at least your advisor must know the terms and risk implications in the documentation. It could be the difference between getting paid back or losing it all. If you have any doubts, have an objective third party, like your lawyer or accountant, also review the details.

THE 2007–2008 DEBT CRISIS

In the last few years, I have been frequently asked why the 2007–2008 crisis was so painful and why it took so long for markets to recover. After all, we saw other crises in our lifetimes where liquidity returned more quickly.

The 2007–2008 debt crisis made us question the core structure of our financial system. When a market suddenly determines that stocks are overvalued and the stock market crashes, we can still have a quicker recovery. After all, everyone knows stocks are risky; they go up and down. But bonds are supposed to be different. They aren't supposed to crash and become unsalable for who knows how long; they are supposed to be safer. We depend on them to be the safest part of our portfolio. A crash in the bond markets scares us much more, and it takes much longer for the markets and for investors to emotionally recover.

We also have major national governments with too much debt to service. Investors have long counted on these major countries to be run in a fiscally responsible manner and their debt was typically risk free. If and when another crisis in the debt markets hits again, it also will be quite serious and will take a long time to recover.

The actions you should take to minimize damage to your Investing Pocket are:

- Have a broad mixture of asset classes, especially including equities. Although in debt crises the equities markets also get hit, they tend to recover faster.
- Don't panic and sell off all your bonds and bond funds at the height of the crisis. Although it could take some time to recover, I have observed that so long as the core portfolios of the funds are sound, the bond values in the general, diversified, fixed income portion of the portfolio will come back.
- The Devil's in the details: You can't always trust the labeling of a product implying that it is in a safe asset class as automatically meaning it is in a low risk class. How do you and your advisor safeguard against such misleading labeling?
- Make sure you or your advisor reads the fine print in the prospectus and verifies it with what truly independent sources say about the product and the product category, especially if it is a new and innovative product placed in a safer category.

Ask your advisor the following questions:

- Have you independently verified that inside each debt fund there are not a lot of high risk credits, i.e., overleveraged companies in risk of failing?
- What is the liquidity of these instruments in the fund? Are there multiple market makers of these underlying instruments? Or even better, are these instruments listed on an exchange? Do they have broad trading support to create accurate, independently calculated prices? Is it really a very liquid market for these underlying securities?

EQUITIES

As noted in Chapter 8, equities in general are designed organically to grow. The volatility risk and the chance of losing all your money normally occurs when you buy individual stocks. Companies can, indeed, go broke, and admittedly, individual markets and stock prices can go down and stay down for a long time.

The categories of equities can be quite varied (see my website for complete list the equities sub categories). The important thing to remember is you can further decrease long-term volatility in your portfolio by purchasing a variety of different types of stocks and investing styles. One of your fund managers may focus on value stock picking while another may focus on small-cap weighted growth stocks. Just make sure you don't bet only on one category within equities.

Index versus active managers: One of the big debates in our industry over the past few decades is which is better, buying an index fund or index ETF (an exchange traded fund that trades like a stock on a bona fide public exchange such as the New York Stock Exchange. Each fund contains the specific instruments to ensure exposure to the fund's particular objective). Or is it better to buy an actively managed fund?

Today, index funds and index ETFs cover virtually all the major asset classes. However, it is the equities class that has been the lightning rod in the debates between active versus passive fund management.

Passive or index fund management means that rather than an active fund manager carefully selecting which stocks to buy and sell, the investment management company merely buys either all or a representative sample of the stocks in a particular market, and weights them according to their relative value in the market according to their chosen benchmark or index. That way, you are assured of being able to participate in the growth of the market, but have little chance to outperform or underperform the market.

Advantages to Passive versus Active

- Most portfolios are broadly diversified. From a risk standpoint, you are participating in the entire market across multiple companies and sectors and your fund will not substantially underperform the market or index that you have selected. What you see is what you get. For you and your advisor, you don't have to worry about an active manager changing the investing profile of your fund and thus, ending up more overweight in a style than you expected. The typical index funds track quite closely to the overall market index they are replicating

- Fund operating costs are lower. Transaction activity is quite low, so you will not generate a lot of trading expenses in a fund. Conversely, there are some active funds that generate additional trading costs in excess of one-half of 1 percent, or 50 basis points a year. You don't always see it in the breakdown of costs, for instance in the case of NASDAQ or OTC securities[8]; the trading costs are normally embedded in the net price you pay/receive in transactions. As direct and indirect transaction costs do change periodically, it is always wise to review the comparative full costs of fund alternatives with your advisor.

- The management fees are typically half or more in index funds, as the management company does not have to pay for expensive fund managers. Many index funds and ETFs based off of indices have management fees ranging from 15 to 80 basis points, whereas actively managed equity funds typically range from 80 to over 160 basis points. Depending on the exact structure, which you can verify with your tax advisor, your tax costs can be less.

Advantages to Active over Passive

There are also advantages to having at least some of your equity portion invested in a selection of active managers:

- **Indexing can be just another style.** To understand the value of mixing in some active managers in your overall equities portfolio, it is important to understand the inherent weightings structure of most index funds. Indexing is in reality an investing strategy. In fact, several major stock market indices are weighted and thus, perform similarly to a momentum growth blue chip stock picker's style, meaning the largest stocks in the marketplace have the largest percentage in your portfolio. So, if a major company's stock has a high P/E ratio[9] and is in a high-growth situation, this stock could be weighted more heavily in your selected index fund.

Conversely, your small company value or low priced stocks could have a very lower weighting in your portfolio. Although there are now new index funds to ameliorate this disadvantage, one must simply remember that indexing actually can perform similarly to single active management strategy, for instance, like an actively managed high growth, blue chip stock weighted portfolio. Thus, in the spirit of broad diversification of investing styles, you can also mix in at least a few active managers along with some of the newer categories of index funds.

By definition, when many index funds rebalance, they are buying more stocks that have already gone up in value and selling stocks that have already gone down. Since the goal of fund management is to at least try to do the opposite—buy low and sell high—there is an understandable reluctance of many to invest only in passive management. I should add that there also have been recently a few passive or index managers that have structured their process to minimize this negative effect.

Remember also that index lovers will argue that on average active managers don't outperform index managers, which is true. However, you may get more breadth of investing styles by mixing both active and passive.

- **Some asset subclasses lack a developed, liquid index.**
There are many exposures in the world's stock markets that are attractive but do not yet have a large index or ETF funds to access that exposure or the pricing of individual instruments in that market may be artificial; an active manager can be the only way to ensure a more accurate exposure in certain asset subclasses.

In the more illiquid markets, index funds and ETFs can actually be more risky. This point is seldom talked about in the literature, because in recent years, there have been few crashes in the lower volume exchanges. It is important to remember that although index fund management has existed with few problems over the last 40-plus years, several newer ETFs and esoteric index funds have not been around too long, so we don't know how they will actually perform in an extreme meltdown of more illiquid exchanges. The advantage of active managers is that they are not required to constantly track so closely to an index. If a particular stock has terrible liquidity, the index or ETF could still likely have to buy it. However, the active manager can and often does choose to stay out of any stock that he chooses, in particular illiquid stocks. This flexibility can be advantageous in a volatile market. When active managers get nervous about the stability of a market, they can simply have their fund hold, for instance, 10 percent cash as a cushion for liquidity in case there are a lot of customer redemptions. Yes, it can result in underperformance of your fund versus the index; however, the liquidity of the active fund due to its flexibility can be an attractive attribute of active funds. Of course, you want to make sure the active fund you are investing in at least has a track record of taking such liquidity precautions. It should be also noted that some of the more advanced index and ETF managers are also attempting to mitigate this problem of potential illiquidity in some markets.

- **Certain Asset Classes do better with Active Management.**
  There are some areas where actively managed funds can potentially outperform index funds. For instance, in high yield and Emerging Market bond funds, the top three quartiles of actively managed funds tend to outperform their corresponding index funds.[10] The majority of these active managers have been better able to stay out of the bonds that are especially bad performers.

Selective strategies by some managers have been shown to have long-term persistence in outperforming indices. One of the key disadvantages of many active managers since the early 1990s is that, in order not to end up in the fourth quartile in performance, they have increasingly just mimicked their index or benchmark. They do this because they don't want to risk performing substantially worse than their index and then be fired. On the other hand, since their fees are higher, investors end up losing because the fund is no different than the index, so the funds on average will perform worse than the index due to their higher fees. Plus, as an investor, you didn't get any further diversification. However, a select group of managers has purposely deviated from the mean, often by concentrating their funds into stocks that don't track the market and focusing on selecting a smaller group of stocks. The result is a higher return over time than the index. Dr. Martijn Cremer at Notre Dame University has done some excellent work in following these fund managers and has created an Active Share Index. This index measures the percentage of the fund's weight-adjusted portfolio that differs from its benchmark. Depending on the time frame, this style of fund management has often beaten their benchmarks in excess of 1 percent per year while the "closet index" active funds have typically underperformed their benchmarks by nearly a half a percent.[11] As Sean Stannard-Stockton of Ensemble Capital and other successful Focus Fund style managers have said to me, "By concentrating on just 25 to 30 stocks and absolute return for investors, it frees me up from worrying about the index and trying to constantly manage 100 different stocks." Although it is hard to predict if this trend will continue and naturally, the fund managers have to be proven good stock pickers, it has continued to work for the above managers for over 20 years, though it is not yet being tracked by either Morningstar or Lipper. Most important for investors, this fund style will give your further diversification of styles, unlike a lot of the standard, broadly invested active funds. It should also be noted that the strategy is hard to do for large funds as they will be limited to primarily picking large corporate stocks if they try to run a concentrated portfolio.

Since your number one goal in the Investing Pocket should be broad diversification to increase returns while decreasing risk, carefully constructing with your advisor a combination of both passive and active managers can accomplish this goal while still keeping your overall costs lower than if you went with only active managers. Even if the philosophy of your advisor as well as your own personal preference is to go predominantly with indexing in order to keep your costs down, mixing in a small portion, such as 20–30 percent, of your equity allocation is fine over the lifetime of your portfolio. Just keep in mind that it has been proven in a number of studies that lower cost funds are a larger determinant of better overall performance than other methods.[12]

There's little advantage to you from mediocre active fund managers who merely replicate the index metric they are being measured against, then charge you two or three times more than the passive fund equivalent. It is clear that loading up your portfolio with a lot of expensive funds that are merely "index huggers" or "closet index funds," as they are called, should not get too much allocation in your Investing Pocket.

COMMODITIES

A broad array of specific commodity types can help diversify your commodities exposure. This category generally is divided into three broad categories (visit my website for the detailed list of commodities sub asset categories):

- Metals, both precious, like gold and silver, and industrial, like steel and copper
- Minerals, as in oil, natural gas
- Agriculture, like pork bellies, grain, even forest products

What is critical to understand is that in the case of many commodities, they don't grow in value. Despite what the "gold bugs" advertise, it is best to keep only a small portion of your Investing Pocket in such assets. After all, in the case of gold, it just sits there, and in fact costs you money every day as you have to pay for storage. However, gold and other commodities store value, and in certain markets over your lifetime, they can be an excellent way to diversify your risk. It is wise to spread your commodities investments over more than just gold or oil. For instance, at least in agricultural commodities, they can be sold for consumption. In terms of commodities index funds, you do want to make sure that the fund is not over concentrated in just one or two of these dominant asset types, as they overwhelm the relative valuation in these categories. It will likely ameliorate your risks if you also have some broader exposure in such asset subclasses as silver, timber, food categories, and the like. A good advisor will help you arrive at a more balanced package of commodities exposure.

DERIVATIVES: OPTIONS, FUTURES, SWAPS

Up until now, we have been covering asset classes that have direct exposure to financial or commodity assets. Derivatives in and of themselves are representative of other underlying assets. They derive their value from other asset classes. Options and futures are based off of a particular stock, or stock market or a bond category. In certain instances they can help an investor and a fund manager in obtaining exposure that is otherwise difficult to obtain by buying the direct instruments in an asset class. They also can be used to help you hedge risks. Derivatives run the gamut, from low risk hedging instruments to extremely high risks, as illustrated below.

The confusing part for many investors is that there are so many terminologies used in the derivatives world. And unfortunately, products containing derivatives are often positioned by marketers in the industry to be lower risk than in reality. (As with the other classes, see my website for further detail on derivative products; often these products are not meant for the Investing Pocket.)

Derivatives are like pain killers. They can be extremely helpful in decreasing risk. But they can also be highly volatile and hurt your performance when used incorrectly. The good and bad with derivatives such as options and futures is that they can make an investment safer or riskier depending on how they are placed into a fund. Thus, more than any other asset class component, you or your advisor needs to understand intimately how derivatives are being used in any of your underlying funds. As to using derivatives yourself, they generally do not have a place in the Investing Pocket; it is quite difficult for the average investor to discern the true risk level of each type of derivative, so it is best to view this product category as primarily for the Trading Pocket. For the average investor, it is best to shy away from direct derivative investing completely.

Image 12.1   Continuum of Risk in Derivatives

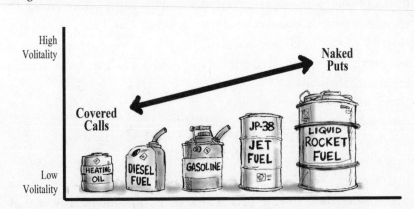

If the prospectus or product definition mentions the use of derivatives, it may be ok as some of the best run major funds in the industry do use derivatives as part of their investing strategy. However, I recommend you ask the following questions of your advisor:

- What is the likelihood of losing much of my principal? How can a loss transpire?
- Is it an OTC derivative? (This is a derivative structured by the broker-dealer rather than a listed option or future sold on a registered exchange.)
- If it is a structured derivative product, is there only one broker committed to making a market in this instrument?
- Is there any scenario where I could lose more than my initial investment?
- How is your advisor and the broker compensated on this product versus other, more standard products, like buying or selling a stock or bond?

For the average retail investor, I generally do not recommend having too much exposure to products that rely solely or primarily on derivatives to enhance your yield. I especially caution you against products that contain customized derivatives, as opposed to listed futures and options. Having a listed exchange behind the underlying options and futures gives you more protection and liquidity as well as a better gauge to measure the true value of what you have purchased.

The beauty of investing today is that most of your underlying funds don't need to apply excess derivatives exposure in order to give you broad diversification in your portfolio. There is already enough diversity of choices available to you without having to purchase products that are so complex even most advisors have trouble deciphering their risk.

INVESTMENT VEHICLES FOR EXPOSURE TO ASSET CLASSES

The advantage of using investment vehicles for exposure to asset classes rather than buying each stock or bond individually is that you can invest less money and yet get the same broader exposure. For instance, for as little as $3,000 in many cases, you can buy a diversified bond or stock fund. Whereas, if you tried to buy the individual stocks or bonds, you would have to invest perhaps over $200,000 to get the same broad exposure. These investment vehicles come in a variety of flavors.

Mutual Funds, Open End

Public mutual funds use different names in each country. In the case of the United States, "40 Act Funds" derive their name from Congress's passage of the Investment Company Act of 1940. This law, with amendments added over the years, has resulted in enough protections for investors that it encouraged people to invest. *Open end* means you can place the order buy or sell at any time, and you will receive a price calculated overnight based on the prices of the underlying securities at the close of the markets at the end of the corresponding trading day—so called forward pricing. This daily pricing of the fund makes these products easy to understand their current value. The disclosure/reporting requirements and daily liquidity, along with other restrictions yet coupled with enough flexibility to adjust to changing markets, all have been major contributors to the growth of investing. Other countries have also introduced and refined their primary public fund vehicles. For instance, in the UK—and through their former colonies around the world, including Hong Kong, Singapore, Australia, and New Zealand—they have adopted their local versions of what are called unit trusts and have met with similar acceptance across a cross section of retail investors. Similarly, in Europe the SICAVs and UCITS funds[13] have attracted millions of retail investors. Thus, for most investing in your Savings and your Investing Pockets, these open end mutual funds that are publicly registered with the SEC and other regulators are the standard investing vehicle of choice.

One risk I should point out is with large, long-existing US public funds. Due to the tax treatment on these funds, you do need to have your advisor review the amount of hidden tax potential liability that can lie within the fund. There can be a scenario where the fund drops suddenly in value right after you buy, and then there are substantial redemptions resulting before the next tax reporting period. The result is that you literally can lose money in the value of the fund and also have to pay taxes due on the fund if high redemptions occur. It is a rare scenario; however, it is a risk inherent in the old and large funds that you and your advisor have to examine. (Note: Morningstar now provides some tax information that offers at least a partial view into this issue.)

Mutual Funds, Closed End

Originally, this type of investing was quite popular and dates back to the nineteenth century. In this structure, the fund is listed on an exchange and sells just like any other stock. Since the fund is closed or the total amount of money inside of the fund to invest is fixed, the price is simply based off the supply and demand for the fund. Thus, even if the stocks inside the fund are worth $100 million, the fund may be only valued on the exchange at $95 million or at a discount from its liquidation value. Conversely, there have been times when some closed end funds actually sold at a premium, for instance, if the underlying securities were difficult to buy on their own. However, due to the fact that the fund structure is closed, many of these closed end funds do sell at a discount, which has negatively affected their popularity especially when they are initially offered. Given the rise of open end funds, closed end funds have become less popular.

Exchange Traded Funds (ETFs)

Ironically, ETFs are actually similar to closed end funds in that they are also registered on a bona fide exchange, except that they are open to buy and sell and fluctuate in size every day. They typically sell at a price similar to the underlying securities inside of the ETF. They have become popular because they are so easy to trade and normally reflect the exposure to a particular market they are replicating. Since they trade like a stock, the transaction costs are often minimal, and the ongoing management fees have been fixed to a low level to attract customers. This favorable pricing has also fueled the explosion in demand.

However, there is a risk not often discussed that does lie with the less liquid ETFs and those ETFs that employ leverage, particularly in markets where the underlying liquidity could dry up quickly. To date, there have not been any disasters; after all, ETFs are relatively new. However, when you buy ETFs in, for instance, some narrowly traded emerging markets, a significant gap could happen quickly between the price and liquidity of the ETF and the price of the underlying stocks. This gap can occur in spite of arbitrage activities in the case of troubled markets. Thus, in some of these low liquidity, high volatility markets, an open end actively managed mutual fund may be a better or safer way to obtain the exposure you desire.

Outside of these exceptions, ETFs have become popular for good reason. They garner exposure to a variety of larger, more liquid asset classes and they are so cost efficient.

Private Placement Funds

Normally such funds are not sold to the public as they do not have the same strict disclosure and other restrictions on them that are on publicly registered funds. For that reason, I generally recommend they not be a large part of your Investing Pocket, even if you are given an opportunity to invest in them. However, for more affluent investors, these funds may have a place in the Trading Pocket.

Real Estate–Direct Ownership

Real estate comes in many forms, not just in owning your own home. There are many advantages to buying your own home and taking advantage of tax considerations and the possible long-term appreciation. After all, you have to live somewhere; you might as well have your abode double as an investment. However, it should not be included as a part of your Investment Pocket, given the concentration of risk and times of illiquidity.

Home ownership has been great for many, including myself, for decades now. But going forward there are some concerns about overinvesting and overleveraging in your own house:

- Weak demographics may limit types of real estate in certain areas that will increase in the future.
- When you own a home, you have both high geographic, even local concentration and high liquidity risk. So, if your biggest

asset is your own home, you need to build up other unrelated asset classes in your Investing Pocket as soon as you can.

Real Estate Investment Trusts (REITs) and Funds of REITs

A real estate investment trust, is a company that owns and operates income-generating real estate assets. In addition to owning your own home or renting out properties you may own, REITs can be an excellent way to get exposure to investment oriented real estate without the concentrated geographic and investment risk of buying the real estate directly. And even better for the average retail investor, REIT funds give you a broad diversification across, for instance, hundreds of buildings located in dozens of states and countries. Their risk profile varies greatly, from speculative property and development funds carrying considerable risk but higher target returns, to REITS containing only existing, already leased high quality buildings, making them lower risk but still able to yield a return that can be higher than bonds. Because of the growth in variety of the various REITs and REIT funds, even small retail investors can now garner domestic and global real estate exposure and yet still have liquidity, meaning you can generally buy and sell the REITs much easier and more quickly than if you own the real estate directly.

Annuities/Investment-Oriented Life Insurance Products

This category mixes underlying asset classes in with a life insurance component. Annuities are often considered separately from life insurance as you are primarily receiving a return during your lifetime. The attractiveness of these products is that they often sell you on a guaranteed capital return, though not always in the case of the variable return products. In addition, the insurance industry worldwide over the past century has done an excellent lobbying job with their related governments. They have been able to secure tax advantages in their products that are not available in standard mutual funds. Unfortunately, a lot of the tax advantages intended for customers are eaten up in additional fees charged by the insurance industry over and above what people would pay for a fund. Insurance has a place in most every family's overall financial plan, especially when the bread winner has a family to support while he is working. However, in several countries, there clearly have been more insurance products sold than is needed in a financial plan. Back when there were few products available to affect proper diversity, the insurance products did provide more of a role. But in today's world, an investor has more choices and does not need a large amount of this category in his Investing Pocket.

When evaluating this category, make sure to consider all the fees you will pay, that liquidity is limited without a further discount, and the investment returns net of fees have been typically mediocre, when compared to open end mutual funds. Regarding the guarantee products, this guarantee actually ends up costing you a considerable sum of money each year when all costs are considered. Conversely, if you invest your own money in a non-guaranteed diversified portfolio of funds over your lifetime, you will be able to earn your money back with high certainty, so why lose the additional embedded cost of 1.5 to 2 percent to the insurance companies each year when you don't have to? They can guarantee your return when the payout is so far away, but you can in effect do that yourself by investing and holding a broad variety of asset classes for the long term. In the final analysis, having a small portion of your total investment money in in this category may be fine. In particular, an experienced financial advisor can find certain annuities that may fit well into your specific financial plan when taxes are considered. In these cases, it is important to comparison shop by looking at the prices of what the full service insurance brokerage companies charge on these plans versus the discount brokerage firms, just so you know what you are paying. In the final analysis, more than 10 to 15 percent of your total Investing Pocket in such products can start to be an unnecessary drain to your overall long term return.

ALTERNATIVES ASSET CLASSES

Of all the categories, Alternatives can mean very different things to different experts. Some advisors look at alternatives in a narrower manner, defining them under: Hedge Funds, Venture Capital and Private Funds only. Other advisors view Alternatives as a broader category also covering: Real Estate, Commodities, even art and collectibles, as well as various types of limited and master limited partnership structures. Thus, it is difficult to say that the entire broadly defined category is either good or bad for your portfolio or how much you should have in Alternatives as it depends so much on the definition you use.

Furthermore, the Alternatives category can contain the same underlying asset types as in the traditional stock and bond asset classes. In these cases, your advisor has to consider any overlap of exposures from the Alternative category into assessing the level of exposure you have in each asset class.

Since we have already covered the major asset classes above, let us here focus on the narrower sub categories of Alternatives not yet defined.

Alternative Investments: Hedge Funds/Venture Capital and Private Equity Funds

In this category, money managers have the advantage of minimal restrictions under their limited partnership agreements with investors. Depending on the details of the agreement, they are allowed to invest in private companies, start-ups, and, in the case of hedge funds, a variety of listed and structured derivative products as well. These alternative investment vehicles are primarily for accredited investors, high net worth individuals and institutional investors that meet the regulator-determined set criteria of considerable financial resources and investing experience. There are specific minimum requirements by the regulators to limit small and inexperienced investors from buying such structures. Also, the minimum investing size is often quite large, in excess of $500,000, so it is above most investors' advisable limits for a single investment. Recently, there are public funds being introduced that have funds in this category as the underlying investments. This allows access for the retail investor to participate in these different styles of investing. However, the total amount of fees can be quite high, and the liquidity can be limited as well. Normally, when accredited investors buy into this category, their money is tied up for a decade or more.

Managers in this sub category often claim their funds are an excellent way to further diversify your investment because their

Table 12.1   Correlation Among Asset Classes, and Annual Returns and Volatility of Major Asset Classes, May 2008 to May 2013

Correlation Among Asset Classes						
	S&P 500	S&P P/E Index	Hedge funds	VC	Annual returns	Volatility
S&P 500	1.00	0.91	0.87	0.97	3.3%	18.7%
S&P P/E		1.00	0.84	0.87	-4.0%	36.2%
Hedge funds			1.00	0.87	3.6%	8.5%
VC				1.00	-1.4%	29.6%

Source: S&P 500, iShares, S&P P/E index, HFRI, Dow Jones VC Index

funds do not to correlate with standard public asset classes. However, research has recently shown this claim may not be always true.[14]

Note that there are times when certain Alternatives can co-vary closely with the standard asset classes, recognizing that the above table is only for a short period of time.

Yet the hedge funds and VC structures definitely cost you more, with fees ranging from 1.5 to 2.0 percent annual management fees, plus 15 to 20 percent of the upside gain in the fund going to the managers. Also, this structure of paying the fund manager an additional performance fee can encourage more risk taking than is in the more standard funds as the risk/reward is quite asymmetrical in favor of the fund manager, meaning if there is a gain, the manager gets 20 percent of it; if there is a loss, the manager does not directly share in that loss. Also, the survivor bias in this category is quite large. You simply do not find out how many of the management's previous funds were not successful.

To top it off, although hedge fund managers often profess to be able to earn considerably more than more stable, boring public funds, our own analysis and the research on this category does not back up these claims. Given how much money has poured into this category, I would be surprised if this overall category on average does not underperform over the next decade when additional fees are considered. This is especially true of fund of funds, which are funds that contain only other funds, given that they have underperformed in good years and yet still suffered in bad years. The additional fees eat up any of the advantages.

Despite these disadvantages, I can understand why accredited or large investors may still like a portion of their overall portfolio in this category. In the future, there may be at least some non-correlation with certain alternative funds versus public funds and other traditional money management investment choices, which could give you further diversification. However, the excess fees will more often than not eat up the excess returns that the funds promise. Given its extra costs, and its illiquidity even for accredited investors, this category should represent a small portion of their total investment. Any more than 5 or 10 percent should really be classified as a Trading Pocket investment.

OTHER FUND VEHICLES

Limited Partnerships (LPs) and Master Limited Partnerships (MLPs)

Limited partnership vehicles are available only to qualified investors to invest in a range of asset classes. On average over the decades, I have seen more fees paid and heard more stories about money being lost here than in many other categories. Even when these LPs have paid back a return plus capital to investors, often an investor would have made no more money than if he/she were in more liquid and lower fee products. Even though there are tax advantages, when you look at who benefitted on your tax advantage, the product makers took a lot of that advantage in their additional fees. In these products, it is especially important to see who is advising you to buy these products and how exactly he is compensated. Since the industry makes so much more on these products, you don't have to think hard about why a salesman could be aggressively pitching such products.

There have been good LPs sold in the past; particularly, some knowledgeable, affluent investors have made a good after-tax return from some LPs. Still, they are often products that belong in the Trading Pocket for sophisticated investors, given their lack of liquidity (often no viable option to sell less than ten years) and their complexities.

Over the last 20 years, the industry, notably via publicly traded energy firms, has also developed master limited partnerships

(MLPs), which have become popular with even the average investor given their attractive high yields. Although they have worked well for many investors, the recent high valuations and the concern about quality deterioration with some newer MLPs means you should exercise a degree of caution with them, despite the high yields. I don't suggest keeping too high a proportion of your total portfolio committed to this category. Work closely with your independent advisor on the due diligence before considering a purchase. In addition, as of this printing, there are certain tax advantages, for instance, to MLPs wrapped inside of Exchange Traded Notes (ETNs) which could be quite attractive. However, given how frequently the tax code and interpretations are changing, it is best each year to check with your tax advisor to make sure you understand the current tax treatment of each investment vehicle in your portfolio.

Target Date Funds

Target date funds are like mutual funds in the hybrid category that keeps on changing the asset mix (stocks, fixed income, cash equivalents) in its portfolio according to a selected time frame that is appropriate for a particular investor—usually retirement and other major life events. They are often ideal products in IRAs and 401ks, given their long term nature. These funds have the attractiveness of adjusting their risk profile as you age from a more growth oriented portfolio to a more stable and income oriented portfolio. You do need to learn just how much and at what times they adjust the equity/fixed income proportions as funds do vary. Also, you want to take these proportions into consideration when analyzing your entire portfolio. In general, these funds can lessen the task each year for you and your advisor in annually decreasing the risk level of the portfolio as you age. They are especially attractive for small investors that can't afford an advisor, as the fund does the rebalancing for them. Although these are important advantages, it is important for investors to still review the fund up front and ongoing to make sure it operates as you intend. Also, although several of these funds have acceptable levels of fees, some of these fund types have been known to be excessive in their fee structure. Thus, the overall fee structure—management fees, upfront sales charges, and ongoing selling fees—should be compared with similar standard mutual funds in the same category.

Unit Investment Trusts (UITs) or Closed End Bond Funds

Although not as popular as before, these are closed funds where, up front, a fund company places a particular group of similar long-term bonds into a fund structure and markets them as a fixed maturity fund. As the fund matures, your interest rate risk declines as the individual bonds get close to maturity. It also has the advantage of spreading your individual bond risk across multiple bonds. On the other hand, they have lost some of their appeal, because if you have to sell out before maturity, you can lose in the discount on the fund.

Wrap Accounts

As mentioned before, these accounts were launched by major brokerage firms in response to customer and individual broker demand for a program that does not entice brokers to trade in your account. Simply, the customer pays an annual fee to the broker for the account, plus the fund management charges that go to the fund company, and that is all. Each time the broker and the customer decide to change a position, there is no charge. Because many investors like that they are on the same side of the table with their brokers in terms of recommendations—as the broker and the brokerage company are paid the same, irrespective of trading frequency—this account structure has grown considerably over the past 25 years. The one word of caution is that investors should still look at the underlying fees in each fund to make sure they are similar to other public funds available. Fortunately, most of the major brokers have a wide variety of choices for funds, so it should not be hard for the broker-advisor to help the investor select a favorable fund.

Another attraction to this kind of account form is that unlike fund of funds, the investor and the broker-advisor can customize per their and your personal preferences.

There are two popular forms of wrap accounts:

1. **Separately managed accounts:** In these accounts, rather than consisting of mutual funds inside the wrap account, the investor and the broker select a money manager together. In this case, the individual securities are bought and sold directly inside the customer wrap account, so there are no fund management administrative charges. This form of wrap has some advantages in that overall fees can be lower, and the account in certain instances can give you more flexibility in that with some accounts, you can restrict what types of stocks you do not prefer. You are protected from fraud as the broker and money manager only have limited trading authority; they can't transfer any money from the account without your advance instructions, and you will also independently see every trade when you receive the brokerage company's trading confirmations. Still, as with any account, you must monitor the account and check the references of both the broker and the money manager.

2. **Mutual fund wraps:** In this type of account structure, the underlying instruments inside the fund are mutual funds rather than individual securities. The advantage to a customer is the additional security of knowing that underlying assets are publicly registered funds that must operate under the regulations of the 40 Act. The disadvantage is that the fees can be a little higher due to this multiple entity structure, and you have no ability to customize each fund.

Do It Yourself (DIY)

Naturally, there are investors out there who like to do all their own stock and/or bond picking. In and of itself, there is nothing wrong with this process. It has the advantage of limiting your cost, as you can use a discount broker and you don't pay the additional cost of an advisor in order to keep your overall costs to a minimum. This type of investing can even be considered to be in the Investing Pocket rather than only in the Trading Pocket, assuming the DIY activity is a small percentage of the total pocket and your investing portion is truly diversified across many sectors. *However, you should look at yourself as merely one of many managers you utilize inside the Investing Pocket.* That is why, often, a DIY money manager (or his/ her spouse) looks at the DIY portion as classified inside the Trading Pocket; this way, the family does not put too much money at concentrated risk and looks at outside money managers as receiving the bulk of their investment money.

CONSTRUCTING YOUR PORTFOLIO?

After you have decided the total target amount of money to put to work in each asset class, your next step is to decide what investment vehicles to buy. You and your advisor should exercise a certain level of care when selecting individual funds and other products to construct your overall portfolio for two reasons:

1. **Inadvertent overconcentration:** Just like the mistake my doctor friend made, if you simply slap a lot of funds together and do no analysis as to what is contained in each fund, you could end up not so diversified. You want your advisor to do the extra analysis across your portfolio of funds to see what your exposure is to specific asset classes across the variety of funds you own.

2. **Sloppy product selection:** Sadly, I have often heard from advisors who inherited an account from a novice or uncaring broker who had rightly told the customer that they should be broadly diversified. But the broker-advisor then simply threw a lot of mediocre products with high fees into the portfolio and said, "Don't worry, you are diversified." The customer ended up with a lot of poor-performing, overpriced products. This example is similar to what caused the 2008 mortgage-backed subprime crisis. Salesmen and bankers and ratings agencies all said, "Don't worry; the portfolios of mortgage-backed securities are broadly diversified." Yet many of the loans in certain portfolios were terrible. If I take a different can of garbage from each major city in the world, I will then

have a well-diversified mountain of garbage. No matter how diversified it is, it is still garbage! The same goes with the product selection: You have to put a certain amount of care into what you put into your portfolio. You don't have to be perfect at it, but equally, you don't want to take the selection process for granted.

The Basic Fund Criteria Used by Investors and Their Advisors

When evaluating index funds for your portfolio, there are a few issues you want to consider:

- There is a "Goldilocks" dimension to choosing index funds of the right size: not too small, not too large. Depending on the asset class, you don't want to buy the smallest funds available in this class, because there are scale advantages to building an index fund that can make a small fund too costly. Also, small index funds and ETFs do run the risk of being shut down in the near future. Conversely, the largest index fund in the asset class may be so large that it is difficult for the fund to sell out positions as they are so large, selling each position in the fund can actually move the market and negatively affect the price. More importantly, the older, giant index funds can have a large portion of unrealized tax gains that you could get stuck with. A good advisor can help you decide which funds would not have large, unrealized tax gains.
- Buying index funds from investment companies that are among the larger firms managing indices can be advantageous for you. Experience in the entire process of running index funds can result in lower costs and safer operations, which benefits you.
- When evaluating ETFs, likewise stay away from the smallest and in some cases, the largest funds and ETF management companies—though there can be exceptions to this guideline that your advisor can help you with. Liquidity of the ETF, i.e., how large is the daily trading volume, is important if and when you want to sell; the more liquidity the better if you want to sell all of your position quickly.

In both ETFs and index funds, as with all active funds, the funds expense is a major factor. There are certain index funds that are simply priced too high relative to the standard funds available in the market place, so make sure your advisor explains why each particular fund is the best value for you. It is also worth a little time to independently check on internet sites the various costs of each fund, just to make sure you are hearing the whole truth.

For the active management of your portfolio, how do you and your advisor evaluate which companies and which funds to buy? Most of the criteria for selection of active funds was covered in the risk and product definition chapters. Later on, I will list the detailed questions you can ask your advisor about his selection process, just to make sure he is doing proper due diligence. Next, we will examine how to incorporate international options into your overall portfolio to help you further decrease risk and increase your return.

THE LESSONS UNIQUE TO DEBT

1. **Bonds and bond funds on average can be safer, but not always.** Make sure you or your advisor examines the details.
2. **Bonds don't rise much more than inflation at best.**
3. **Bonds and bond funds are great tools for diversifying a portfolio and for ensuring current income.**

THE LESSONS FOR ALL PRODUCTS INCLUDING EQUITIES

1. **Diversification is now easier.** Using diversification to decrease risk was not easily accomplished in decades past due to the limited availability of product choices. Now, it is relatively easy, even for the average retail investor, to find a variety of active and passive products to accomplish the attractive broad exposure needed to keep risk at bay.
2. **Understand the pros and cons** of each asset class and product vehicle you use to purchase such exposure. Utilizing index funds and ETFs are beneficial to keeping your costs

low. You and your advisor still have to analyze each product and its contents to make sure you understand all the likely risks and costs.

3. **Don't over focus on trying to pick the best funds.** It is quite difficult to anticipate which funds will do the best. Instead, spend more time on getting the overall mix of asset classes right.

CHAPTER 13

BEYOND BORDERS

Understanding How to Invest in International Markets

The world has gone global, but how global is your portfolio? The last step before learning how to construct your financial life plan is becoming comfortable with how the new global dimensions of investing can fit into your portfolio.

The Three Pockets approach of using diversification and time works so well for the safe investor for two key reasons. First, countries have emerged out of the undeveloped stage and are now viable economically. Through most of the twentieth century, all we really had to choose from for a chance for reasonably safe, long-term growth was the United States, Canada, Western Europe, and Japan. In the twenty-first century, we can add 20 to 30 more countries, depending on various criteria, that have reached a critical mass of minimum acceptable investment standards. The diversity of these new countries makes them extremely attractive from a standpoint of decreasing risk. They are spread across the world and often are not dependent on the same economic forces at the same time. The range of opportunities in the last two decades has exploded. Their diversity now represents:

- Virtually every continent in the world.

- More countries have now received a decent credit rating meaning they can obtain even more capital for accelerating their growth. Of course, these countries will need to stay on the right track and continue to use newly available money for properly growing their economies. However, for cautious investors, it now means they can augment their bond portfolios with bonds from selected growth countries that often yield better than in the United States, Japan, and Europe.
- A package of several growth countries also covers many categories of commodities, from scarce minerals to foodstuffs to energy. And they now have the capability to access the expertise, technology, and capital to exploit these resources.
- Larger and younger demographic growth countries that have a supply of inexpensive and flexible labor.
- A large base of skilled and educated labor. These growth countries can now produce a myriad of globally competitive products and services.
- The emergence of the network age means many countries can now be competitive in technology-oriented services that in the last century were not possible. The velocity of information and ideas and even education allows countries to become globally competitive much quicker than last century.
- Large populations that have entered the consumer stage and can be attractive markets for mature developed countries' products and services.

Another key reason is that dramatic growth of a variety of investment products are now readily available to anyone. This dramatic growth has only begun to take advantage of the opportunities. Just 20 years ago, retail investors rarely had cost-competitive access to fund managers that were able to take advantage of such innovations as:

- A continuing global convergence of regulatory, corporate governance, securities exchange, and accounting rules that allow for more accurate assessments of each country's progress and global comparative status.

- Refined indices that gave growth to ubiquitous benchmarks, index funds, and ETFs covering individual countries, regions, and global growth country themes.
- Quality information on each country covering macro statistics, more consistent and professional individual company accounting, publicly accessible financial news, and other information enabling both fundamental and quantitative style[1] fund managers to access global information on all the growth countries at the click of a mouse.
- Hundreds of active fund management firms, many with local offices spread throughout the growth countries, that can now analyze each company, governmental entity, and other local factors on sight. Equally important, many of the analysts and executives are from these countries and have been educated by global universities and companies.
- Global corporate and government bond funds that only a decade ago did not have the supply of creditworthy bonds from which to choose. In addition, regional and global infrastructure funds have now given growth countries further access to capital to address key roadblocks to further advancement in an economically disciplined manner.
- Global specialty products such as REIT funds and funds of REITs, allowing investors to obtain real estate exposure across the globe—not be limited to the United States or Europe. Investors can even choose the risk profile that fits their particular needs, for instance, REITs investing primarily in AA-quality and above residential apartments, or commercial buildings in Asia or in Latin America.

But why have so many Western investors and even advisors still not adjusted their approaches to more actively include growth countries into their overall portfolios? For me, my personal encounters opened my eyes to the new global opportunities for investors.

RISK, LIKE BEAUTY, IS IN THE EYE OF THE BEHOLDER

Back in the mid-nineties, the US stock market was on a fundamental and historical value basis, among the most attractive it had been in a long time. The earnings growth of many companies had been substantial, and yet their stocks prices were quite reasonable. On a relative basis, given that the Dow was only around 3,000, the United States looked like a good place for sophisticated, affluent Asian investors to have at least a small portion of the total investment pool. Yet it was a surprisingly difficult sale to wealthy investors in Asia, especially versus other fund ideas. I asked one very smart, wealthy Malaysian investor why he owned no stock or bond funds with American exposure. He rubbed his chin for a while and finally mumbled, "Those big American companies like GE, IBM, and Ford have been doing well for a long time already. How do I know they can continue? And they are so far away, whereas I pass this canning company on my way to work in Kuala Lumpur. Every day I see them; they are growing. I know them. It is much safer to buy their stock."

You can see it is not just in America and Europe that familiarity with an investment is often what makes people feel more comfortable with risk. Naturally, any investor not intimately familiar with what is going on in countries that are 6,000 miles away may consider such a stock or a bond more risk than the investment deserves.

BREAKING ROCKS

Around that same time, I spent a few days in Shanghai investigating the practices on the Shanghai Stock Exchange. During my tenure as CEO of Jardine Fleming Unit Trust, we used this exchange for much of our trading in China; I wanted to make sure we understood business practices, trading and clearing operations, and compliance standards. At the end of this trip, I went to dinner with the vice chairman of the exchange. We had gotten to know each other quite well over the past year, so I felt comfortable drilling him with detailed questions about the specific practices and monitoring techniques of the exchange to identify trading infractions. At the end of dinner, and after a few bottles of Shaoshing wine, he looked up at me and said, "Look, Tim, all these technical questions you have been asking me the past two days, the truth is I don't know half of what you are talking about!" He then looked around to make sure no one was listening and then exclaimed, "While you were getting your MBA at Harvard and training on Wall Street all throughout your 20s, I spent 12 years breaking rocks in Manchuria on a comrade work team to build roads! I didn't start my formal education until I was in my late 30s. And most of my colleagues are in the same predicament. It is going to take us a long time before we can meet your standards."

I contrast this story with a trip just seven years ago, to the same exchange, meeting with a new and younger man having the same title, vice chairman of the Shanghai Stock Exchange. I could quickly tell this man knew what he was talking about in how to run a globally competitive exchange in terms of the complicated trading rules and compliance. Later over lunch, I asked him about his background. He had received his MBA in the United States and interned at Goldman Sachs before coming back to China. Throughout the last decade, I heard many similar stories from regulators as well as senior company executives in China, India, Brazil, and Indonesia. In less than 15 years, throughout the growth countries, many of their top institutions and corporations added highly skilled executives that can compete with the best of Western talent. After all, they were often trained by the "Best in the West." Unlike the nineteenth and early twentieth centuries, when England, Europe, and the United States were progressing into the industrial age, the global immigrant working population is now quite mobile and working for firms all over the world. And a much larger segment than before arrives on our shores with better educations from their home countries. This constant ebb and flow of talent across the globe has resulted in a transfer of information and expertise at a speed never seen before. Yet for many retail investors in the West, their image of these now powerful growth countries still remains one of legions of poor workers breaking rocks to make a road. Although their progress is far from over, as a whole, many of these growth countries are now at an investible stage.

It is not surprising so many retail investors still have a bias against investing little or nothing into growth countries. Even many Western analysts have often missed this global economic revolution. Since 2000, I have closely followed what the average reporter and even the global stock analysts say about many emerging markets. From the beginning, most all I heard from pundits were various combinations of "China is never going to make so long as it is communist. You can't trust 'em," or, "This recent growth in the emerging markets is just a temporary thing. Their governments are weak and will undoubtedly collapse."

Over the last five years, I have continued to hear: "Yeah, China has grown, but now they are due for a massive correction"; "The violence and these corrupt dictatorships are so bad it is still too dangerous to even consider any of these countries."

Given the amount of bad news on average we in the West have received over the past decade, if you told the typical educated American that in the year 2000, Brazil, Russia, India, and China, known as the BRICs countries combined represented 3 percent of the world's GDP. Then, asked them what does the combined GDP of the four countries represent today as percent of global GDP?

Over the past year, I have asked Americans and Brits this question on several occasions. The range of answers I typically get is between 5 and 10 percent. Just for fun, cover up the next paragraph in the book and take a guess.

Now, uncover the answer.

Today, the BRICs countries alone represent roughly 20 percent of the world's GDP. Never in history have we seen such a rapid economic and social revolution.[2] Three billion people moved from next to nothing in global output to more than one-fifth of the world's production. Going forward, the more "country neutral" global investment analysts are seeing that BRICs countries will continue to grow as a group—likely more than the United States, Europe, and Japan group. Furthermore, the next 11 to 15 growth countries after the BRICs will likely grow even faster.

The projections from leading financial institutions over the next five years, and others, are projecting within the next ten years that growth countries actually represent the majority of global growth. Even with any modification of these projections, the category of 20 growth countries has become too important to ignore.

Let's step back and think about any variety of sample portfolios. If you are told there is a group of asset classes that will likely garner 60 percent of the world's growth for the next two decades, would you think that having only zero to 5 percent of your money

Fig. 13.1 Emerging Markets' GDP and Market Capitalization Forecast (to 2030)*

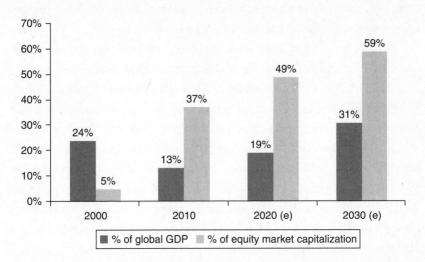

Source: IMF, MSCI, Goldman Sachs Global ECS Research estimates (Equity market capitalization is based on percentage of MSCI All Country World Index.)

* The emerging markets (EM) sector is too important and too powerful for the average investor in the West to continue to miss out on.

in that portion of asset classes would make any sense? It would actually be a risk to your portfolio to leave out that group of asset classes. Yet that is exactly how the majority of retail investors view the emerging market. It is time to change that strategy.

Interestingly, many institutions realize this change and are taking advantage of it. Greg Ryan, an experienced executive at a major financial institution, recently told me what he frequently hears from the more sophisticated institutional investors. "It used to be that we all compared ourselves in terms of performance to the S&P 500. Now we know better; we spend much more time looking at how we are doing versus the MSCI World and FTSE global indices.[3] Many institutional investors recognize that they can't get sufficient yet steady growth from just investing in the United States, and many realize that they need more exposure to the emerging markets (EM) countries. Yet still today, many institutions are underweight EM countries. And in the case of retail investors, we have still not seen as pronounced a shift to global and EM investing.

If you are in your 40s or early 50s, and if you would like to find a path to safely grow more than merely 2 or 3 percent a year over inflation in your combined portfolio, it will be difficult to grow your portfolio safely over the next three or four decades without increasing your weighting of growth countries.

It is natural that the news we hear on the corruption in EM countries versus industrialized countries would scare the majority of investors. However, the financial services industry and the media have not done a good job in separating the more investible countries from the dangerous countries in the EM world. Higher quality, advanced-growth nations are lumped in with the poorest nations, at times in anarchy. Singapore and Taiwan really have little in common in terms of investment risk with Syria and Chad. Yet Singapore and Taiwan are erroneously considered by some to be EM countries and lumped in with Syria and Chad. If an investor is to become comfortable investing in countries other than the United States, in Europe, and Japan, it is important to refine and segment this massive and varied world. To many, especially to older investors, seeking diversification by including higher risk countries in the mix feels too risky.

In the twentieth century, we classified the world in two categories: developed and developing nations (or sometimes termed *emerging markets* even though some countries remained far from emerging). The developed countries were seen as safe for investing, while EM countries were considered attractive only to the active risk-seeking investor, but that is all changing.

EVALUATING COUNTRIES

To directly address these profound changes, I reviewed much of the research created by several of the most reputable country analysts in the world.[4] By assembling a set of consensus criteria, and looking at what all the different approaches contribute to our understanding, I put together a summary of what elements are critical to evaluate so the average investor can quickly understand how countries can be ranked in terms of risk and opportunity for growth.

The country classifications show more detail than in many financial models to highlight the choices and the questions you and your advisor can discuss. Fortunately among the various top analysts in the field of country identification and segmentation, there is a lot more agreement than disagreement as to the general or core criteria for segmentation.

Both the criteria and the weightings can change over time, and it is important to at least annually review the country mix. By weightings, I mean the percentage of recommended allocation of investment to various countries. In addition, even if a country has a high score on most criteria and weightings, there are times when a single criterion can "knock out" the country from your investing mix, for instance, if a civil war breaks out.

Perhaps the most important point to mention is that over the next 20 to 30 years, one or more of the better countries will likely fail to meet expectations. However, given the diversity, breadth, and number of countries, there is a high probability that the majority of the countries will perform at or near what is projected. Even if growth countries as a group underperform the continued high growth expectations of global analysts, growth countries as a whole will still grow at a faster rate than developed countries.

Summary of Criteria for Ranking the Economic Prospects of Countries

Political Environment

A country needs a basic level of political stability and certainty for its economy to grow. It also needs a governmental structure that encourages economic growth if it has any chance to improve the lot of its people.

It is also in this topic of defining a favorable political environment that there is much disagreement across the world. Indeed, many in the West have erroneously believed that if a country is not operating in a Western-style democracy, it cannot improve and become stable. Yet we now know that our Western Greco-Roman invention of democracy is not necessarily internalized in Asia. There are too many economies across the world that have grown throughout the decades yet took very different political and economic paths to success.

After living and working in several countries, I have learned that, irrespective of the political structure of a country, there has to be some minimum level of commitment to encouraging investment and commerce by government authorities for consistent progress. Even in countries where there was an absolute dictatorship in place, so long as at least a minimum level of capital was able to efficiently flow back into the growth of the economy, and there was a minimum critical mass of society that had a commercial mind-set, the country could grow and improve its population's lot in life.

To be provocative, I should also add that becoming a Western-style democracy does not automatically mean you have a stable government that will lead to rapid growth. We all watched in dismay over many decades as India, one of the world's oldest democracies, operated in near anarchy and economic deterioration. It was not until the 1990s that we saw a mind-set of commercialism finally emerge in a segment of the population and even parts of the government that could allow India to progress. Even today, we see the country move two steps forward followed by one step backward as it entered into the more advanced growth countries stage. The Arab Spring, which encouraged a big change in Egypt, proved that becoming a more democratic nation does not necessarily create an immediate safe political and investment opportunity.

Legal/Regulatory Structure

A minimum level of political stability potentially can allow for the modernization of a variety of legislative, regulatory, judicial, and market oversight structures to support the growth of the financial system and the overall economy. Fortunately, there has been much innovation on the regulatory front, as more than ever before, the regulators of many countries are in constant communication in order to develop what is increasingly a global standard of regulations. Each country reserves the right to make its own laws, but there is more pressure on individual countries to follow best global practices. This convergence of thought on a variety of rules and practices puts more pressure on each growth country to comply with a global regulatory standard. At the same time, the knowledge transfer across regulators covering the myriad of specific complex rules necessary to govern a modern economy has made it easier for these officials to know what to do. They utilize their ready access to all the other countries' officials and rules; thus, they don't have to try and invent everything themselves.

By way of contrast, as recently as the mid-nineties, my colleague and I were meeting with a senior official at the Ministry of Finance's regulatory division of a Middle Eastern country. The official claimed with great pride that they now had a modern and properly regulated financial services industry. I was jet-lagged and barely able to stay awake, so I let my colleague do all the talking. Just as I was about to doze off, my colleague had one last question for the minister. "We have had difficulty getting a hold of the rules and regulations governing the securities industry. Could you help us get a copy of your rules?" The minister's bushy eyebrows arched as he exclaimed, "Of course not! We never share such rules with anyone. You will have to talk with one of our accredited lawyers and he will handle it all for you!" I was now wide awake as my colleague then asked him why it was not appropriate to let either his citizens or foreigners read the actual laws and administrative rules. The minister looked at us in astonishment, "We can't publish the rules. Otherwise, if everyone knew the laws, we couldn't change our mind!" Despite being created nearby, it seems the ancient Code of Hammurabi, where greater access to codified laws was first allowed, was not adhered to in this particular country. My colleague and I decided not to set up a subsidiary there. Fortunately, today, due to this open communication across more trained regulators and the ready access to multiple countries' laws, such secrecy of laws is becoming more rare in all but the most frontier of economies.

Today, by comparing open standards across countries, investors and analysts can more easily see which governments are advanced enough politically to support investment as well as oversee a regulatory structure that protects consumers and investors, yet does not overly restrict the ability of businesses to operate. Key metrics that fund managers and other experts look for: rules and regulations governing the conduct of trading; settlement and custody; shareholder rights and protections; and an efficient and trusted banking system. These and other regulatory and industry structures covering international trade relations and foreign exchange activities all need to be in place, and adhered to, before a country can move forward. Only when institutions, corporations, and individuals believe this basic governmental infrastructure is in place can they risk capital and invest in an economy.

Corruption

Most countries have varying degrees of corruption, including your own country. You only need to look any given day at the news in the United States or Europe to read stories about executives, politicians, and even judges getting caught disobeying laws and paying officials off. Corruption is a constant and never-ending battle. Fortunately, much attention has been applied to the understanding and classification of what corruption really means, and how to rank countries in terms of their level of corruption. There are many sources of data, but one that is especially easy to understand for the average investor is the Corruption Perceptions Index (CPI) created by Transparency International.[5] CPI reflects the views of observers from around the world, including experts living and working in the countries and territories evaluated based on the perceived level of public sector corruption. Without doubt, there is a certain amount of subjectivity in identifying and weighting all the criteria that go into measuring and ranking each country in order to create any corruption index. Many people will have differing opinions about the classifications and are even critical of how they assemble the data. In the case of Transparency International, CPI measured public sector corruption on a range of 100 to zero for the 2012 edition, with zero being the worst. Transparency International's study on corruption further delves into the details covering each industry for which it creates other measurement tools, such as a Bribe Payers Index, 2011 in which more than 3,000 business executives from 28 leading economies give their views on the extent to which companies from their countries engage in bribery abroad. Another tool is the Global Corruption Barometer, where in 2010 and 2011, more than 100,000 people in 100 countries were asked about such specific issues as: frequency and reasons for paying a bribe this past year, attitudes toward reporting incidents, and their views of their government's efforts to fight corruption.

Some will be surprised by the results of Corruption Perceptions Index of 2012. Some countries in Europe such as Greece scored no better than Brazil, China, and India; Russia ranks even lower than Vietnam. Interestingly, Hong Kong, Barbados and Japan are ranked less corrupt than the United States. A nation's size does seem to matter. From my personal observations, countries with large populations both developed and growth countries, generally have a bigger problem controlling corruption than do the smaller countries. It is clear that just because you are buying investments in one of the developed countries, never think that corruption doesn't exist. It potentially impacts your investments in every country.

Investors have long invested in countries that score a mediocre or poor ranking on the corruption perceptions index. Yet many of these investors have frequently made a considerable return on their money. Foreign operating companies as well as investment managers that are legitimate and obey laws have also operated in countries that do not score high in suppressing corruption, yet still made considerable money for their shareholders.

What many of us in the investment industry are looking for is at least a concerted effort on the part of the government and the local industry to fight corruption. Even though it takes a long time and is never fully expunged, is the country at least making a genuine effort to improve? For me, seeing and verifying this genuine effort counts for something. Take the examples of three countries/territories in Asia: Hong Kong, Taiwan, and South Korea. Thirty years ago, these countries were struggling with corruption as they worked toward a more advanced country level. But unlike some of their Asian counterparts, they were making a considerable effort in the uphill battle to contain corruption. Though there was not sufficient

Table 13.1 Stock Market Performance in Selected Asian Countries* vs. S&P 500[†]

	Taiwan	South Korea	Hong Kong	S&P 500
31 Jan. 1980	100.0	100.0	100.0	100.0
30 June 2013	1776.3	894.1	1431.4	1407.0
Annual returns	9.0%	6.8%	8.3%	8.2%

Source: Global Financial Data

* Contains index data from Taiwan SE Capitalization Weighted Index, Manila SE Composite Index, Korea SE Stock Price Index, and Hong Kong Hang Seng Composite Index.

[†] Index base at unit of 100, the index of the following country equity markets.

quantitative data at that time, regional experts had a rough idea of levels of corruption by country. If your personal corruption screen was overly strict, perhaps you would not have invested in any of them and would have missed major investment opportunities, given their growth over the past 30 years.

Thus, for the Investing Pocket, it makes good investing sense, as well as good moral sense, to keep out of pervasively corrupt countries. At the same time, there are plenty of investing opportunities in the growth countries that have, to greater and lesser degrees, kept corruption at bay.

Infrastructure

Basic foundations in financial services, telecommunications, energy, transportation, and technology need to be in place if a country has a chance to advance. However, when you visit some of these growth countries, you may see primitive levels of infrastructure in several areas of the their economies when compared to your own country. When you step off the plane in a growth country, you need to look at their world through a different set of lenses. Each country has its own advantages and faults.

Even if a minimum level of infrastructure is in place, most fund managers around the world need to see a minimum size of equities and bond markets before moving the country up the rungs of the classification ladder. For instance, if the total market capitalization of the combined public companies of a country is not over $30–40 billion, most global investors won't follow the market closely. Investors want the ability to sell easily, so the free float, or amount of stock that is truly available to trade, needs to be at a minimum level of over 25 to 30 percent of the total market's capitalization for investors to feel comfortable in buying securities in a country. In addition, both the government and the major corporations must demonstrate that they can pay back the debt on a dependable basis. This should lead to improved credit ratings for both the country and its corporations. Once the rest of the world sees the country's basic infrastructure, as well as the financial market's size, liquidity, and credit worthiness, are all at a minimum level, then a country can move up to a more acceptable investment grade status.

Macro-Economic Metrics

A country can reach a higher rung on the country classification ladder if it has a favorable balance of payments (it is able to sell to other countries at least as much as it wants to buy) and has a resulting strong currency, including multiple currency reserves, and keeps control of the government budget without excessive taxes. Another key consideration for analysts is the amount of foreign direct investment flowing into the country; it can tell you just how attractive this country is to the rest of the world.

Natural Resources

Having natural resources that the world craves is a major advantage for a country. However, it is equally important that the country itself is able to take maximum advantage of these resources and invest the proceeds back into the country. Conversely, if the resources are removed by foreign companies and only a few citizens ever can reap the benefits, and the rest of the local population receives no benefits, then the country may remain in the lower rung of the ladder. Australia, for example, has just about every kind of mineral demanded by the world. And more importantly, they are able to further refine many of these natural resources which adds value before they are shipped overseas, so much of the profit remains in Australia. Brazil has also brought its local population many advantages out of their agricultural and other resources. On the other hand, several African countries have been able to garner only a small portion of the value added from their resources. Just because the country has natural resources does not automatically mean it is on the road to progress, either for its people or for retail investors in the Western world.

Conversely, what has impressed me more over the last 40 years of travel and work overseas is the number of countries that thrived with no natural resources, such as South Korea, much of China and India, Taiwan, and Singapore. Yet there was strength in their weakness, as their people knew that they personally had to work harder to become their countries' only natural resource. A large source of hardworking, young, inexpensive labor has catapulted many a country from poverty to wealth, which leads us to the next heading.

Population Factors

There are a near infinite variety of ways that a country's people are evaluated and compared to others. Naturally, relative elements such as education or literacy levels, health statistics, work force participation, and income distribution contribute to the evaluation process.

Particularly in the case of population analysis, delving into details and not just looking at macro averages is important to gauging investment opportunities in a country. Unfortunately, many of the models built for country indices weightings and country ranking frequently miss the more important, although less exact, measurement criteria. When you just look at general averages, you often miss major opportunities.

Just how misleading can averages be?

The "averages" mistake often made in investing is to rank countries simply by looking at average GDP per capita. In the case of the giant growth countries, you would neither have predicted nor today could understand these countries' growing economic power and investment potential just by looking at GDP. In China for 2011, the average GDP per capita in international dollars (Intl $)[6] was approximately $6,100. Yet with giant population growth countries, like China, there is actually a country within a country. Geographically inside China, in just three key provinces—Tianjin, Beijing, and Shanghai—there are well over 150 million people with the GDP per capita over Intl $20,000 per year. Similarly, in India, though not as wealthy as China, cities like Mumbai, Bangalore, and Hyderabad had nearly 100 million people with an annual GDP/capita in excess of $10,000[7] in 2008, while the average of India was only $4,000[8] as of 2012.

These already emerged areas inside China and India are powerful, successful economic centers in their own right, and make up the bulk of investing opportunities. Yet, if you only looked at the low averages of GDP or income per capita of the entire nation, you would not know of the exciting economic revolutions that have already taken place in multiple regions.

Quality of the Companies

Many a good-performing fundamental investment manager barely looks at the country level. They focus more on looking for good companies, and for the most part don't care what the address of the headquarters is. If the manager ends up with more stocks in one country versus another, it simply grew out of finding better companies at cheaper stock prices in that country. The approach has a lot of merit; from the bottom up, the manager makes sure the stocks of the right companies are purchased at the right price relative to other stocks in other countries. I also like this bottom-up view as part of one's overall criteria, because if analysts are underweighting a country because there are not many attractive, long-term stocks, it likely says something about the entire country. It is OK to buy funds from sound, long-performing managers who follow this approach. But you and your advisor should also be looking at the country level as well, and making sure your overall portfolio of funds has a diversified mix of countries

For short-term trading in and out of countries, you may choose to make some small bets in your Trading Pocket. Much of how a country will do in equity performance for the next 6 or 12 months has to do with global money flowing in and out of one country versus other countries and the short-term performance of local currencies. I have seen a country doing well on all of the above criteria; however, because there is strong momentum in the global markets investing elsewhere, short term, capital can flow out of even quality countries, to be invested elsewhere. But for the truly long-term investor, there is little worry; countries that have met the above quality criteria and have many good, globally competitive firms operating inside them will, over time, get recognized in increasing long-term value.

Company Domicile versus Revenue Sources

Several fund management companies have recently argued that an investor can get plenty of international exposure to the emerging market growth just through buying into American companies that sell a lot of their products overseas. Naturally, if much of a company's revenue is coming from outside the United States, then as an investor you are getting exposure to the great growth coming out of the EM markets. In addition, many high growth foreign companies have listed on the London Stock Exchange, the New York Stock Exchange, or the NASDAQ. So, you don't have to leave the borders of the United States or the UK to garner sufficient exposure to attractive foreign markets. After all, aren't markets increasingly converging?

There is much logic to this argument. When working with your advisor, you can choose funds especially targeted to buying stocks of companies with a high percentage of foreign revenues. However, it may still be insufficient in terms of making sure you are taking full advantage of the overseas opportunities for the following reasons:

- Many great foreign stocks are not listed in London or New York, and you will miss the appreciation of these stocks if you are only buying US companies.
- Even though you buy American companies that have foreign revenues, you are missing all the foreign companies that garner revenue in their own countries.
- The stock prices of foreign operating companies will at times be a better value than those listed in New York or London. Thus, you achieve greater diversification by buying US companies with large foreign revenues as well as foreign-registered and -domiciled companies.
- Although particularly in the short term during times of sharp declines, it looks like markets are definitely converging, there remain many examples of countries where stock markets over time operate quite differently than in other countries.

THE FIVE COUNTRY CLASSIFICATIONS FOR THE TWENTY-FIRST CENTURY

One of the hindrances keeping people from investing more outside of the developed countries is that many analysts and even indices and funds simply classify the world as either "developed" or emerging. However, when you apply more granularity to the analysis of countries, you see that there are many other country investing opportunities above the emerging category. Below is my attempt at further segmentation to help you and your advisor in your investing analysis. Please see my website for a constant update in my country classifications.

1. Mature Countries

These have established though often older infrastructures, and stable economies though often aging populations. Here we include the United States, Canada, Western Europe, and Japan. For the most part, they remain advanced, and select countries definitely have opportunities for growth over the next decade. Notably, the continued competitiveness of US industry and its emerging energy independence make both the United States and Canada attractive long-term investment markets. In addition, the UK, Germany, and much of Scandinavia have done a solid job remaining globally competitive and financially able to maintain their economic viability. I find it very encouraging that several countries, even after they had matured and even lost power, were able to reinvent themselves. For instance, the UK lost its mantle as the world leader at the beginning of the last century. Yet by 2007, just before the European crisis, the UK actually made more income per capita than the United States. The euro crisis negatively impacted all of Europe, but still the UK reinvented itself, became more inclusive in allowing a variety of nationalities and foreign companies to succeed in their country, and was able to regain economic strength. This is a testament to societies never giving up trying to improve the lots of their citizens.

Though some mature countries will continue to reinvent themselves and succeed as the United States has done, a valid concern remains regarding selected mature countries' rapidly aging societies and high levels of debt. In particular, the lack of fiscal and monetary responsibility makes several of them no longer such automatically safe investments over the long term of your portfolio. Your advisor will need to conduct periodic analysis on these at-risk mature countries. History has shown us that when countries begin to fail economically, it is not necessarily well telegraphed; Witness the sudden financial crises early this century in the "PIIIGS" countries (Portugal, Ireland, Italy, Iceland, Greece, and Spain), which caught most investors flat footed.

At present, in addition to the above mentioned PIIIGS, one should also follow closely the economic signals coming from Japan, Austria, the Benelux, and even France; these governments often are virtually antibusiness in words and actions. Given this dangerous combination of aging population, negative or limited economic growth, extremely high national debt, and pension obligations, it may be safer to keep investments in these countries to a minimum. At the same time, countries can improve their fundamentals, as evidenced the past few years in Ireland. Sometimes the global market may be too skittish to increase their improving companies' stock and bond valuations, so your advisor and/or the underlying fund managers may see a good buying opportunity and increase their weightings in such countries before the valuations return to a higher, more normal level. Predicting when countries' values will improve is extremely difficult to do consistently. However, you should expect the fund managers of your multi-country funds to monitor relative country performance and ensure over the long term that you do not become inadvertently over weighted in risky countries, even if they are classified as a developed nations.

2. Advanced Growth Countries

This category includes Hong Kong, Singapore, South Korea, Taiwan, Australia, New Zealand, Israel, and Chile, a group of nations that by most criteria are often more healthy than many mature countries. By a variety of criteria, many of these countries are considered financially and economically strong and actually contain some of the world's lowest risk investment opportunities. As a group, they are slowing down in growth, and some are even beginning to feel the impact of their own aging societies. However, a basket of advance growth countries stocks are likely to show a higher average growth than a basket of only mature countries.

I have taken great pleasure in observing how smaller countries, almost city-states like Hong Kong and Singapore, were able to create a consensus in their societies to put together rapidly a national strategy for development. In particular, Singapore could almost be called Corporate Singapore, as they systematically analyzed a variety of markets and chose where they could be the most competitive. Their logistical successes in air passenger and freight and sea container management are the envy of the world, and have become ideal models for far away city-states like Dubai as well as other North

Asian ports such as Keelung, Taiwan; and Pusan and Incheon, South Korea. I remember in the late seventies seeing how much Singapore and Hong Kong were investing in their giant container yards and wondering if these facilities would remain so busy once neighboring countries were able to similarly automate and improve their harbors. They have; both ports have continued to dominate the region over the last 30 years in the cost-efficient movement of goods. These smaller countries have also forged a connection between their schools and commerce to ensure an educated supply of relevant labor skills to grow their economies. I have seen similarly impressive education/technology/commerce coordination in other countries, such as Ireland and South Korea, as well as in cities/provinces like Hyderabad, India; and Shenzhen, Guangdong, in China. They have become far superior to the outdated educational systems in Japan, France, and the Mediterranean countries.

In the case of Australia and New Zealand, they have used their highly skilled labor forces and advanced corporate entities to take full advantage of their plethora of natural resources.

An undeniable phenomenon in creating both advanced growth and growth countries is the positive influence of massive immigration. This is a controversial statement to many; we often hear complaints across the world about how immigrants are ruining the entrenched local society, taking jobs away from youth, costing additional money in welfare, or increasing police force budgets to combat the rise in crime. Yet over the years working in such cities as Taipei, Hong Kong, New York, Silicon Valley, Los Angeles, Miami, London, Sidney, and Vancouver, I have observed that immigrants by far bring a strong economic vibrancy to a country. They are hardworking and ambitious as a group, and quickly become contributors rather than a drain to their newly adopted cities. This population shift has fueled the rapid economic growth of America, Canada, Australia, China, Taiwan, Singapore, and many others. Even Dubai, although it has experienced high volatility in recent years and needed help from its "older cousins" in Abu Dhabi, actually has become among the most economically vibrant countries in the Middle East. Over 80 percent of the population is immigrants.

3. Growth Countries

This group of some 15–20 countries—notably including BRICs, Turkey, Mexico, Indonesia, Thailand, Malaysia, Hungary, South Africa, Czech Republic, and Poland—is especially attractive to investors because they have already reached a critical mass to continue growth. Over the past decade they have shown higher growth than mature countries and, by many of the criteria listed above, have a strong chance to continue on their growth path. Many will likely show a GDP per capita growth rate over the next one to two decades or perhaps double that of many of the mature countries. In addition, as a currency basket, the currencies of these countries should remain an attractive balance to the world's key currencies. Their interest rates should be higher than those in mature countries because they are growing, yet as long as their fundamental fiscal monetary policy remains sound, along with a positive balance of trade, their ability to pay back debt can remain better than many mature countries.

Deciding which countries should be considered growth versus emerging growth is the subject of much debate. At the end of the day, in terms of your personal portfolio, you and your advisor often will ultimately decide on which countries belong in which category in your portfolio. I shall try to shed some light on why many of the less biased analysts believe that these countries listed below should be considered growth countries despite individual areas of weakness.

China and India: Both countries have suffered considerable volatility; some years they spring forward with amazing growth, only to be stopped by such problems as lack of coordination between government and industry, inflation, income imbalances, or dramatic currency fluctuations. In addition, due to their massive sizes, they continue to struggle with reining in corruption. However, we should remember that the United States, the UK, and other advanced nations went through the same struggles. And building each country's infrastructure—not just in buildings and roads but also in technology, energy, communication, and organizational skills—is likewise a constant challenge to manage with critical obstacles delaying progress.

To keep a proper perspective, we should again remember that in America, we lived through many deep economic depressions as we reworked our economy to become more efficient. Even in more recent times, we need to remember our own lapses in keeping technology up to speed with progress. In studying my own industry, I learned how, in the late 1960s, we had to shut down the NYSE (New York Stock Exchange) every Wednesday as the industry could not keep up with the massive "Paperwork Crisis." Over 100 broker-dealer NYSE member firms went out of business. China and India have experienced similar crises, yet now they have more automated stock exchanges than the NYSE. In fact, the earlier a country entered into the developed stage, the more backward its stock exchanges and central clearing organizations are today. China, India, Turkey, Thailand, and Taiwan all have long had fully automated stock exchanges, many with de-materialized stock certificates; meanwhile, the United States still keeps the archaic structure of traders on the floor of the NYSE.

It is important to remember, even with our own economic history, growth never went straight up without any recessions or crises. So, why would you expect it to be any different in the growth countries? It doesn't mean they shouldn't be invested in.

I believe China and India should be included in your growth countries portfolio because of the sheer size and growth rates of their economies as a percentage of the global economy—because each possesses "country within a country" advanced regions with a significant population of an upwardly mobile middle class and a selection of quality public companies available.. You may want to underweight one or the other, but not including them would leave a large hole in the risk-and-return balancing of your portfolio.

Brazil: For years, I had no personal interest in investing in Brazil. It seemed it would never come out of its malaise. But starting about ten years ago, my fund managers and analysts visited company after company in Brazil and saw an economic revolution begin to percolate. Similar to Mexico, the returning "knowledge workers" from the United States and Europe helped the country right itself. Plus, Brazil has vast reserves of natural resources; when China began to drive up the demand, and thus the price, of these resources, Brazil was able to become a major beneficiary. With a GDP per capita approaching $14,000, a population at 200 million, and an average age of only 29,

Brazil should be able to maintain a strong long-term growth rate, albeit with bumps along the way. And with its number of creditworthy companies and listed stocks, it deserves a place in the growth countries category.

Russia: This country is a more difficult call, and I can understand why some analysts would leave it out as a growth country. Corruption remains an epidemic in all sectors of government, commerce, and society. The population remains stagnant at less than 150 million; however, it has a segment of society that is among the most educated in STEM[9] in the world. We don't know how many of the educated elite will stay or return, but there is also in Russia at least a small virtual country within a country," with a critical mass of many highly educated and experienced people and several well-managed companies. Whether it will rise above corruption still remains to be seen, but given its size and its vast supply of natural resources, it is worth placing them at least marginally in the growth countries category. It helps to have a historical understanding of countries like Russia. Only 160 years ago, they emerged from serfdom, and it has been just 20 years since the Soviet system collapsed. It can take time for such a country to create a sufficient social infrastructure to keep corruption at bay and allow broad competition in a global market.

Eastern Europe: In 1975 when I was a young banker traveling through Europe, it struck me how different the eastern bloc countries' economic levels were. East Germany, Czechoslovakia, Poland, and Hungary were much more advanced than Romania, Bulgaria, and Albania. In many countries, the life had been sucked out of their societies under the weight of Soviet domination. For example, in 1969 while on the way to study in the Soviet Union, I saw that Warsaw was literally an army base for Soviet troops, with over a million Soviet soldiers milling around. It is no wonder that even though it has been nearly 25 years since the Berlin Wall crumbled, many former Soviet bloc countries have still not fully recovered.

Still, some countries have been able to more quickly recover their old economic glory. The Czech Republic is probably most notable in its status as a true growth country. Few people realize that in the 1920s, Czechoslovakia was among the seven most dominant economically advanced nations. It makes sense that along with the Eastern part of Germany, the Czech Republic could recover the quickest. However, there remain serious vestiges of the old communist ways. For instance, it still scores surprisingly poorly on the corruption scale. It does deserve growth country status, along with Poland and Hungary, due to its advanced labor force and ability to properly exploit its connections with the European Union. The former Soviet republics, as well as the rest of Eastern Europe, however, remain far behind.

Mexico and Turkey: Both have had citizens work overseas in the United States and Western Europe. Though many have immigrated permanently overseas, many have also come back home and brought their saved up capital and, more important, their training and expertise. With this commercial mind-set and knowledge, they are transforming their countries into growth countries. You may say correctly that Mexico is too corrupt still, and that violence makes it dangerous to operate a business. Yet underneath this turmoil is a growing base of solid skills and a new population determined to excel. In Turkey, despite its proximity to massive political unrest and rising debt, the country has laid a solid foundation for commercial growth.

South Africa: This is another one that is a difficult call, but by enough metrics, it belongs in the growth countries category. Despite a large portion of its 50 million people living in poverty, it does possess a "country within a country" with 20 percent of its population reasonably well educated and possessing a strong economic natural resource base. However, its high debt and the debt's effect on its currency is a bit worrisome, so many analysts prefer to keep their exposure to South Africa more modest than many other growth countries.

Please remember one final point of investing in the growth countries. I am not saying that one or more of these countries won't fail to meet investors' long term expectations. In fact, you can count on at least a few failing. However, you can probably say the same about one or more of the mature countries. The safest route is to own a broad, multicountry basket of geographically diversified investments.

The basket, even net of any individual country failures, will grow at a much faster rate than the developed "old" countries.

4. Emerging Growth

This group of countries has shown promise, and often in the past, it has been predicted that they will emerge. However, for a variety of reasons, they have only made partial progress. Individually, they deserve a small allocation of your investment dollars, primarily for those under 50 and with an appetite for risk. Indeed, some analysts expect at least a few of them to become growth countries in the coming decade.

The Philippines is an excellent example of why you have to wait to see concrete signs of economic advancement before committing your own dollars to investment. In the 1970s, the Philippines was considered to be the next country to emerge. Considerable dollars and global business attention flowed into the country. Major US universities opened up satellite centers; for many in the press and in international agencies, it was the darling of the emerging countries.

When I first visited Manila in 1978, I had many well-educated friends from the Philippines back in the United States and just assumed I would see firsthand a country on the cusp of emergence. The purpose of my visit was to identify sound manufacturers throughout Asia. On my last day there, I met with the president of a well-respected company and toured his facility. He was Western educated and was quite impressive as he spoke so intelligently about the world of economics. After an engaging and expensive lunch, we drove in his chauffeured new Mercedes Benz to the factory. At first I was impressed with the sophisticated equipment his factory had obtained, thanks to investment support. However, it still remained in its original wrapping, dated as arrived six months prior. As we toured his plant, the CEO could not answer even the most basic questions regarding operations. I discovered the only reason all the fancy machinery was still in its original wrapping was that no one knew how to assemble and operate it. I left that evening for a flight to Taiwan, disappointed that despite all the resources the CEO had, there was no quality production yet coming out of his plant. Early the next morning, I met with a competing firm an hour outside of Taipei. The owner of this factory had his daughter take me out to his factory in an old Yue Loong taxi. I met the owner in an alcove on the factory floor, working where he could see firsthand all plant activities. There was little time for niceties; he immediately started to show me his entire operation. There was no fancy machinery because he had built most every machine himself. After three hours of review, there was not one question in which he did not have full command of the answer. He had built his active business personally, and he and his crew were focused solely on making the best possible products at a reasonable price. You can imagine who I was more interested in doing business with. This story has happened time and again. Taiwan succeeded while the Philippines languished. Over the next two decades, Taiwan received next to nothing in financial and political support while the Philippines received far more financial and intellectual resources from the rest of the developed world.

Today, it may be worth moving the Philippines into the emerging growth category and out of frontier markets for one reason. Over the past 40 years, millions of hardworking Philippine workers have gone overseas to work in foreign companies and study at Western schools. Although some will stay overseas, others are remitting valuable foreign currency as well as returning home. And just as we saw in Mexico, Turkey, and Brazil, this massive foundation of talent is likely not going to let its country languish.

Pakistan: Some global analysts consider this a growth country, given its size and a base of educated talent inside the country. However, given its level of corruption and economic and political disorder, I feel it is better left in the emerging growth category.

Indonesia, like the Philippines, has not yet reached the critical mass stage of economic development. However, fueled largely by the increased demand from China and elsewhere, coupled with a marginal improvement in the political environment, I feel it is worth placing in the emerging growth category. One promising development for

Indonesia, as well as for all of Southeast Asia: Two years ago, I spent a lot of time with my fellow fund managers in mainland China. Due to the one-child policy established in 1979, many factories were having difficulty finding enough young, cheap labor. I was surprised at the volume of Chinese companies that were setting up manufacturing facilities through Southeast Asia as well as the subcontinent. This plant migration from China is becoming another positive for other nearby countries.

Columbia and Peru are following a similar pattern to Mexico; various economic metrics show they have strong potential. The *United Arab Emirates* (UAE) and *Morocco* are among the more interesting countries in the Arab/Muslim world. They both possess a small number of quite successful publicly listed firms and are making progress to improve the economic prospects of their people. However, given the extreme volatility of this region, they remain in the emerging growth category while many neighboring countries remain in the frontier category.

Nigeria is a tough call. On one hand, it has strong reserves and controls its own oil production. Its currency and reserves are surprisingly strong, and the government has committed to continue to invest in the advancement of the country. With a population of 170 million people, it is the seventh-largest nation in the world and is also one of the last sources on the globe for a vast source of young, cheap labor. At the same time, it is a political powder keg; given the recent turmoil in the north of the country and with its neighbors, it is wise to keep one's investment here small. However, as long as your portfolio is already quite diversified, I understand the attraction of an 11 percent government-guaranteed interest rate from a country that already has such large hard currency reserves.

5. Frontier

The rest of the world, some 100 countries, falls into this category. Many of these countries may never emerge in our lifetimes. At different times, one or another of these countries showed promise. However, for a variety of reason—including politics, corruption, lack of any infrastructure—they have been unable to progress.

Countries that were once at a higher level can slip into this frontier classification. An example of just such deterioration is Argentina, given political developments over the past five years.

There are selected countries in the frontier category that are still in the "highly speculative" stage, but look quite interesting from an investment standpoint and could progress up the ladder in the coming years. These "interesting" frontier countries include Bangladesh, Croatia, Slovakia, Mauritius, Sri Lanka, Egypt, Qatar, and Vietnam.

Each country has its own unique issues. For instance, *Egypt* has a segment of its population and economy that is clearly a "country within a country." Companies in Turkey have found several ways to utilize the people resources of Egypt by operating a variety of subsidiaries, creating an Egyptian version of the *Maquiladora*, the name used to describe a similar phenomenon in North America where US firms set up manufacturing and assembly plants and service centers along the Mexican border. This trend has not only resulted in improving employment in Mexico, but also in transferring skill sets to Mexico. The only reason Egypt was moved down to frontier status is that its political situation has become so volatile in the past few years that one should look at Egypt strictly as a country for your Trading Pocket, at least at this point.

Vietnam is showing rapid economic growth fueled by a young and dedicated labor force along with a growing population. In a few decades, Vietnam may have more people than Japan. Also fueling this economic prosperity are firms from other countries such as Singapore, Japan, and China, which are moving many of their facilities to Vietnam. Today, there are few public stocks with trustworthy accounting and corporate governance, and corruption is far from under control, but it is definitely a country to watch and may be more broadly investible within a matter of years.

Like emerging growth countries, this category is especially interesting for investors under 50 years old. At this age, you have enough time to withstand the high volatility in these frontier countries and reap the long-term, high growth chances. Selecting active managers in this category rather than index funds may be more attractive as the fund managers can focus in on the countries and companies that show the most promise with the least risk.

THE LESSONS FOR INVESTING
BEYOND YOUR BORDERS

1. **Selected developed countries remain attractive.** There is a selected subgroup of countries in the developed world where it still makes sense to invest. Especially interesting are the United States, Canada, UK, and Germany, as well as selected assets in Scandinavia and the rest of Northern Europe. The rest of the developed world is "TBD."

2. **Don't be afraid to invest in the better emerging markets.** There are especially attractive investments in the lower risk categories of the advanced growth and the growth countries. Expect these better countries to suffer the same booms and busts that we in the West still experience. But that is no reason to minimize your exposure.

3. **Emerging market investing is not hard:** Given the breadth of quality fund managers around the world covering the growth country categories, investing via mutual funds is now much easier than before. These higher quality growth categories should now be considered a core part of your Investing Pocket portfolio, not just for speculation and market timing in your Trading Pocket.

4. **Lastly, no matter how much you may disagree, investing zero or only a tiny amount into growth categories of the world is the wrong answer.**

CHAPTER 14

WHAT ABOUT YOUR PERSONAL PORTFOLIO?

How to Build and Monitor Your Portfolio

"THE BUNNIES, THE SNAKE, AND THE OWL," AS TOLD BY JAMES MCMAHON

One morning, two little bunny rabbits woke up to discover that their mother was eaten by a snake. They were so frightened and didn't know what to do. The older bunny brother said, "I know, the owl is so wise; let's ask him how we can protect ourselves." So they went to the large tree nearby and asked the owl what they should do. "It is simple," replied the old owl. "All you have to do is turn yourselves into a ferocious dog and the snake will be scared away." The two bunny brothers thought for a moment and then asked the owl, "But how do we turn ourselves into a dog?" The owl spun his neck away and scoffed, "I concern myself only with matters of strategy and policy. I do not bother myself with the details of execution."

Doesn't it peeve you when you want specific help on how to invest and all you get is some general strategy that doesn't actually help? I have listened to exasperated investors complain when they get no practical help about the details of actually putting together their overall portfolios. There are brokers who simply want to sell you something, but they can't really help you figure out where their recommendation fits with what you already own.

It's important to go through the essential steps of how to put together a portfolio of investments for you, and what to do on an ongoing basis. In the next section I will cover more on advisors, including how to decide whether you need them, and if so, how to use them. To help you get started, let's assume for now that you are working with an advisor or counselors in assembling and executing your life investment plan.

You and your advisor will both have your own ideas, and I want to leave as much flexibility as possible; many roads can lead to long-term financial success. Independent financial advisors are just that, *independent*, meaning most every advisor will have different but strong opinions about what you should and should not do. The purpose of this book is to lay out a framework so you can better understand and evaluate how advisors structure a portfolio of investments that meet your personal objectives and views. More than anything, at the end of this chapter I want you to know the key steps to building a safe portfolio and how to avoid any roads that will put your plan in financial danger.

STEP 1. HOW MUCH DO I NEED TO INVEST TO COVER MY LATER YEARS?

The first question you need to answer is how much you and your spouse need to invest now, and for as long as you are working, in order to have enough money to support both of your lifetimes. Remember my great-grandfather? Start by recognizing that your money really needs to last until you're both in your nineties, just in case one or both of you lives that long. Then, decide what kind of lifestyle or spending rate you can afford. Then, considering taxes, inflation, and other costs, you want to back into a periodic investing amount that allows you to reach your target.

As you can see below, there are several models for financial planning available that are either free or quite reasonable that you can use to help in your planning. These models take into consideration many important factors, such as:

- Expenses that you have to save up for before you retire, like college planning and down payments for a house.
- Determining what are the required expenses versus which ones are discretionary.
- What are the tax rates in the state and country you live in, and what will be the impact?
- What other assets do you have? And what are other liabilities that you must cover?

Your financial planning process can be approached in two ways—do it yourself (DIY) or with the help of a financial advisor. Even if you prefer to use a financial planner or advisor to help you with this planning analysis, it is wise to at least take a look at a few models. There are various websites that offer financial planning tools to help users keep track of and plan for their complete financial life. These sites act as a starting point or a warm-up tool to financial planning. A quick review of just a few popular websites shows that these can be a good starting point for simple tasks such as assessing an investor's retirement goals, the effect of taxes, and figuring out a high-level overview of how to structure investment, spending, and saving to achieve them. Following are just a few examples of frequently used DIY plans.[1]

E$Planner (basic.esplanner.com), from Economic Security Planning, offers an easy and free plan. The basic version of E$Planner helps an investor enter his/her family details, current and projected salary before retirement, retirement age and assets, and other factors. The tool generates information on an investor's sustainable living standard and allows a user to build scenarios based on change in salaries or housing move or retirement-account contribution to figure out the impact on living standard. The basic version recommends annual amount of discretionary spending, savings, and life insurance coverage for an investor. The program includes important details on taxes, inflation, and Social Security benefits that other free financial planning tools tend to leave out.

GoalGami (www.apps.goalgami.com) is another tool that helps users determine the most appropriate investment plan based on their household balance sheets and financial goals. It helps users in building scenarios based on what-if events related to changes in income and expenses to ascertain how the changes affect their lifetime goals.

Betterment (www.betterment.com) is a goal-based financial planning tool that suggests a portfolio construction approach based on a user's goals. It walks a user backward in the steps required to meet an end goal. Betterment calculates the chances of achieving a user's objective from the information on initial deposit, monthly savings, and time horizon that a user provides. There is also a slide bar that allows users to change the allocation of their assets between equities and bonds to see the impact on returns.

If you choose to use an advisor that also does financial planning, they typically have more advanced tools that can allow you to refine your projections even further. For instance, one tool that I reviewed from Advisor Software Inc. is used by over 600 advisors around the United States and can factor in projected growth of a variety of stock markets around the world as calculated by global investment analysts, so you can better see what the effect of investing in growth countries will do to your portfolio.

At a minimum, most people like to first take a quick look at a basic scenario, e.g., If I start putting money into my Investing Pocket now, how much will I be able to take out each month when I am in my retirement years? Here is a simple scenario: Let's say I am now 45 years old, and I can put $1,000 a month into investing until I retire at 65. Then, after retiring, I begin to take out $2,000 a month, including accessing my retirement tax advantaged accounts. Now that my house and car and kids are no longer an expense, I can live on much less. Plus, I may well be receiving Social Security (assuming it is still valid in 20 years.) and even a modest pension from my work, so $2,000 a month may be all that I need from my Investing Pocket after retirement. Let's also be safe and assume a conservative

Fig. 14.1   Investing in a Portfolio with 5 Percent Returns

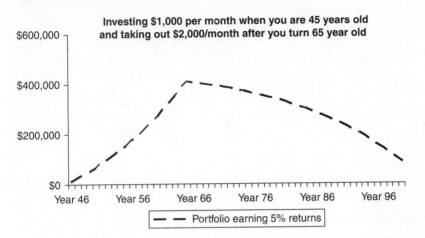

blended portfolio that only is able to earn 5 percent (1 percent less than the projected minimum 6 percent we shall discuss below). For how many years can I take $2,000 a month out of my Investing Pocket before I run out?

As you can see, my money will likely outlive me; even at 100 years old, I still have over $100,000 extra in the Investment Pocket.

The above projections also assume an inflation rate of approximately 1 to 2 percent. If inflation turns out to be higher, then your returns might also be a bit higher in the long-term. If inflation is lower, then your return will be lower, but your purchasing power will offset this decrease. As to evaluating funds, whether or not you happened to pick some top performers versus average performers is not as big a deal in your long-term performance.

Now, let's assume that I decided instead to never invest in a broadly diversified portfolio and just left the money in the bank. Thus, over the years, I only earn 2 percent a year, or just about what inflation is. For how many years after retirement will my money last?

As you can see, by leaving my money in the bank only at a 2 percent yearly return, I will run out of money at age 77 or 12 years after retirement.

Just earning the additional 3 percent over the bank interest or 5 percent per year in the diversified account meant the difference between running out of money while I am still alive vs. having enough money for as long as I live including extra for any medical costs.

Fig. 14.2   Investing in a Portfolio with 2 Percent Returns

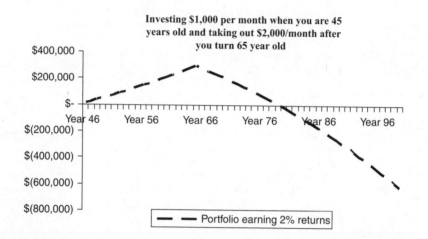

Why use only 5 or 6 percent? What can you assume as an average annual return over your lifetime in a diversified Investing Pocket?

All too often, there are some advisors and salesmen that promise annual returns far more than can be realistically delivered, especially if the next twenty years don't look as good as the past twenty years. The answers I have heard rank high on the list of biggest lies or exaggerations, right there with people's height, weight, and length of commute. If you properly mix the variety of asset classes we have covered, your blended return over the long haul in the Investing Pocket will be modest, in the 5 to 8 percent per year range, depending on how conservative you are and how future decades perform. Given the last century of data, one can assume that some of the more conservative asset classes will only return to you 2 or 3 percent, while more volatile growth asset classes over the decades can average north of 8 percent.

In fact, using the last century of data in the below graph, if we just invested in a blended portfolio of 60 percent equities and 40 percent fixed income, the return would have been 8.1 percent per year.[2] I chose this period of long term investing because it runs right through the worst investment time of the last century, yet your diversified portfolio would still have grown sufficiently. The safest approach in planning is to calculate in the 5 and 6 percent range just to see what

Fig. 14.3 Investing in a Diversified Portfolio of 60 Percent Equities and 40 Percent Fixed Income (1903–2012)

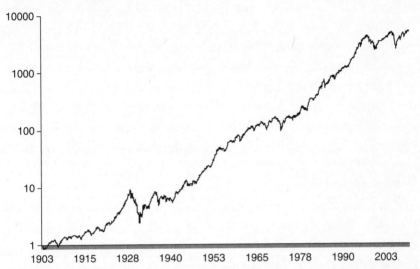

Source: Global Financial Data (returns are displayed in log scale to show the variations in early part of the century)

would happen in a diversified portfolio if things did not go nearly as well this century.

There are two very critical points to recognize. First, given that you have decades of investing in your life financial plan, you will not be in negative territory later on when you are in the drawdown phase of your plan. In the interim years, if times are bad, even for a decade or more, the diversity of asset classes and geographies and the amount of time allowed for investing means that you can safely count on at least this modest amount of growth over time. It is always better to look at the future as a range of outcomes rather than a single number because the future is never so exactly predictable. Second, although a 5 or 6 percent return may seem to be a boring annual return—not like many of the claims you have heard in the past—the compounding effect coupled with the broad mix means that you can count on it. Any higher numbers quoted by some in the industry may come with considerably more risk than they mention.

You may ask why you need to have extra at the end of your life. You might think, "I have a poor family health history; I probably won't make it all the way to 100." Maybe true, maybe not. But there is one additional factor to be considered in today's world of financial planning that makes planning much harder than in the past: *the cost of your health care*. Not only do you need to be saving much more than the past due to the likelihood of living longer, but predicting your total health care costs have become among the biggest challenges to determining how much you will need as you get older.

Many people don't want to think about the last years of their lives. But it is important to financially come to grips with what really may happen to you and/or other members of your family. Allow me to cite just a few real-life examples of the range of health care costs.

Helen Passes

My mother died last year, just three months shy of her ninetieth birthday. From the time she was 65 until 85, she was by choice quite frugal. Each year she spent less than $25,000. Her only vices, as she called them, were buying used books and cheap items at the dollar store for her grandchildren. Every so often, my brother Dan or I would take her to a used bookstore so she could get a "book fix," or "joke gifts" for the kids. Just before turning 86, it became clear she could not be on her own anymore. My brother worked full time, and I was working overseas most of the time; we had no choice other than for her to move into an assisted living complex. As her dementia became worse, we had to move her into a facility that could care for her on a 24-hour basis. Fortunately, every day after work, Dan would visit her to make sure she was being properly cared for. The costs climbed from $4,000 to 6,000, and then to $8,000 a month for the last six months of her life.

As is often the case, her last months were rough and quite stressful on my brother. Fortunately, I happened to be home just before she passed. It was hard for all of us to watch her suffer, but the hospice care was outstanding. I named her caregiver the "Helen Whisperer" after the book *The Horse Whisperer*; we in the family could never tell her what to do, but she always did whatever he said. On her last night, she sensed the end was near and looked up at me and said, " I am scared. I don't want to die." Then, after a little shot of oxygen, she said, "Well, what are we going to do now?" I told her golf was out of the question, and she laughed.

One of the most difficult issues financially that we all have to wrestle with is that you don't know when the person will die, even when the end looks near. In the case of my mom, later than night, she passed away.

What I experienced with my mother has helped me understand what people can expect financially in their later years. The total cost of her care the last three years was over $200,000. Fortunately, I could cover the cost, and the care was much better than average. We are lucky in that regard. But I wonder how the average family could have covered such a cost.

I have a colleague whose father's Alzheimer's is so bad they must spend close to $20,000 a month on around-the-clock care; he actually remains healthy, so this type of care might well be needed for who knows how many more years. Her mother felt guilty about not being able to take care of him, but the physical and mental stress of taking care of her husband had put her own health at risk. Luckily, they have the funds, but what would happen in the average-income family that doesn't have an extra half-million dollars to pay for such costs?

On the other hand, another friend just told me about his father at 86, an ex-produce man, telling his sister an old joke about a head of lettuce. Just as he finished the punch line, he had a massive heart attack and died on the couch. He had never been to a hospital, and the total cost of his health care was zero.

A well-known epidemiologist and health care cost expert, Dr. Walter Stewart, recently told me something he learned in his research: "When they interview people in their 60s and ask them about how long they want to live and how do they want their final medical decisions handled, the most frequent response is, 'I don't want to be a burden on my family.'" My brother and I heard that from my mother, so we told her the place where she was living only cost us $800 a month. Only then did she stop complaining. Similarly, when my colleague's father resisted going into a long-term Alzheimer's care facility, the family also lied and told him it was a good deal, only $600 a month. Only then did he agree to go.

None of us wants to be a burden on our family or society, so what amount do you aim for to cover your health care costs? The cost can range anywhere from zero to $500,000 or more in today's dollars. Today, there is a much higher probability that people will need full-time care for their later years than was needed in previous generations. When I was ten years old and my father took me to Europe, I saw the high proportion of men and women as young as their 60s barely able to walk. Now, we get new hips and knees. Similarly, before the new heart meds became so popular, many often died before Alzheimer's or dementia could set in.

I don't tell these stories to depress you, but rather to simply point out that a larger number of us will possibly need expensive assisted care in the future, and we need to recognize and budget for it.

But what cost for your health care do you aim at? The short answer is as much as you can. If you don't spend it, at least your family can inherit it. Even with investing in long-term care insurance, I think that if you can possibly add another $100,000 or more as a target to reach, as I did in the above example, just for the extra care you may need, you will be able to sleep better now.

Other Factors Affecting Your Financial Plan

Other factors that go into deciding what your long-term target should be is the real estate you own. Real estate can become quite illiquid in down markets, so if you are relying on this asset as a retirement tool, it is best to sell a bit earlier, since it is hard to know when you will need the funds. On the other hand, if the family decides to wait and sell the house only after either you or your spouse dies, there can be significant tax advantages, depending on the country. Thus, as with many decisions, your long-term financial plan should be closely reviewed with your tax and estate advisors. Some people consider counting on a reverse mortgage, but with these plans you must borrow the entire amount you will need for the rest of your lifetime upfront; thus, you have to pay a lot of extra interest expense now on money you will spend over the next ten years, which will further decrease your nest egg.

In designing your investment plan, come up with a figure to put into your Investing Pocket each month so it can keep growing right into your 90s, plus cover your later year's assisted living and health costs. If you have a decent amount of home equity, you may not need to add additional health care funds into your Investing Pocket.

If you would like to try different iterations of how much to put in and what to expect in your later years, I have developed a few basic tools on my website, www.timmccarthy.com. I look at these models as merely a starting point; it is much better to go through the full-blown financial planning process either by using the financial planning tools available on the web or, even better, working with a financial planner or investment advisor. That way, you and your advisor can further refine your targets and get an even better idea of where you are heading.

STEP 2. THE WEIGHTINGS OF YOUR INVESTMENTS

You have an idea about methods to help you decide on the target amount you need to be putting in the Investing Pocket each year. The next task is finding how you and your advisor decide how much to put into each asset class, and when.

There is an entire subindustry developed around building "optimization models," quantitative models that carefully analyze the past performance of various asset classes and tell you what your exact weighting should be in each class. However, after reviewing so many of these models and watching them over time, I find they frequently do not work much better than the simple allocation guidelines we will review below. Just because one or more asset class has performed one way for the past 20 years does not tell you how they will perform over the next 30 and 40 years. Remember the case of gold; it did nothing for 20 years, and then suddenly exploded. Also remember that past models do not take into consideration how much growth countries have improved, nor how old mature countries have become.

It reminds me of what an old carpenter once said to me: *"Don't measure with a micrometer if you are going to mark with a wide pencil and then hit with an ax!"*

Dan Kern of Advisor Partners said it more elegantly: "Many of these optimization models are trying to create the illusion of precision in an area that simply can't be predicted so accurately."

So, how do you weight asset classes? As a rough start, it is okay to factor in your personal preferences as well as some of your advisor's preferences. I say this first, because even if I didn't, most of you would still do it anyway. It is your money, not mine. However, it is best not to be too radical or rigid in your asset class weightings. For instance, rather than completely rejecting one asset class or another, it is much safer for you to think in terms of adjusting the range of how much to invest in one class over another. If you still really hate investing in emerging market (EM) countries, rather than put zero into this broad category, simply put the minimum amount recommended below. That way, if you happen to be wrong, you won't be too wrong.

The simple methodology for the relative weightings in each asset class is often done by the market size or total value of one asset class versus the size or total value on another. For instance, in the case of stock markets, a weighting may be the total market capitalization of the United States[3] versus the rest of the world's stock markets. Or in the case of bonds, the total nominal value of bonds of one country versus the rest of the world. (See below asset allocation example.) There are other basic guidelines worth discussing in the following sections.

The Ratio of Equities versus Bonds or Fixed Income Is Often Determined by Your Age

In other words, if you are older, you should gradually own a smaller proportion of stocks and more bonds in your portfolio, because in your older years you want less volatility. Dr. Andrew Rudd, chairman and CEO of Advisor Software, says, "The ratio is not so much a function of your age as your own personal financial needs and wants. If you might well need the money sooner, for whatever reason, then you may well want to have a higher ratio of bonds. On the other hand, if you have enough to live off of and you want to grow your family's long-term wealth, you may keep much more in equities than your age may indicate."

In my personal opinion, since people need more growth due to living longer, and because the risk of equity volatility is ameliorated by the long number of years you are investing plus the breadth of countries in your portfolio, you can have a higher proportion of equities than is often recommended for a conservative portfolio.

In the case of bonds, it is also important to mix up the types of bonds in your portfolio, from sovereign to corporate-rated bonds and even at times buying a small amount of bond funds focusing in on lower-rated bonds and asset-backed bonds. However, the more volatile types of fixed income exposures should be kept to a minority of your total bond portfolio if you are retired.

The Country Allocation for Equities and Bonds

This is the subject of much debate, as you saw in the previous chapter. Traditionally and in many indices, the weighting is done by the relative existing or past market size of each country versus the rest of the world. The most well-known example is the MSCI World Index.[4] However, the problem is that in this index investors are underweighted in the countries that are clearly growing faster. The research done on the expected GDP growth over the next five or ten years[5] gives us the ability to weight the countries that will likely have a larger percentage of the world's total GDP. It can be expected that those higher growth markets will over time have stock markets that will give a higher return.

Some traditionalists argue that in the past, GDP has not predicted stock market growth; however, in the distant past, many emerging markets did not have exchanges that are as well run and as liquid as they have become this past decade; therefore, GDP growth will be a better predictor of better stock market returns going forward. Most investors like to more heavily weight their own country for a variety of reasons, many of them valid. For instance, you may wish to have more exposure in the country in which you expect to retire. It is perfectly OK in normal circumstances to even double-weight the exposure to your own country if you live in one with a smaller stock market, as long as you make sure to at least keep a healthy portion of other countries in the portfolio. In the case of the United States, because so many US stocks also gain from their international revenues, it may be fine to have as much as half of your total equities exposure to US stocks.

As to your allocation across currencies, part of this diversification is already inherent in your country allocation into international bonds and stocks. Currency exposure is unique in that it is the one type of class that is purely zero sum, meaning that when one currency goes up, another currency must be going down. Make sure you have a broad exposure to a variety of currencies, especially from countries that have strong fundamentals in currency reserves and are fiscally and monetarily sound. It is no longer an acceptable risk to have all your exposure in just one currency. No matter how powerful you think your country is, it is still a lower risk to your long-term portfolio to have some other currency exposure. Today, due to the growth and increasing strength of so many countries, it is relatively easy to have a broad basket of different currencies. As you age, you will want a larger weighting in your home currency in order to decrease the volatility of your portfolio. However, you are exposed if your own currency falls considerably versus currency of other countries.

Dr. Rudd gives an excellent example: "Your Consumption basket, even as you age, remains exposed to other currencies. Much of your food, the cost of the building materials in your dwelling, and many other products and services you use are often priced in another currency." Like it or not, if your home currency deteriorates dramatically, it will likely inflate dramatically the cost of many items you need to consume. You and your advisor should review your portfolio and have an approximate understanding of your overall direct and indirect currency exposure to the various currencies embedded in your portfolio, either through money markets and bonds, or through stock funds.

Commodities Are All Assets You Can See, Kick, or Touch

These include precious and other metals, agriculture, timber, and energy. You and your advisor will analyze direct exposure in these commodities as well as indirect exposure—investing in heavily dependent commodities-exporting countries and in companies dedicated to commodities, like mining and oil companies. There are a variety of direct and indirect ways you can garner exposure to commodities. There are also nontraditional commodities that can be at times attractive to your portfolio in small quantities, like art or other collectibles. Now, even water can be a tradable commodity in some countries. It is wise to have at least a little exposure to commodities, because in times of crisis this category can hold its value. Some commodities index funds tend to overweigh either gold or oil and have hardly any of other commodities such as food, timber or other metals. It is preferable to select a commodities fund that includes a larger portion of all the commodities. However, given that this category does not organically grow as does a stock or a bond, keep the exposure in your Investing Pocket to less that 10 to 15 percent maximum, but with a minimum of 3 to 5 percent.

Real Estate Exposure

This comes in two forms: your own house or the direct investments you have made; and in REITs, REIT funds, or real estate limited partnerships you own. In the case of your house, if you have a lot of equity in your home or homes, e.g., half or more of your total assets, then you may not need any more exposure to REITs other than perhaps 3 to 5 percent in, for instance, global REITs. However, if you do not have much exposure personally to real estate, then it may make sense to have as much as 10 to 15 percent of your total equities exposure in REITs and REIT funds for further diversification.

Insurance and Annuities Policies

Depending on their structure, these can also be a form of investing. They typically operate in a similar fashion in your return to bonds, except that these policies are not so liquid without paying a penalty. So, if a large percentage of your total financial assets are in insurance products, it needs to be factored in as being part of the larger fixed income class of assets. There may be exceptions, however; if the variable annuity, for instance, is exposed to equities markets, the policy's value should be counted in the equities portion.

To conclude: Up until this chapter, I have tried to get you comfortable with the fact that you don't have to worry about getting the allocation and weighting of each asset class exactly right. After all, given how uncertain the economic world has always been, it is impossible to achieve perfection in asset allocation. However, it is understandable that many advisors and customers will still want to carefully construct their allocation mix.

STEP 3. ACCUMULATION AND MONITORING

As we discussed, the "trickle in, trickle out" method is one of the most effective tools in decreasing risk in your Investing Pocket. And as you accumulate positions in each of the asset classes, you can monitor what you have already bought.

Frequency of Investing

Concerning how often you should buy funds, naturally the lowest risk approach is to buy a little each month. However, for many people it is too inconvenient, and also hard to make the minimum investment required in each fund unless they have a systematic investment program. The good news is that there is very little additional risk if you only make new investments every quarter; even if you don't get around to purchasing but once or twice a year, it will have little negative impact on growing your money and keeping your risk low over your lifetime. The most important rule to follow is, Don't invest a significant portion of your money into risk asset classes all at once. If you do, you can run the risk of bad timing, whereas if you are investing a little all the time over decades, you take the timing risk out of your portfolio.

Also, don't worry about buying all the individual assets class at once. For instance, in one quarter, you can buy a domestic index fund, and then the next quarter you can buy an international actively managed fund, and then the third quarter you can buy a medium-term international bond fund. Over the decades, it won't matter much what interval you actually purchased what particular asset class, especially if you build up the exposures to all the asset classes relatively evenly. By alternating what you buy at each interval, you are incorporating the strategy of diversification.

Where possible, I advise you to sign up for automatic reinvestment of your dividends and interest income. That way, you are continuing to build up your positions over time.

As part of the monitoring process, an advisor may help you time more optimally what you are buying by looking at what sectors are particularly low valued at the time, using the standard value comparison metrics discussed above. For instance, if US stocks are at their all-time highs but most of the analysts don't like the international growth stocks category—and these overseas markets are selling at low prices relative to their earnings and book values—then your advisor might recommend starting to build up your international portfolio. A year or more later, if US stocks come down, then your advisor may decide it is time to buy more of the US market, or buy a US REIT fund for further diversification.

My own view about timing markets even on the margin is that even most experts are unable to know the right time to buy/sell. It is especially true when deciding when to get into the markets. What I have personally noticed over the decades is that most of the time, it is too hard to tell if a crash or a sudden rise is imminent. In most times, you are simply better off to continue to trickle in and not worry about the timing. However, occasionally there are markets that are clearly oversold or overbought.[6] And only in those cases has it made sense to adjust your accumulation on the margin. Recognize that you will still likely miss at least part of the timing just due to how emotional markets are. It is when a market is at its best value when most everything you read and hear says this asset class is terrible. As to the kinds of metrics you and your advisor use to judge when markets could be overvalued or undervalued, please review the valuation metrics covered in Chapter 12.

It is critical not to misinterpret this recommended long-term accumulation strategy with trying as an attempt to time markets and go in and go out every month or quarter. That introduces way too much needless risk into a portfolio. After all, what if you are wrong? I am talking about buying slowly over time and holding these positions over a period of decades. This is not your selling strategy. That comes much later in life.

Furthermore, as part of the ongoing monitoring process, your advisor is gauging where you are underweight, and overweight, and is normally balancing your portfolio by buying over time more of what you are underweight, rather than selling what you are overweight. I am not saying "never sell, only buy!," but selling should be rare. An exception would be if a particular asset class has risen so high that it has outsized the rest of your total portfolio; your advisor then may want to reduce the portion of the massively overvalued asset class a little and put the money into a lower-valued class. I must emphasize though that this should be a rare event; in the Investing Pocket, you don't want to get into the TAA (tactical asset allocation) game, where there are frequent dramatic adjustments as you or your advisor constantly try to time the market and make big bets on one asset class versus another. This strategy generally loses and adds needless risk to your Investing Pocket.

Up to now, I have been talking about investing a little each year because many people can only put so much money to work at a time in their Investing Pocket anyway. But what do you do if all of a sudden you have a large amount of money come to you that you want to invest? Maybe you inherited a significant sum, or received your pension in a lump sum—or after reading this book, you decided that giant pot of money sitting in the bank needs to be invested pronto. It is important not to put all your money at one time into any risk asset class. Even if you give the investment advisor the total amount of money to manage, it is best to instruct him to leave a large portion in the safe, low-volatility asset classes, like money funds, and only invest portions at a time into the risk asset classes. For instance, you can instruct him to increase your investments once a quarter over the next two, three, or even four years. That way, you will incorporate the power of time diversification into your portfolio, just in case the markets suddenly go down right after you put a major portion of your assets in. Don't worry that you may miss part of the investment opportunity by straddling your investing into the various markets. After decades of market exposure, any opportunities you may have missed at the beginning will become immaterial to the end outcomes. Besides, by stretching your investing process out over three to four years, you will be assured that you were at least partially right in your timing because some of your money was invested during this period.

As you and your advisor monitor your funds' performances within each asset class, you may decide to sell one fund and replace it with another. It could be that the fund management company has lost a lot of good managers, or that your advisor may think a fund might be soon shut down due to the AUM shrinking, as our research has shown.[7] However, these sell transactions should be infrequent. Your average or normal holding period for your funds would be mostly 5 to 15 years.

Also, if you are in the accumulation stage and only have a small portfolio, it will be difficult to tailor your investments to a particular country or customized investing strategy. Not to worry. If, for instance, you are buying an actively managed fund with a broad investment charter, like an international stock fund, it is the job of the fund manager to select from a variety of EM and developed markets for you. So over your lifetime, you shouldn't be at that much of a disadvantage versus the larger investors.

High net worth investors, especially those with Investing Pockets over $1 million to $3 million, can work with their advisors to customize their portfolios to more precisely fit their particular investing philosophy. For instance, they may want to weight the growth countries more than the mature countries, and since they have enough money, they can buy multiple funds and ETFs to accomplish the investor's exact strategy.

In your monitoring process each year, you are not just looking at how each fund is performing. What is most important is to look at the entire portfolio and see if you are still on track to meet the withdrawals you are planning in your later years.

As you enter your 60s, or your 70s, you will naturally need to slowly adjust your investment strategy. At these intervals, it is best then to be selling small portions of your riskier asset classes over the decades and either use that money for your monthly expenses if you are totally retired, or place that money in shorter term, bond asset classes. In sum, you want to keep that image of the sloth I described before in the back of your mind. Don't make any large sell or buy movements at any one time.

STEP 4. YOUR AGE: REFINE YOUR ALLOCATION BY WHERE YOU ARE IN YOUR LIFE

For many people, the most powerful driver when building and managing a portfolio is their age. The simple reason is that as you get closer to withdrawing the money, you have to adjust the portfolio so that sudden market fluctuations won't damage your long-term target return.

Of course, there can be many other drivers that can be equally important depending on your personal situation. For instance, you may be wealthy enough that you won't need all the money you are investing and know that a certain portion will go to a charity, or to your kids. In that case, even though you are, for instance, 70 years old, the portion of your portfolio to be given away may be managed as if it were for a person or entity much younger than you are, for instance the way someone in their 40s would run their portfolio. This is because your children or the charity won't need or be able to even spend this money until long after you have passed away. Therefore, this portion of money you won't ever personally spend can be managed less conservatively. Let's look at three different age categories and the typical decisions that need to be made during each. At the conclusion of each section, I give sample global portfolio allocations for someone in each age bracket. In these scenarios, I give ranges so that in the case of equities, if you are at the oldest end of these age brackets, you might want to have the range more at the lower end, whereas, if you are at the beginning of that age bracket, you might want to have your equities exposure at the upper end of the range. I believe these recommendations should be a range rather than a single number to allow for the personal preferences of the investor and the advisor.

Image 14.1   Sample Allocation Across All Three Pockets

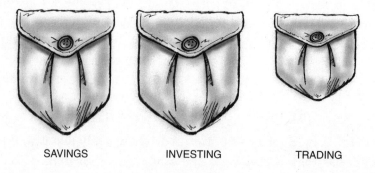

SAVINGS   INVESTING   TRADING

Key Factors in Allocation:

- Once you start out, the Savings Pocket must first be filled per the minimum levels you set. For instance, do you have emergency funds covering at least four to six months' expenses? After this preset amount is reached, you can begin to add to your Investing Pocket.
- The Investing Pocket should take the bulk of your additional funding. However, after you retire, you may want to slowly increase the Savings Pocket proportion in order to decrease your overall risk level.
- **You do not need to put any money in the Trading Pocket.** This pocket ensures that if you must take additional risks or insist on trying to time markets, you limit this activity to your Trading Pocket, which should be a minority of your funds.

**General Guidelines by Age: Up to Your
Mid 50s: Start Trickling In**

In this age bracket, many of you are likely still paying a mortgage, have kids in college, maybe even have to pay for your own parents' health care. It is hard to think about your own long-term investing needs or even have the ability to save up enough for an Investing Pocket. However, as you saw in the above examples, the earlier you can start putting in even a little money, the more robust your plan can be. There are two powerful reasons why. First, the further you are from starting to drawdown your funds, the more aggressive you can safely be in weighting the asset classes. The net effect is that you will get a higher return per year on the overall portfolio if you can begin to invest earlier in your life. Second, the power of compounding really is maximized when you can have your money growing over 30 years or longer. Remember that example in Chapter 8 about how much equities can grow over multiple decades.

Indeed, even if in your 30s you can start to put just a few thousand dollars a year into your Investing Pocket, the equity growth and the compounding effect will make you much happier in your later years. I would even say if you can start such an investment process in your 20s it would be even better.

Savings Pocket: As said above, the first thing you have to do is build up an emergency fund. Depending on family size, age of children, and job security, ideally you would like six to nine months' pay or expenses here, with an absolute minimum of three months. When your future income is highly uncertain, you might want a year's expenses in this pocket.

As you are still young, you can have some slightly higher-yielding short-term funds in this pocket. Just don't have the majority of the money in a short-term fund that is not easy to understand, like a fund loaded with complex derivatives or containing more risk than a standard money market account (MMA).

Although you may not have a lot of money, try to have at least some money in a second institution, either another bank or broker just to watch any SPOFs. One bank can hold your savings account while a brokerage account elsewhere can contain your money market fund.

Investing Pocket: At a minimum, make sure to take advantage of IRA and 401(k) limits and opportunities (in other countries it is often called an ISA, or investment savings account, which allows your money to grow tax free). We don't get many opportunities in our lives that are such gifts, so take advantage of it every year. Then, after funding your IRA, if you have even a little bit of additional money to add to your Investing Pocket, even a few thousand dollars, you are ready to talk to someone about your investing options. If you are too small to have an advisor, I recommend either using a reputable internet broker or using those brokers or banks that have access to a trained investment person to whom you can ask questions, even if it is on the phone. Typically, low-cost firms often won't give you firm or committed advice. However, they can help in what I call guided discovery; their more experienced reps can tell you the pros and cons of each product so you can tell for yourself how much of one risk versus another you want. It is best to visit a few offices of different brokers or banks, just to get a feel for which ones you are more comfortable with. I recommend finding a rep in the firm that has had at least ten years' experience, even if it is a discount brokerage firm. In the world of investing, you really want the person helping you to have personally lived through a couple of investment cycles, just so you know they have seen what can go wrong. In Part III, I will explore the advisor selection process.

As to the sequence of buying, it is best to start out with broader fund charters because the amount of money you are putting to work is small. This is also the time to invest in more aggressive growth stock funds, like small company stock funds, funds that are investing in frontier and emerging countries, and high-yield and moderate-rated corporate bond funds. As you can see in the below recommended asset allocation sample by age bracket, when you are still young, you can take advantage of volatile asset classes that over the long run yield considerably higher returns.

Trading Pocket: Especially when we are younger, it is tempting to go for it and try to make quick money by trading. However, build up your Investing Pocket before you start trading. As a very rough rule of thumb, always have far less money in your Trading Pocket than in your Investing Pocket. The money you are gambling with in this pocket should only be the money that you can easily afford to lose. Remember, as you get into your 50s, you might not be able to make it again. If you get a big bonus, take advantage and fund your Investing Pocket. You need it to keep growing, because unexpected things can happen in a career and you may not be able to work as long as you would like.

Mid 50s to Early 70s: Accelerate your Investing Pocket Funding

Your retirement age is now within sight. It is critical that you begin to put away a larger amount of funds into your Investing Pocket. These are often the high-earning years of your career, so it is wise to make sure you have amply funded for your long-term needs. If you receive a large bonus, first fund the Investing Pocket before you plan other discretionary expenditures. For many, it is difficult to know exactly how long you will be able to keep making your high income. I have seen investors early in this stage of their lives think they will continue to make their high incomes up until 65—but their firms may have other ideas.

Also, many individuals in this stage have investments in other structured plans, often connected with their work. Their 401(k) plans may have a limited group of choices for them, or they may even be in a defined benefit plan where their corporation has selected an outside manager. In addition, they may have considerable exposure to their company's stock. Or their family may have set up a trust that has exposure to various asset classes. Lastly, you may have purchased a fixed return or variable life or annuity product that has underlying asset class exposure. It is very important to know what underlying asset classes you are exposed to so that can be incorporated into the percentages suggested in the chart. You don't want to inadvertently double up your bet in one asset class. One frequent example I see is that a person owns a long-term, guaranteed fixed return product, which will therefore closely correlate with the risks and returns of a long-term bond fund. Yet, the person may then also own a larger portion of his/her own managed portfolio in bonds as well. Thus, the investor ends up with double the exposure to bonds and not enough exposure to equities.

If you have a considerable estate—over $5 million in financial assets plus a lot of real estate with little or no mortgage—it may be worth it to hire a trust attorney to review your life financial plan as well. If something happened to you and your spouse, remember the IRS takes a big a portion of your estate. At the same time, some complicated trust structures can be more bother than they are worth to use as you manage your investments, and you might not like the loss of flexibility. So, balancing out all the various factors, including what is a major nuisance to execute over time, is the right way to think about estate planning.

Regarding all your advisors—tax and accounting, investment, lawyers, even doctors—it is important during this period to line up advisors that are younger than you. Check to see who the young partners are coming into all your counselors' practices. I have this problem now: Half the doctors I trusted are now retiring. I like that two of my own investment advisors each have very competent, experienced 40-somethings that will take over their practices when my contacts retire. This is especially true of trust attorneys: By the time your estate is being settled, it would be nice if you dealt with a person that was closer to the age of your children, rather than buried alongside you.

Savings Pocket: Normally, this pocket should remain at a steady level, because additional funds should be put into the Investing Pocket to get the growth you need. However, it is certainly ok to have a full year's expenses and some emergency money in this pocket.

If you have any extra money beyond what you are putting into your Investing Pocket, accelerate the payoff of your house loan. By the time you retire, it is most prudent to have virtually no debt. People often get wrapped up in trying to keep tax-deductible interest to decrease their taxes. However, all too often, the net of the deduction relative to what you are actually getting paid in the Savings Pocket can actually be less of a return for you. So, it may be better to get rid of the extra debt.

You may have saved up to a point where you are reaching the upper limits of FDIC insurance in any one of your bank accounts. If so, open up a few bank accounts at multiple banks to avoid an SPOF. If you haven't already, now would be the time to also put a portion of your Savings Pocket money in one or more MMAs at either a brokerage firm of the brokerage division of a bank.

The top mistake people make is that they don't start investing because they think the times are too uncertain. So they leave all or most of their money in the Savings Pocket and they miss the growth. Worse, interest rates often do not keep up with inflation, so you lose the purchasing power of your money over time if it is not invested in a broad package of risk assets.

Investing Pocket: Until you retire, this pocket should remain in full growth mode because you and/or your spouse likely have 30 or more years after you stop working for your money to last. Even after you retire, keep any adjustments to your portfolio to a minimum. The image you want in your mind is that you will slowly spread out your rebalancing over the decade after you retire. During that time, you and your advisor will begin to:

- Move out of frontier and emerging growth markets and more into growth and advance growth markets, in both debt and equity exposures.
- Slowly decrease any weighting of your exposure to the more speculative high yield fixed income funds in place of investing more in rated debt instruments.

Table 14.1 Sample of asset allocation recommendations for the Investing Pocket

Age range	40–54	55–71	72 or older
Equities	**60–90%**	**45–65%**	**20–40%**
Home country	25–35	20–30	10–20
International equities			
Other developed countries	10–15	8–12	5–10
Growth countries	12–22	8–18	3–10
Frontier countries	8–18	3–8	0–3
Fixed income	**12–30%**	**20–40%**	**40–75%**
Developed (incl. Home)	7–20	13–30	35–60
Growth markets	5–10	7–12	5–15
Frontier markets	0–5	0–3	0–1
Real assets	**10–20%**	**8–15%**	**5–10%**
Real estate			
Home country	5–12	4–10	3–8
International	3–8	2–5	1–3
Commodities	3–8	2–5	1–3

- By the end of your 60s, it may be wise to adjust your equities portfolio to have less of the growth stock and small company stock exposure. In place, you can cultivate those funds that have more dividend yield.

Trading Pocket: By the time of retirement, it is most important to have your Investing Pocket fully funded. If there is excess money left over, even after allowing for possible expensive health care/assisted living costs, then have fun if you want and enjoy the game of trading stocks. Though the odds of winning are not great, they are a lot better than Las Vegas.

A note of caution: I have seen many instances where a little extra money resulted in people losing way too much money. Sometimes, a speculative investment can pull you into further obligations that end up digging deeply into your Investing Pocket. So be careful with your money here; you can't make it again. Remember, the "sunk cost" concept, which means that if you have lost money on an investment, don't make the mistake of throwing good money after bad. Better to accept your losses and move on than think you have to put more money into an investment to save it. Also, remember that you can use this pocket as your stress release valve; if you panic one day, don't touch your Investing Pocket, just sell out your Trading Pocket and put the money in your Savings Pocket.

Over 72 Years: Don't Adjust Too Much Too Soon

I chose 72 years as the next life stage because after having several conversations with various gerontologists and psychologists, it seems that at 70 many people still think they are young. But for some reason, at around 72, people begin to realize they are not so young anymore. And, since more people are working later, at least part time, they don't necessarily have to dig deeply into their Investing Pockets until they are into their 70s.

There are a few "must do's" I should highlight for this section. If you haven't already done it by this age, you can no longer delay getting your estate plans in order. It is just too irresponsible to leave it alone any longer. One of the saddest and most frequent occurrences I see are people leaving it up to their kids to decide how their estates should be divided. It puts too much pressure on the surviving spouse and virtually guarantees there will be permanently damaging arguments in the remaining family. It is your job to settle the division of assets now, in your will. You will have a much higher chance of better family harmony after you pass. Even if one or another member is unhappy, it is better that you are blamed rather than your children blaming each other. Also, especially if you are wealthy, I advise you find a third party not slated to inherit anything, and much younger than yourself, to act as the trustee or executor. This person can act as the voice of reason and ensure your estate is properly handled.

The second hard choice you need to make in your financial life plan is at what point, should you give up managing your assets? It is one of the most difficult personal decisions in many people's lives but it is so much better to decide in advance before mistakes are made. And then, you have to stick to your original plan of when to turn over the responsibility. My mother wisely did this. Driving was becoming more stressful for her, so when she turned 81, she announced that at her next birthday she would not renew her license; she also decided not to look at her finances unless my brother or me were present. It was hard for her at first, but she knew she had done the right and safe thing. Starting in your 70s, periodically take cognitive tests so you know you can continue to oversee your investments. Even if you are still functioning well, it is important once you are in your mid to late 70s to involve the person who will eventually take over the function of managing your investments before it is too late.

I realize this is an emotionally difficult process to face, but it is the responsible thing to do. An old friend of mine's dad was a stock exchange floor trader and remained in the job long after Alzheimer's had set in. Since he owned his own seat on the Floor, he could still trade on the Floor. Eventually, after money was lost, his sons had to go around to all the other traders and say, "Don't accept his orders without checking with us." It was a financially dangerous situation, and even though you are probably not such an active trader, you still don't want to have any chance of putting yourself in a similar situation when it comes to managing your financial assets. Along those lines, many brokerage firms are so concerned about their liability that they won't take trades from people over a certain age without an additional connected person also approving those trades. The brokerage firm just can't assume the liability. So, way before you get to this stage, it is wise to turn it over to whomever you trust to manage your money. I will have more on the issue of whom to trust in the next chapter.

The Savings Pocket: In this stage of your life, your Savings Pocket should slowly be taking in funds from your Investing Pocket in order to decrease your volatility risk. The sloth philosophy should still rule. No sudden changes in your portfolio; only gradual shifting of assets into your saving pocket and into short- and intermediate-term fixed income and variable interest rate products and funds.

The Investing Pocket: It is critical this pocket continues to grow. Given that you are already 72, and if you are in relatively good health, you or your spouse may still have over 20 years of good living left, which means that even with volatility in the markets, 20 years still means that a lot of the volatility will be smoothed out for the portion of your money still exposed to risk asset classes.

During this period of your life, within each risk asset class, you are switching to lower volatility investments gradually each year and buying a larger proportion of assets that kick off current income, like dividends and interest income, to cover your monthly withdrawals. These investment types within each asset class also have lower volatility on average because they are coming from companies that are more mature and can afford to pay higher dividends.

In terms of country allocation, it is during this period that the proportion of mature countries and advanced growth countries becomes the dominant proportion of your risk assets in equities and bonds. I would not move it to all home-country assets, because you want some exposure to other countries equities, bonds, and currencies in case your home country develops serious economic problems. You also may want to keep a small portion of your assets in growth countries and emerging growth countries in order to maintain some growth that is also a bit of a hedge against inflation. The frontier countries portion can shrink to zero to decrease your volatility. Likewise, in this stage of your life, high yield and other unrated bond categories should be eliminated due to risk.

In this life stage, I suggest putting the bulk of assets in publically registered mutual funds, or if you are buying directly stocks and bonds, it should be with an advisor that you have already known for at least a decade. This is not the time to buy private products, like private limited partnerships, not under the strict rules of the SEC; the due diligence is harder for you to verify, and the illiquidity is not something you want in your portfolio. Even if a salesman claims there is liquidity, unless you can independently verify the product can be easily liquidated at a reasonable price, stay away. One quick test is to see if the underlying instruments or investment have a quoted price on an exchange or public quoting system, like NASDAQ.

The Trading Pocket: Provided you have the extra funds and don't need any more money to support yourself and your family, even if you live to be 100, trading is tempting. After all, you now have the time to study the markets. Just make sure you involve the person who will eventually assume the oversight of your investments. Keep such activity in a separate account from your Investing Pocket, just so you won't be tempted to move more money out of your Investing Pocket and into your Trading Pocket. You may be saying, "I know this already!" But I have seen so many financial disasters happen to older people who lose their life savings that I must restate this warning.

- Many financial planning models consider all your financial assets in a single pocket. Since I view the Savings Pocket as simply the amount you need to keep for emergency or short-term expenses, and the Trading Pocket as purely a discretionary pocket, I have confined the above suggested ranges to only your Investing Pocket. If you decide to indulge in speculative or trading type activities, it should remain a small portion of your total investing program unless you are so wealthy you won't need to draw upon that money. Normally, the Trading Pocket ranges from zero to 15 percent of all your Pockets in order not to jeopardize your long-term investing plan.
- Short-term fixed income, including money market funds and bank accounts, is factored into the amount you want in your Savings Pocket.
- Multiple traditional asset allocation models use various other mechanisms to calculate the portion of equities. For instance, among the most popular and simple rules of thumb is to subtract your age from 110, giving you the amount of the equity portion in your portfolio; your advisor may have other acceptable ideas. Every individual has different opinions and life circumstances, so I thought it better to give you a broader range of the total proportion of equities. However, other approaches should at least fit inside this broad range.
- The amount in your home country versus other developed nations is a function of personal preference plus the size and opportunities in the country where you live. For instance

advisors in smaller countries like Ireland or Singapore consider the home country to include the entire European Community or the Asian Region, respectively.

- Growth countries' economic exposure is also partially included in developed market stocks due to the source of a portion of the growth countries' revenues embedded into many of the developed countries' domestic stocks. For instance, McDonald's and Ford Motor Company have massive overseas operations and thus participate in the growth of foreign markets. However, this may not be enough exposure to growth countries, as you are missing major companies not listed in the developed country. For instance, if you only bought stocks listed on the NYSE, you would miss many local public companies in growth countries that do not have a ADRs and GDRs[8] on the NYSE.

- Within the equities portion, you and your advisor will determine such further divisions as growth stocks versus value stocks; more conservative high dividend stocks versus appreciation-oriented stocks; small companies versus large companies; or industry-sector-focused stocks versus stocks across all sectors. In each case, the former choices are for the younger aged investors while the latter choices are for the older investors that are looking for lower volatility.

- Regarding fixed income or your bond allocation: It is wise to mix both corporate and government bonds; in certain economic cycles, some government bonds can be ever riskier than corporate bonds.

- Regarding your real estate allocation: If your home is a large portion of your assets, you may set the home country allocation to real estate investing to be at the minimum, since you already have direct exposure to real estate via your home.

- Commodities should be broadly invested across precious metals, industrial/commercial materials, energy, agricultural goods, and timber. Make sure not to be solely exposed to just oil and gold; they tend to dominate certain indices.

- Note that the category covering hedge funds, venture capital, and private equity funds is normally not in the Investing Pocket. As discussed before, given the high fees eating into your returns coupled with the fact that this category at times correlates more with the traditional classes than has been advertised, it is not a critical category for the average investor. Also, as a group they have not outperformed more traditional classes. However, high net worth investors may decide to further refine their allocations and invest a small portion into this category; up to 5 percent of the total portfolio could be OK. However, given its illiquidity, it would better fit in the Trading Pocket.

OTHER KEY QUESTIONS WHEN DECIDING ON YOUR PORTFOLIO

What if I Come Up Short in My Plan?

First off, don't panic and do something stupid in investing. Second, it is not all bad news; you know where you are, and unless you are already in your 70s, you have time to make adjustments. Let's talk about what you can do to shrink that gap:

Shrink your expenses now. Work on your expenses now and eliminate any discretionary items you can until you see your long-term financial plan is more in line with where you want to be in your later years. Due to the compounding effect, money invested in your 50s will grow substantially over the next 20 and 30 years.

If you have children and you are spending your retirement money on educating them now, the result will be that you will need their help when you are old and out of money. Not a cool place to be. Rather, your college-age children can work part time, apply to more reasonably priced colleges, and take on a modest amount of debt themselves. After all, it will make them mature faster, and let's face it, we all know the unlikelihood that spoiled children will take proper care of you in your later years.

Rethink what you are going to do in your 60s. Either delay retirement, or if that is not possible, at a minimum, think about what part-time or lower stress job you can do until you are, for instance, 70 years or older. The good news is your expenses will likely be lower because your kids are raised and you no longer have a mortgage. So, you don't need to make as much money.

Fig. 14.4   Investing in a Portfolio with 5 Percent Returns

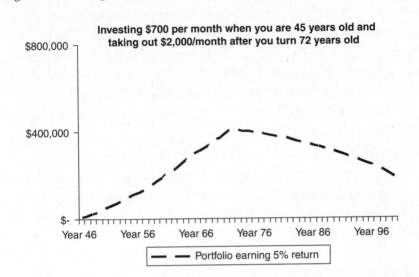

Don't take any money out of your Investment Pocket. Working even a little after retirement can delay touching the Investing Pocket. This gives you three powerful advantages. One, it gets you out of the house so you won't be bored to tears. Two, the funds in the Investing Pocket can keep growing, keep compounding. Three, you can keep your portfolio longer in a growth mode as you are lengthening the time horizon of the money. By delaying the time to begin withdrawing money, the profile of your Investing Pocket can remain on the same growth trajectory as when you were in your 50s, even though you are now in your 60s. The impact of having a more growth-oriented portfolio means you may garner an additional 1 percent return per year throughout that period, and compounding through that period. Thus, when you delay the withdrawal assumptions, you will likely see the amount of money available to you for your later years increase substantially, perhaps enough to take away your shortfall.

Above is just such an example of this idea:

If you do not withdraw until 72, and start investing about $700 per month when you are 45, then you will end up with $190,000 in your portfolio when you are 100 years old, compared to a deficit of $625,000 if you started withdrawing immediately after retirement.

Can You Accept a Little More Risk in Your Portfolio?

Up until now, we have been talking about the lowest possible risk scenario to grow your money. However, if you are still coming up short, you can consider adding a little more risk into your portfolio in a measured way. Yes, you increase slightly the chances of an eventual shortfall; however, you will be surprised how little risk such a move can actually be to your long-term portfolio. Just remember, don't take any sudden steps in your Investing Pocket, and don't invest in some get rich quick scheme. Don't worry, by employing these measured recommendations below, your portfolio will *grow with the least amount of added risk to your long-term plan, but likely with a much better return*. Examples of increased return measures you can employ without adding unacceptable risk:

Increase the equity portion of your overall portfolio. So long as you continue to work at least part time for a few more years and do not start withdrawing any money in your Investing Pocket until you are 70 or so, your volatility in a broadly invested equity portfolio will be substantially reduced. And a larger equity portfolio can easily bring you an additional 1 or 2 percent in compounding annual return.

Increase the portion of your portfolio in growth, emerging growth, and even frontier countries. The volatility of your portfolio will increase marginally, although for periods of more than a decade, this increased risk impact should be minimal. And since this is a broad basket of countries, even with some of the countries failing, the overall basket is still likely to grow a lot more than a basket loaded with mature countries only.

Consider substituting a larger portion of other income producing assets in place of a more conservative allocation to the fixed income or bond portfolio. Such examples can include small amounts of income-producing REITs, convertible bonds, high dividend large company, more conservative preferred stocks, and bonds. Also, providing your advisor does a good job in due diligence, you can add a small portion of the independently high-rated, asset-backed portfolios available. Also, your advisor can run a series of scenarios so you can refine your projections to fit your unique financial situation.

I Have Shorter Term Goals to Meet. How Do I Plan For Them?

Understandably, especially through your late 20s, 30s, and 40s, you will have to save up for target expenses that have much shorter horizons than your retirement funding. These needs include such expenditures as a down payment for your house or your children's college education.

It is best to set up separate Investing Pocket accounts, as these needs will have separate horizons. For instance, if your child is not expected to start college for ten years, then you have a time horizon of funding that lasts for 10 through 14 years. The portfolio will look similar to the ratios of a person just after retirement:

- More fixed income or more medium-term bonds of up to 10 and 12 years held to maturity
- Equity exposure in the more conservative areas such as dividend stocks from major established companies
- Overall exposure from mature and advanced growth countries

Although the return will likely be lower than your long-term retirement Investing Pocket, you will have a higher chance of not losing any money in this specific Investing Pocket that has shorter term goals. Also, take advantage of all the tax advantaged programs many governments allow for. That way, you can be growing the portion of the money that you have otherwise had to pay in taxes.

IRAs, 401(k)s, ISAs: How Should I Handle Them?

This is a simple answer. Delay as long as the government allows you before withdrawing any of the funds. This money is growing without being taxed yet. Just think of it as the government letting you have the money to make income on it all those years before you have to pay them back. It is a gift, so take advantage of it. Also, depending on the advice of your advisor and other counselors, you may want to consider delaying the withdrawals from your Social Security account.

How Do I Decide About Socially Responsible Investing?

Personally, I have been interested in this topic for a number of years. Over the last decade, while I was at Nikko Am, a number of us had a genuine interest in creating funds, such as an Eco Fund, a Water Fund and a World Bank Green Bond strategy focusing in on responsible investing. I have learned over the past decade that there are a lot of investors that sincerely want to invest in this category. However, it is important to note that most investors expect a good return on their investments as well. After all, it is not a charitable contribution. It is your Investing Pocket we are talking about. As Dennis Clark of the Shelton Green Alpha fund says, "People want responsible investing done responsibly." Meaning with their Investing Pockets, most people want both: socially responsible investing and no sacrifice in their return. Thus, when considering such funds, you want to make sure the fund management company is returning to you a competitive return and, at the same time, buying stocks in companies that have a good track record in corporate governance and are responsible to their communities and operate to an ecologically protective standard. They should supply sufficient details before you and your advisor make the decision.

THE LESSONS FOR BUILDING YOUR PORTFOLIO

1. **Do the plan now. Don't wait.** You need to know where you are and what you are aiming for.
2. **Start funding the Investing Pocket now, even if it is only a small amount of money.** With "trickling in," there is no need to wait for a better market. Make no sudden moves in this pocket.
3. **Plan for emergencies.** Factor in some emergency money needed in your 80s, just in case your health expenses are high.
4. **Weighting matters.** Work carefully on the weightings of your various asset classes, but don't worry that it will not be perfect.

PART III

FINDING THE ADVISOR YOU CAN TRUST

After learning about how to grow your money in a safe way, you can also understand why so many people choose to select an advisor to help them put together and monitor their investment portfolio. Fortunately, over the years, I have met thousands of outstanding advisors, professionals who are highly trained and genuinely look out for their clients' best interest. But for many investors, finding a good advisor, someone who they can trust, can be a daunting process. The following chapters are structured to help you with the selection process as well as how to work with your advisor on an ongoing basis.

CHAPTER 15

WHO IS MOST DANGEROUS?

It's Who You Least Suspect

One afternoon, my mother and I were relaxing and she said to me, "How did you survive working in a place like Wall Street? Who could you trust in such an environment?"

I smiled. "It started back when I was three years old. It was one of my first memories. You said to me that I had to get my tonsils out at the hospital. If I was a good boy, you would get me anything I wanted. I told you I wanted a puppy, a German Shepherd puppy, like Rin Tin Tin on television. You readily agreed. All through the pain of the operation and recovery, I just kept on thinking, 'It is worth it. I will get my puppy.' After I came home and felt better, I asked about when I could get my puppy. The next day you bought me a little German Shepherd puppy—a stuffed animal! That's when I learned two things: 1. Don't trust anyone, not even your mother. 2. Get all agreements in writing. (Even though I couldn't even write.)"

She adamantly denied it until I reminded her how I used to try and feed my stuffed puppy Wheaties every morning. Then she paused and said, "That's right. I did do that to you."

In hindsight, I should have never told her. I had to comfort her for the rest of the day so she wouldn't feel so bad, and my brother was mad at me for bringing it up. Later on we laughed about the story and how we did finally get a Collie (like Lassie).

I have often felt it ironic that the people who love us the most are at times the very people that may lie to us—like a child making a desperate parent say anything just to quiet them down or sooth them through a traumatic moment.

While working on Wall Street, I have heard many stories about investors losing money and getting ripped off, and all too often, it was by people whom they knew well, especially relatives. It is not a comforting story, but since it has happened so often, I felt compelled to mention it at the start of this chapter.

MY GERMAN BUNNY BOSS

My first direct experience with fraud in the financial services industry goes back to 1975 while working as an analyst in a bank in Germany. My boss, Herr Hase (ironically, it means "bunny rabbit" in German) was the number two in the branch and extremely well respected. I was assigned to make sure the files on his deals were in proper order. One day I stumbled upon a loan he had made on behalf of the bank to his Panzer club, of which he was the director. He and his friends had a hobby of restoring World War II military vehicles. The problem was that the loan was long overdue, and there was no sign-off from any other officers in the bank, a direct violation of house and regulatory rules. I reminded him several times that the loan needed to be paid back, or at least the documentation put in proper order, but I was ignored. I told the branch manager, who, despite being a personal and longtime friend of Herr Hase, was furious because he had repeatedly and sternly warned Hase to repay the loan immediately. Herr Hase never did. In my final report I mentioned this problem, and within days internal auditors came in and investigated Herr Hase. It turned out he had over a million dollars in fraudulent loans. I learned two important lessons about trusting people when it comes to money. One, even people with great reputations can still commit serious fraud. Two, it is difficult for good, longtime friends to believe a friend will commit such crimes. So, the ability of someone to give you an accurate, unbiased reference about their friend can at times be jeopardized.

Over the years, I have learned many other key lessons from closely observing various frauds and rip-offs.

The recent news has been full of financial fraud and abuse. We have seen a wealthy board director, the former CEO of McKinsey, convicted of insider trading. Probably the worst fraud in recent years was the Madoff crime. In the mid-nineties, I did a fair amount of trading with Bernie and Peter Madoff's company. These two very intelligent individuals taught many of us in the industry valuable insights and created many trading innovations on the brokerage side of the business. What do these frauds all have in common? To a man, they were already successful, had all built careers with clean reputations. Why was it that after so many years each of them became so desperate they would risk it all so unnecessarily, would ruin so many lives?

I knew many of them through the times when they were actually committing the crimes. I'm sure they didn't just wake up one morning, look in the mirror, and say to themselves, "Today, I think I am going to rip off a bunch of people." It seems that it starts as a minor infraction, but it grows larger, and then they can't get out of it.

I can't begin to fathom why they do it, but what I do know is that there are people we know well and have trusted for years that we think could never commit a crime. But no matter how successful they have been, how many good people vouch for them, they can still rip you off. What is your protection? As the old adage goes, trust—but verify. Trust—but cut the cards.

When selecting an advisor, have an independent third party check on things for you, to verify if what you are seeing makes sense. It is also good to check with people that know them well, but remember, even they can get fooled by a smart-talking and, up until then, reputable close friend. Independent verification is often difficult to get right, so even if you get comfortable with a person whom you have known for a long while, or is in your family, or has made you money in the past, continue to check on him and how he is handling your money.

Unfortunately, there are no guarantees, no times when you can fully rest, even if the money is sitting in the bank. In the spirit of SPOF, always be looking, and remain suspicious. Don't drive yourself nuts with paranoia, but a dose of skepticism is your only friend when it comes to money. What specifically can you do?

- Talk to people who know the person and company with whom you are thinking of investing. And not just their friends, but also people who know him or the firm and don't have a vested interest. In the many cases of fraud I have personally reviewed, close friends could not bring themselves to report the infraction.

- Make sure you receive independent verification from another institution that your money or investments are there, in your or your estate's name, and that the value is independently verified by outside processes, such as a reputable trust bank or custodian. In the case of working with an advisor, the firm he is associated with should be a regulated entity, like a brokerage firm or a bank, where the custody of your funds is in safekeeping.

- Never write a check or wire any money to a person. Always make sure you know the institution and the account your money is going into.

- Periodically recheck your references. Checking only once at the beginning is never enough. People change.

- No matter how tempting, never have all or most of your money with one person or entity, just in case something goes wrong.

- Make sure your verification and the information you receive is truly independent. Your accountant, attorney, other investors, regulators' publicly available information, even other businesses that he or she deals with can become the independent verification you need to determine who to work with. If something feels awry, stay away. As mentioned above, even successful, formerly honorable people can rip you off. But with shady people or people with a reputation for committing even minor infractions, you naturally have a much higher chance of losing your money.

THE STORY OF CLIFFORD IRVING AND HOWARD HUGHES

What do I mean by truly independent sources of information?

Back in the early seventies, Clifford Irving, a published and reputable author, created a scheme to write a fake autobiography from made-up interviews with Howard Hughes. Hughes was a recluse at the time, and Irving thought he could pull it off by doing massive amounts of research before presenting the book to McGraw-Hill. In order to make sure the book was valid, McGraw-Hill verified most of the information by going into the Time-Life library, which they owned. What they did not realize was that Irving had gleaned most of the information for the book in the same library. Naturally, the information in the book checked out. Just after the book was printed and distributed to bookstores, Howard Hughes surprised everyone by calling his old friends in the press and letting them know it was a fraud. Irving served 17 months in jail.

This story is relevant to investors because you will hear what you think is independently verified information, yet it is all coming from the same source. And often, people who don't know you may not be willing to say anything other than, "Oh yeah, he is a good guy"; they don't want to take any personal risk by offending the person in question. In any case, you need to ask more specific questions, such as:

- How well do they know this person?
- Have they ever heard anything that would concern them?
- In what areas is this advisor better than others? (Implying that in the other areas, the advisor may not be so good. So, you can use this questioning technique to ask the follow-up question, "So, he/she is not so good at the other areas?")
- Do they know anyone else you can talk to who knows this advisor well?
- Would they put their mother's money with him?

I have often found that visiting the advisor more than once can tell you a lot about the person. Before you give them your money, see how they do with simple requests for further info; for instance, ask for sample reports. If the advisor is annoyed or doesn't actually follow up, that tells you a lot about how he will be after you are a client. Also, don't transfer all the money over to the advisor at once, but rather spread it out over at least three months. That way, you get a chance to see that everything is working well as you will receive a written confirmation independently back from the brokerage firm or bank that your money is now in your name at the institution before you send over any more money.

REGULATORS

Fortunately, regulators have improved considerably the availability of the histories of registered persons and firms in the industry. It is well worth the extra effort to check out these reports; you can do it online. In the United States, such sources include:

Securities and Exchange Commission (SEC, www.sec.gov): The SEC is the official federal agency of the US Government in charge of protecting investors and maintaining order in financial markets. It also has a helpful website for checking out both brokers and investment advisors. In their computerized database, the Central Registration Depository (CRD, http://brokercheck.finra.org), you can review information about firms and their representatives. As to independent investment advisors, you can visit the SEC's Investment Adviser Public Disclosure site (IAPD, www.adviserinfo.sec.gov). I especially like the fact that you can review the actual Form ADV and see what the advisor has committed to do to the regulator. In particular, if the advisor claims to be "fee only," that means he is obligated by the SEC to only take compensation from you, the investor, and will not be paid by any of the product suppliers. In this way, you can be better assured the advisor's recommendations are not unduly influenced by a particular fund provider.

Financial Industry Regulatory Authority (FINRA, www.finra.org): FINRA is the industry's private self-regulatory authority responsible for protecting investors under the rules of the SEC. On their website, a section called Broker Check allows an investor to see a broker's history and firm to better gauge the reputation. The site also includes other useful tools: a "Risk Meter" to judge your investment risk profile, a description of Professional Designations, an Investor Alert, a Fund Analyzer, and a Retirement Calculator.

Securities Investor Protection Corporation (SIPC, www.sipc.org): After reviewing the above information, always check to see whether both the brokerage firm and its clearing firm are both members of

SIPC, which provides limited customer protection if a brokerage firm becomes insolvent. Review the specifics of what you are covered for. SIPC's list of questions to ask advisors and brokers is quite helpful. The questions cover specific experience, school and employment history, registrations, clearing firm information, related companies, reasons for product selection, payment methods, and history. Also, make sure to ask for the Form ADV copy, just to verify what you may have already seen on the regulatory websites.

State regulators: Each state typically has a site for state licensed investment advisors that are not large enough to be regulated by the SEC. If your advisor is not SEC registered, it is definitely worth checking the site in your state to verify your advisor's registration and history.

AARP (formerly the American Association Of Retired Persons, www.aarp.org/money) and **Certified Financial Planner Board Of Standards** (CFP, www.cfp.net): Both are valuable websites for further quick education tools. With a variety of valuable help tools, the AARP has a quick checklist for reviewing financial professionals, tips on guarding against fraud, and updates on the latest scams to watch out for. The CFP has an easy to read yet complete guide from A to Z in how to utilize a financial planner.

Federal Deposit Insurance Corporation (FDIC, www.fdic.gov) and **Federal Savings And Loan Corporation** (FSLIC): Just because you have a large portion of your savings in a bank or savings and loan doesn't automatically mean you don't have to worry. Take many of the same precautions we mentioned above, even when you are dealing with a bank. At present, each depositor is insured up to $250,000 per insured bank. If you and your partner have a joint account, then each of you would have $250,000, for a total of $500,000. Review the details of your coverage on the FDIC website, which covers both FDIC and FSLIC insurance, and you can see how trust accounts, IRAs, corporate accounts, and the like are covered. Also, I recommend you check the site to independently verify the exact name of the bank you are depositing your money into is listed and covered exactly as is listed on the FDIC website. There have been instances in which an institution uses nearly the same name as an insured entity—but is not insured. The site also lists other important information about industry analysis, failed banks, and required financial reports.

Investor's web sites: Fortunately, most established countries now have similar regulatory support sites available for investors. In fact, domiciling your account in a jurisdiction that has strict regulations governing the registration and policing of brokers and advisors is definitely recommended. Irrespective of where you live, you want a globally recognized regulatory authority overseeing your money and the investing process overseen. You will want to verify the same kind of information on your brokers and advisors elsewhere that you can obtain in, for instance, the United States, Japan, or Europe.

The above precautions are necessary and should be followed to better ensure your money will not be lost due to fraud or mishandling. On the other hand, please do not take these precautions as a reason not to invest at all. Irrespective of what you decide, it is dangerous to ignore them—even if you just leave the money in the bank.

LICENSES

There are so many different initials and licenses after the names of brokers and advisors that it can be confusing trying to figure out if the person with whom you are dealing truly has passed the necessary exams. Via the references, make sure you know that the person with whom you are speaking is actually the same person registered with regulators. There is no need to be shy; ask to see the actual registrations and proof that you are talking to the correctly registered person.

What is particularly confusing is that Registered Investment Advisors (RIAs) are registered with the SEC or with their state's securities agency. The advisors must adhere to a fiduciary standard of care for your money as laid out by the Investment Advisors Act of 1940[1]. In essence, the fiduciary standard means the advisor must put the best interest of the client ahead of anything else. Brokers or registered representatives (RRs) working for a broker-dealer come under FINRA, as mentioned above, and operate under a different set of fiduciary standards for protecting investors. Key to the FINRA requirements is their suitability standards. Suitability simply means that the recommendations given to you by an RR must first consider, or be structured to fit, your particular predicament. Thus, under this so-called "know your customer" (KYC) rule, the RR must first learn about your specific financial ability, tax situation, your investment objectives, risk tolerance, and any other unique characteristics before he makes a recommendation to sell you a suitable security. At present, RIA's fiduciary standard is stricter and offers more protection to investors than does the suitability standard for RRs; practically speaking, though, most major broker compliance departments' rules and practices do police their brokers' advice more closely than in the past. There are moves underway via the Dodd Frank Act to make the standards the same; however, it is difficult to predict if or when there will be changes.

If they are an RR, you want to verify that they are registered in the FINRA system and have passed the Series 7 exam, which allows them to take securities orders, or at a minimum the Series 6, which covers just mutual funds and variable annuities. If they are an RIA, they must have either passed their Series 65 exam (Uniform Investment Advisor Law Examination) or they have obtained one or more of the following designations: certified financial planner (CFP), chartered financial consultant (ChFC), personal financial specialist (PFS), chartered financial analyst (CFA), and/or chartered investment counselor (CIC).

Outside the United States, you can find similar required registrations in virtually all developed countries. For instance, in Europe it is call the European Financial Planning Association (EFPA). Also, the Chartered Wealth Manager (CWM) designation is conferred by the Board of Standards of the American Academy of Financial Management (AAFM) and has been adopted in 145 countries.

I realize most people would not want to be bothered with checking to make sure an advisor has the right initials next to his title, but it is important to make sure your advisor is properly registered and has taken all the appropriate tests. There have been instances where a salesperson put in fake initials, lied about his registrations, or even pretended he was someone else. It is always good to talk with either the compliance person in the office and/or with the office manager, and have him verify all the proper registrations of the person you are considering as an advisor.

THE LESSONS OF WHO YOU CAN TRUST

1. **Don't trust everyone.** In selecting advisors, no one should be automatically trusted.
2. **Check everyone out. This is your financial future.** Always go through the systematic process of checking out both the advisor and the firm.
3. **Once isn't enough.** Conduct a periodic independent review of your advisor, as well as broker registration and status.

CHAPTER 16
WHERE DO I GO FOR ADVICE?

Brokers, Banks, Independent Investment Advisors, Financial Planners—Which One Is Right for Me?

THE VALUE OF AN ADVISOR

M any people are comfortable managing their own money. It is certainly possible to do, especially if you have the training and the time and enjoy the process of building and monitoring your portfolio on an ongoing basis. However, despite all the do it yourself (DIY) tools readily available for investors, the majority of customer investment assets are still at least partially managed by Advisors.

During my time at Schwab, with the advent of the internet making direct trading and buying of funds so easy, I assumed that over time, customers would take over running the majority of their money. Internet stock trading exploded the volume, and soon more than two-thirds of all our trades were done on the internet. Yet by the late nineties, when I looked at the portion of customer assets we had in custody, the majority was actually still managed by advisers. Equally interesting, over the last 20 years, customer assets in the likes of Schwab, Fidelity, TD Ameritrade, and E*TRADE have grown exponentially in attracting customers. Yet when you look at where the customer assets came from, it was primarily out of banks. The major brokerage companies had not lost a significant share of investible assets and, in fact, had actually grown in total assets under custody and management. Why did so many people with the majority of their assets, especially with their mutual funds, still want advice in some form or another? Many people like having their own trading or investment account. They may enjoy it as a hobby or want to keep their trading costs down when they make up their own mind about what stocks to buy and sell. But many will also want to make sure the bulk of their long-term investing is done with the help of an adviser. Over the years, I have asked many customers about their reasons for wanting advice. I most often hear:

- The financial planning process looks a bit complicated. I just want to make sure I have thought everything through so I don't make any big mistakes.
- I am not sure about structuring the overall portfolio, about how much of each asset class I should buy.
- In some cases, I know what I want to buy, but I just want to get some validation.
- I have my own portfolio of stocks I like managing. But my spouse doesn't want me to be the only manager of all our money.
- I just don't want to be bothered, especially since I am clueless anyway about how to put together and then monitor a portfolio.
- There are so many different funds out there. I don't know how to evaluate all of them.

CHOOSING THE RIGHT TYPE OF FIRM

Independent Financial Advisers

Over the last two decades, this category, particularly where the Independent Financial Advisors have gone through the process to properly register with the authorities as a Registered Investment Advisors (RIAs), has been among the fastest growing categories of professionals advising on investments. To many in the industry, this has been quite a surprise. In the late eighties, one well-known broker-dealer predicted that the number of firms were going to shrink dramatically as technology, product availability, compliance requirements, and reputation considerations were going to make the small or independent broker and RIA office no longer relevant. Yet the exact opposite happened.

As an investor trying to decide which to use, you would naturally want to know why small independent firms' market share has been growing. After all, in an era where trust is even more of a concern, why would someone want to go to a little firm instead of a giant firm, with millions in capital and a global brand standing behind it?

Big Company Brand Deterioration

In talking with investors over the years, it became clear to me that the major traditional brands in financial services have become severely tarnished. The constant negative headlines about bailouts and executive pay and criminal negligence have weakened people's trust in large brands. Thus, many investors prefer an independent Advisor, whose advice comes from an independent evaluation rather than from a headquarters pressuring them to sell a particular product.

The Compliance Conundrum

Local independent Advisors often win out over large firms because the compliance departments in the big broker firms and banks have been forced to put extreme limitations on what their registered representatives (RRs) can say and do for customers based on regulations. The result is that many investors have turned to the independent RIAs because they feel they can get more straightforward answers on the risks and opportunities of various products. Of course, independent RIAs have to comply with similar rules and regulations. They just do not have to constantly appeal to a compliance department a thousand miles away every time they want to say anything other than the internal, compliance-approved speaking points they have been instructed to say.

Prices Are Often Higher at Large Traditional Firms

Overhead expenses in a large firm are similar to your refrigerator at home; even larger refrigerators end up overloaded with perishables. The giant established firms have had decades to let their bureaucracies grow. Despite efforts to cut costs, it is quite a difficult task when they have 100,000 or more people spread across dozens of countries. Small and independent companies don't have to pay for the high overhead costs of the major firms.

In sum, you can easily understand why local independent RIAs have grown. Their customers feel they have someone to talk to that can level with them and not give them "corporate speak" only. Of course, if you are going to consider an independent RIA, you will have to do the minimum level of due diligence. However, even if you go with a major firm, you still have to go through many of the same reference-checking processes on the actual RR the firm assigns to you to make sure you have the right Advisor.

One additional important step to go through when considering independent RIAs is to follow up with their broker and/ or custodian. In the case of an RIA, you will only give the RIA limited trading authority, meaning they are authorized only to buy and sell in your account. They can neither deposit into nor remove money from your account. Thus, you will need to open an account with the broker the RIA chooses and is agreeable to you. Your money will be deposited directly in the broker, but you will allow the RIA to see the account and to trade in the account. Each time the RIA buys or sells in the account, you will receive independently, directly from the broker, the confirmation of each transaction. Also, on a monthly and annual basis, you will receive directly from the broker your statements showing your positions and your activity. This is critical to your protection. *You do not ever give your money directly to the independent RIA.* You want to make sure you are dealing with a major and reputable broker who is responsible for the custody of your account. When you fund your account, *you will send your money directly to the brokerage firm into an account in your name in which your Advisor has only limited trading authority.* In other words, the Advisor cannot take any money out of the account except where you allow a predetermined fee to be paid. Otherwise, only you can remove money.

This process is important for the protection of your assets, but it is also why the independent RIA business has grown. Investors do not have to worry about their assets, because the RIA never touches them. All the RIA can do is conduct the transactions you authorize; you will independently, through the broker, be able to verify what the RIA does.

Lastly, RIAs—both independent as well as those working for brokerage firms and banks—often have additional value-added reports that help you see where you are in your entire portfolio. These are quite useful, but make sure you also look at the independent brokerage statement you receive; that is your ultimate verification of what is happening in your account.

Broker-Dealers

Unlike RIAs, broker-dealers are allowed by law far more activities that they can perform for customers. What is most relevant to investors is that broker-dealers also have the regulatory obligation to sell customers only those products that most suit customers' needs. Today, we are much more knowledgeable about comparison shopping than our parents were. Likewise, over the past 20 years, many other types of institutions are now in direct competition for investors' attention. Yet the major national and regional brokers have kept considerable market share of customer assets despite the growth of the independent RIA segments and the improved services for the DIY market provided by the discount broker segment. In addition, several fund companies—like Vanguard, Fidelity, T. Rowe Price—have done an admirable job in successfully marketing directly to customers. So why is it that broker-dealers have continued to garner the majority of customer assets?

Flexible and Adaptive

Part of the reason brokerage firms remain a major factor in helping investors is that the firms have reacted to customer preference for a fee structure based on asset size rather than on commissions from trading. When the independent RIA providers introduced fee-only pricing structures, major broker-dealers reacted quickly by offering wrap programs that allowed the customer and the RR to bundle a package of funds and stocks into a single account and only be charged an asset-based account fee with no trading commission charges. In this way, customers do not have to worry that the recommendations from their advisors are based on him wanting to generate more commission. At the same time, many older clients do not want to totally switch over to the managed account or wrap model because they have existing positions they want to hold and don't see any reason to pay extra for those assets to be in a managed account. So, in order to accommodate both the clients and their Advisors, many brokerages do not force them into a single pricing structure. By remaining flexible in response to customer needs, broker-dealers have been able to retain a lot of their customers as well as keep many of their better RRs from pursuing the independent route.

Genuine Respect for Their Advisers

Another important reason for the continued success of brokerage firms is the quality of their Advisors. When customers buy a CD at the bank, they are primarily relying on the fact that ultimately the FDIC insurance is standing behind the product, so the information customers need is pretty straightforward. So long as the salesperson knows the interest rate and duration of the product, and doesn't drool or insult customers when talking to them, customers will be content. However, it is quite different when a customer is investigating risk products. Now, the investor wants to know a lot more about the product and its risk characteristics. The customer must not only trust the product maker, meaning the fund management company, and the product distributor, meaning the broker-dealer; the customer must also believe that the Advisor sitting on the other side of the table really knows what he/she is talking about. RRs and Advisors have to be very good at what they do or people will not entrust them with their money. Not only must they be polite and trustworthy; they also have to convince the investor that they are competent. Broker-dealer management has long internalized this fundamental fact and have structured their compensation systems such that the more assets an RR manages, the more money he/she will be paid.

Today, many brokerage firms separate their list of funds that can be put into their wrap accounts into two categories, approved and recommended. This came about because so many Advisors and broker-dealers did not want to necessarily sell the brokerage company approved funds only as many Advisors have their own view about what funds are best for their customers. Accordingly, they asked their brokerage firm's fund review department to instead do enough due diligence to make sure the fund companies and funds were acceptable; they did not care about whether or not headquarters actually recommended one particular fund over another. The RRs themselves wanted to make that final decision in conjunction with customer discussions.

One important reminder, RIAs are under the "Fiduciary Responsibility" requirement by the SEC, meaning that they always have to do what is in the customers' best interest. On the other hand, RR's merely have to follow the "Suitability Rule" which means that they should only sell products to customers which properly "suit or fit each customer's financial profile." Thus, when dealing with a brokerage firm advisor, it would be preferable for you to select an RR who is also licensed to be a RIA.

Product Manufacturing

In today's world, products are much more ubiquitous than in the past. You can pretty much buy whatever fund you are interested in at any number of financial institutions. However, there are certain products in which national and strong regional broker-dealers, and in some cases, the major banks, have an advantage. In accessing a variety of bonds, for instance, especially at the initial offering stage, because broker-dealers have investment banking divisions, they are able to garner products that are not always so readily available to the independent advisors or smaller brokers and banks.

A Known Brand

Although many global brands have been damaged, investors often will still want to go with a brand they have known throughout their lives. As one investor once said to me, "Better to go with the devil

I know." Regional and national broker-dealers have this additional advantage over independents in attracting investors who want the additional safety of a major brand standing behind their advisor. In addition, although the broker compliance departments can be a two-edged sword because they can be overly strict and cumbersome, many safe investors like the comfort of knowing that major broker-dealers have strong central compliance and product management departments overseeing what the broker's advisors can say as well as approving what products they can sell.

In addition, regional brokers as well as those brokerage firms that have focused solely on sales-force support have had a distinct advantage over the past decade because they did not receive nearly as much bad press. They were not running highly leveraged trading and investment banking operations that required large sums of capital, and thus stayed largely out of the fray during the 2007–2008 financial crises. Over the past two decades, we have seen considerable growth in those brokerage firms that focus their business solely on serving Advisors and their clients. Some even allow their Advisors to keep their own name or to share branding by having both the name of their local RIA practice as well as the name of the sponsoring brokerage firm. In addition to the giants like Smith Barney and Merrill Lynch, there have been several other brokerage firms that have dramatically expanded their Advisor model for their clients. Such successful firms include: LPL Financial, Raymond James, Janney Montgomery Scott, ED Jones, and the independent advisor divisions of Schwab, Fidelity, TD Ameritrade, and many others.

Banks

Since the early eighties, when banks were allowed to get into the discount brokerage and mutual fund distribution business, some of them have become quite competitive in offering investment products and services to their clients. Given their size, their brand, and the power of the capital behind them, one wonders why they have not been more successful in taking customer assets away from the broker-dealers. Even more interesting, why have so many new firms over the last 25 years, both discount brokers as well as asset-management companies, been able to take away billions of dollars of customer assets from them? The answers that I have heard from various investors over the years are twofold.

First, the customer service personnel at banks is on average not as experienced or as talented as that seen at broker-dealers. From an institutional culture standpoint, banks have always been used to having a compensation structure that attracts an average performer. After all, that is all they historically needed to sell: checking and savings accounts, and CDs. With lending, a big part of this marketing dynamic from a credit standpoint is making sure the bank picks the right customers. So, a high-quality advisor is naturally going to gravitate to a broker-dealer or an independent RIA, where he/she can be paid for their superior abilities.

Second, the high cost structure of banks often make them not cost competitive versus discount brokers and direct-sales mutual funds companies. If you are cost conscious, you already know you are likely not going to get the lowest management fee products at a bank. Some banks have changed their structure and set up separate discount broker subsidiaries to compete on price. However, since many banks still have high fixed cost overheads, it is wise for customers to shop the nonbanks before selecting products and advice.

Why, then, have several banks still been able to retain investors?

The Local Factor

Many investors are busy and don't have a lot of time to spend on investing. Since many banks are within minutes of their home and/or work, it is more convenient for them to just stop by the local bank. If that branch happens to have a competent investing advisor, it is too tempting to simply use that branch and look no further.

Sometimes, this local factor does work against the bank. It is very difficult to have top quality advisors in every one of their branches. So, when a bank either has a potential investor talk with an inexperienced person, or has to say, "The investment adviser is only here every Wednesday. Can you come by then?," the prospect loses interest.

Nonetheless, it is worth it for investors to have a chat with their local bank, especially if they have been banking there for a long time. It can be valuable to compare their products, services, and quality of their RRs with other firms.

The Changing Landscape

Over the last decade, several banks have made a concerted effort to pay competitively and attract top talent, especially when they have completely separated the broker or investment divisions from the rest of the commercial bank. Wells Fargo Advisors has merged some of the country's top regional brokers into a single national broker-age company separate from the bank; Bank of America now owns Merrill Lynch. Although Citigroup sold its retail brokerage sub-sidiary, Smith Barney, to Morgan Stanley, Citi worldwide remains quite active in providing investment services to their clients. So, the line of distinction has been blurred in recent years. Regulators wisely make sure the brokerage arms of these banks make clear to their clients that they are separate from the banks and do not give FDIC insurance but rather have SIPC insurance. However, many customers still like the security blanket of knowing a major bank owns the brokerage firm with whom they are dealing.

Private Client Groups

Though some banks merely use this title to deliver mediocre ser-vices, there are a number of banks—J.P. Morgan, First Republic, and Citi, among others—that have done a most credible job in building up a strong team to focus in on the high net worth cus-tomers. Their minimums, though, can often be in excess of $1 mil-lion in customer assets. I have spoken to many affluent customers who have been very happy with the breadth of services they receive in addition to investment advice, such as trust and cash manage-ment. They also like the comfort of dealing with a major, well-capitalized bank.

Discount/Internet Brokers

Since May Day 1975, when brokerage commissions were allowed to float, this industry has become a major fixture in providing products and services to investors. By their structure, they typically are not allowed to make recommendations to investors. However, many of these firms have separate, high-level service call centers that are often quite adept at helping customers in what I would call "guided discovery." Rather than making a formal recommendation, they will ask you pertinent questions, and then, given your answers, they will show you a few different funds or products that could fit your needs. However, the final decision is left to you. If you are the type that prefers more specific recommendations or need to be told what you think you should do, an RIA or full-service broker-dealer will perhaps be more to your liking. One of the reasons why discount brokers have grown is that many people want some help but ultimately prefer to make their own decisions.

There are other reasons so many investors have chosen to utilize this category of providers. Investors who are interested in keeping their costs down often prefer discount brokers. Their cost structures are designed to keep prices as low as possible. As extra expense can dig into your return, the choice of using a discount broker or going directly with a fund company for at least part of your investing can be quite attractive.

Another reason is that since discount brokers do not recommend particular products, they often structure themselves to be more "open architecture," meaning they make a broad selection of products available for customers. For investors who want a lot of choice and want to learn more about all the fees, they should also check out the product selection at a discount broker, even if they are working with a full-service broker-dealer. Often, discount brokers will have the cheapest share class of a mutual fund that is offered by the fund companies. However, wise investors always keep in mind that just as they expect their RR at a full-service firm to be fair, they also want to make sure to properly compensate the RRs for their efforts by directing an appropriate level of business to them.

Finally, in order to meet the demand of more affluent investors who want more specific advice, many larger discount brokers have set up separate divisions to provide services to the independent RIA market. As part of this service, they provide the names of RIA firms they have approved to be a part of their loose affiliation.

Direct Fund Company Distributors

Several investment management companies have also engaged in selling funds directly to retail investors. Companies like Vanguard, Fidelity, and T. Rowe Price among others have helped educate much of the nation in the value of buying mutual funds. Their advantages are:

- Their reps have deep knowledge of their investment products. If you really want to understand the products of a particular fund company, the best phone call to make is to their call center.
- Their pricing is often favorable, typically with no upfront loads and often very low operating expense ratios.
- Recently, several of the direct marketing fund companies have also begun selling other companies' funds, so the product range has expanded.

However, for many of these providers, you do not always get the breadth of product that is available from other brokers and advisors not affiliated with fund management companies.

Life Insurance Providers

Historically, life insurance planners helped many people make sure they were covered in the case of the premature death of the main breadwinner in the family, and in helping clients put together a full-life financial plan. These companies gave considerable training to their financial planners, and their sales processes and disciplined plans helped many a family achieve their financial goals when they reached their later years. In addition, due to their brilliant lobbying of governments around the world, the tax advantages of many insurance products were built into the tax code.

However, in today's world, there are so many other more competitive investing alternatives that one must be careful about putting too much money with a life insurance–oriented planner. In my final analysis, you are paying indirectly through your overall loss of return of as much as 1.5 to 2 percent per year or even more for the insurance bundling. The insurance industry and their reps normally go to great lengths to obfuscate what the insurance component and the investment component actually costs you, but it has been my experience that the true cost to you actually comes right out of your ultimate yield. This means that by investing in a broad package of cost-efficient mutual funds directly, you will likely earn more money in the end than if you did the majority of your investing via insurance vehicles. Of course, it makes sense to have a certain amount of life insurance, but straight term insurance is typically the cheapest, most cost effective way to meet this need.

Other Providers

There are a variety of more specialized providers. These include real estate limited partnership distributors, finance companies selling often high yielding asset-backed instruments, commodities and/or futures dealers.

Some of these firms are legitimate and have been in business for a long time. However, I should caution that for the safe investor, it is better to limit the majority of your investing to the above-mentioned institutions in the previous categories. If you do decide to use the special purpose institutions listed here, it should be confined only to the amount you are willing to put in your Trading Pocket *and not included in either the Savings Pocket or the Investing Pocket.* The reason is that for the safe investor, you have more legal and regulatory protections when you are dealing with a registered and reputable broker, RIA, bank, or insurance company, and your underlying funds are public 40 Act funds.

OTHER IMPORTANT CONSIDERATIONS

Separate Account Managers and Fund Selection Managers

Brokers can have a variety of accounts with an investor. For instance, the customer can choose to manage his own account but use the broker to discuss what he/she wants to do, with the broker then executing the trades.

If you are utilizing an RIA, either an independent or a brokerage employee, where the Advisor is making the buy and sell decisions in the account, there are two primary ways the RIA can provide you the investment service: mutual fund RIAs and separate account manager

RIAs. With mutual fund RIAs, the Advisor focuses primarily on selecting funds for your account as he builds a broad-based, multi-asset-class portfolio for you over time. His fee is typically lower than if he was actually picking the stocks, because he is selecting other fund managers to do the actual money management. In this case, you will pay the advisor fee plus the management fee and the expense of the underlying funds. For this reason, advisers typically select funds that have low operating expense ratios (OERs), because they know it is important to keep your overall fees low if you are to garner a good return. A good advisor takes the time to explain all expenses—his costs, as well as the brokerage firm's, the custodian's and the underlying fund company's costs—to you in detail so you are not surprised by any additional costs.

In Separate Account Manager RIAs, the adviser actually picks the stocks and bonds for you, and thus is acting as both the Advisor and the money manager. This approach can have certain advantages. For instance, assuming you meet the advisor's minimums, he will often allow you to be more selective in what stocks you would like to buy. Let's say you are in the high-tech business and already have a boatload of options from your firm. In terms of your overall exposure, you are more than covered in the high-tech space, so you instruct your adviser in this type of account to leave out most or all of the high-tech stocks. This way, you are able to customize or refine your diversification further. Also, from a tax optimization standpoint, you have more control over what you are buying and selling. Assuming the Advisor is a competent money manager, you can have a more concentrated equity portfolio that can give your more diversification from the index than you can get from many public funds. Although you want your entire global portfolio broadly diverse, there is nothing wrong with selected focus by one or more of your managers in specific asset classes. Lastly, as you are only paying the advisor plus brokerage fees, and not also paying a fund company, you likely can keep your overall costs low.

On the other hand, you have not diversified your money managers in a separate account where the only investment manager is the advisor himself. So, it is best to also add other money managers for the balance of your overall portfolio. In some cases, the advisor will do that with you. For instance, he may help you select other separate account managers or other funds as well.

I personally like to buy my bonds through a separate account managing advisor or RR because it is a nuisance to be frequently buying and managing the maturing bonds myself. Some Advisors, for as little as a quarter to a half of a percent, will analyze and select the individual bonds for you. The advantage of buying the bonds directly versus buying a bond fund is that your own bonds mature, so if interest rates go up, since you are holding the bond to maturity, all you are losing is opportunity interest income. On the other hand, if you bought a medium- or long-term bond fund, the value would likely decline, as these funds are marked to market every day. Of course, if you do not have enough money to put together a properly diversified bond portfolio, you can alternatively consider buying a bond unit investment trust (UIT), which also has a fixed maturity date. This will accomplish the same objective of holding its value, provided you held the UIT until maturity.

SOLUTIONS FOR SMALL INVESTORS NEEDING ADVICE

The problem for many young investors is that they would like to get some solid advice, but they don't have the money the top RRs in brokerage firms prefer or they don't meet the minimums of most RIAs. Understandably, many of the reputable Advisors with a good track record in helping investors prefer clients who have at least $200,000 to $500,000 in investable assets. But what if I am just starting out and have only $3,000, or $10,000, to invest? This is where many independent and bank-owned discount brokers can be an excellent alternative. It is a great way to get started; they are used to helping young customers start out. Of course, you can buy directly on the internet, but if you would like some assistance, you can either call the broker on the phone or stop into one of their offices.

Fortunately, when the investment is small, you can start out by buying a broad-based, even multi-asset-class public mutual fund; from day one, you are broadly diversified. If you are under 45, and don't need the money until your old age, you can then afford to put the money into a more aggressive, growth-oriented capital appreciation fund. It will fluctuate more, but likely after 20 or more years, you will have a greater return. Then, each year you can add to your portfolio by buying a different fund in a different asset class in order to begin the diversification process. Assuming you eventually have over a $100,000, it could then make sense to start a conversation with an Advisor if you feel you need help.

In addition, for many small investors that really feel lost, a fixed-fee financial planner may be a great person to see. For an upfront fee, these planners can help you construct a plan tailored to your personal situation.

MANY PROVIDERS ARE IN EACH OTHER'S BUSINESS

As discussed above, many banks have already bought full-service and discount broker-dealers. And at the same time, several of the larger brokerage firms, like Schwab and E*Trade, now own banks and proactively offer a variety of banking products. And selected major insurance companies have either started or bought brokerage firms. So, although many of my comments above regarding the different types of institutions still hold true, the rapidly morphing competitive landscape makes it difficult to generalize too much about one type of company over another. The name on the door—whether bank, brokerage firm, or other entity—just doesn't tell you as much these days. You should care about the firm you choose and do the proper due diligence on them; however, what continues to be true is that the individual inside in charge of helping you matters a lot.

THE LESSONS FOR WHERE TO GO FOR ADVICE

1. **Use the regulations to your advantage.** Today, you have many more alternative institutions for advice. But make sure both the firm and the actual advisor are under the direct oversight of governmental regulators.
2. **Talk to everyone you can.** It is valuable for you to talk first to multiple Advisors at multiple institutions before deciding.
3. **Relationships count.** Focus on selecting the right advisor to help you put together your portfolio, irrespective of the type of regulated firm he works for. The right person is at least as important as the firm he works for.

CHAPTER 17
THE NAKED ADVISOR

How Do I Select the Right Person?

When I read the book by Jamie Oliver called *The Naked Chef*, it struck me that there were many parallels to what I like to see in a good investment advisor. His approach to cooking was to keep it simple, use fresh ingredients, and have

Image 17.1 The Naked Advisor

a foolproof repertoire of dishes that don't take a lot of time and money to create.

In the case of investing, an ideal advisor keeps the investing process and recommendations simple and straightforward and doesn't overwhelm you with a lot of complicated words. He recommends investment products you can see straight through and understand what the underlying investments are; they aren't loaded with a lot of complicated layers of derivatives and hedges. He has an uncomplicated fee structure and is naturally unpretentious in his approach.

These are the reasons I like a Naked Advisor, and why Naked Advisors add a lot of value for customers. The right ones keep their analyses, product choices, and reasons for product selection and asset weightings all straightforward in their explanations. They take what the product providers and headquarters of distributors push out, and they translate it into simple to understand language for investors.

KEY QUESTIONS FOR A PROSPECTIVE ADVISOR— AND UNDERSTANDING THE ANSWERS

Whenever I start out learning a language, the books or tapes provide a list of useful questions. These would be easy enough to memorize. However, when I would arrive in the country and ask even a basic question, I almost never understood the answer. In fact, it was substantially more work to learn how to figure out the answer than it was simply memorizing the questions.

The same holds true in our industry. In fact, some members of our industry, subconsciously or otherwise, seem to practice making the answers unfathomable. Let's look at the most useful questions you might have, and more importantly, the kinds of answers you would expect. In addition, let's look at what bad and good answers sound like.

First off, unless you already know an advisor to talk to, google a few of the more well-known sites to check out advisors, such as Brightscope Advisors, FApages.com, the Certified Financial Planner (CFP) Board website, and even Yelp, though we all know to take these recommendations with a grain of salt. Over the years, word of mouth has probably been the biggest source of advisor referrals. Accountants and attorneys typically know the more popular and competent independent, brokerage, and bank advisors in your area.

Before you sit down with the prospective advisor, it can be helpful to do the following:

- Think about how much you can put aside and how much you would like to have when you are older. As mentioned in the above paragraph, if you have the time, it is worth checking out some of the do it yourself or DIY websites to have a better idea of your key issues and what you think you want to do.
- Check out the advisor's website, or at least the prospective firm's site, to see what they choose to say about themselves or their practice.
- Go on the FINRA, SEC, and/or state registration websites to learn what licenses he/she already has and check out his/her history.

Even though you may know the answers, start out by asking the basic questions.

Question Category 1: Checking Answers You Already Know

- What kind of education did you receive that is relevant to helping me out in investing?
- How long have you lived in the area?
- Have you had any problems with other clients in their investing or with any regulators?
- Since FINRA allows for complaint records to be scrubbed, have you ever had a complaint that was subsequently scrubbed?
- What kinds of complaints have any of your clients had in the past?
- What are your most relevant professional designations?
- Can you tell me about the rest of your office? Do you have a superior? Partner? Other juniors to help you out? An administrative assistant? What is their experience?

How to interpret: Are all his answers consistent with what you have already looked up or can see when you walk into his office? Did he become defensive in any way about his background? Conversely, don't be overly enamored if the advisor went to Harvard or Stanford; some of the best advisors went to their local colleges. However, you do want to make sure that he has received a thorough academic training in investing.

In the case of the entire office, you are seeing if the advisor works alone, whether he works well with others, or may rely on others to do most of the work. If the advisor is not in the office and you have a question, you need to know if someone else can intelligently answer your questions. If they seem reluctant to give you too much detail, these are not good signals. Also, ask to meet with the office manager if there is one. Since this person sets the immediate tone in the office, you want to gauge how genuine this person is. If the advisor is the head of the office, meet some subordinates to gauge how good of a manager he or she is.

Question Category 2: Delving into the Substance of His Investing

- Is there a particular area of investing in which you are more skilled than others?
- Do you have a particular style or philosophy about investing?
- What kinds of products and services do you frequently recommend? For instance, do you prefer exclusively index funds and ETFs, or a mixture, or actively managed funds? Or do you prefer to do the investing yourself?
- How broad is the universe of funds you select from? Do you employ specific limitations or screening tools?
- What are your recommendations and weightings typically based on?
- How do you view performance? Risk assessment? Can you show me some examples of how your selections have performed?
- How frequently do you turn over the portfolio, meaning how often do you buy and sell the positions in the account? (After all, if they trade too frequently, it costs the customer more money and could be a warning sign that they risk profile of the fund is higher than you would prefer. Normally, less

than one times/year is preferable.) Can you show me some evidence?

- How do you help me decide my tax consequences in managing the portfolio? Are you willing to review the issues with my tax accountant? And how about my trust agreements—do you have experience with trust lawyers?
- What is your view and expertise specifically in international investing?
- What is your view about commodities? Real Estate funds?
- Can you tell me the two biggest mistakes in investing that you ever made?

How to interpret: In this early stage of questioning, jump into the content side of investing, at least to see how the advisor reacts. Does he seem to really know what he is talking about? From these questions, you are trying to find out the advisor's style. Is he a religious indexer, meaning he believes only in indexing and no other types of active investing? Or conversely, does he only choose actively managed funds and not take any advantage of index funds or ETFs? Do you think he is too locked in on one way to do things? Or do you sense he is only picking funds that are easy for him, but may not be the best for you? Is he following by rote simply what some other entity is recommending? If so, you should expect him to understand the rationale behind these recommendations. You would also like to know of other sources, like affiliations or associations that he utilizes in coming up with his approach. Does he bring up the topic of fund expenses before you ask? You would like to see him volunteer at least a comment about costs before you bring the topic up. You want to see how seriously he reviews all fund expenses, because he is analyzing your overall portfolio performance. Does the advisor either talk too much about performance, or too little? Is the focus more short term or long term? You would also like to see the advisor turns over a portfolio of funds very infrequently, every few years at most. What you are also doing with this category of questions is trying to gauge what he chooses to bring up by only asking general questions. And if the advisor tells you he never made a mistake, he is either lying or hasn't owned up to mistakes, so keep looking for another advisor.

Question Category 3: His Clientele

- What can you tell me about your other clients?
- How long has your longest client been with you? How long has the average client been with you? Has anyone left you? If so, why?
- What is your minimum client portfolio size? What is your average? Your largest client size? Do you make exceptions? How do you typically handle family accounts?
- Is it possible to get two or more client references from you? Also, may I talk to the custodian or broker or manager that covers the security and operations of my account?

How to interpret: You are still at the stage where you are watching what he is volunteering to say, or discovering what he is leaving out. It is not often wise to be an advisor's smallest account, nor the largest. You would prefer he not make too many exceptions to bring you on. Likewise, you want him genuinely to want you as a client, but not be desperate for new business. You would love to see long-term relationships with many clients. As to references, sometimes clients don't like to have their names given out. However, a long-standing, reputable advisor will have references for you to check. You are also gauging how accommodating he is in fully answering your questions.

Question Category 4: Fee or Compensation Structures

- Can you list all the fees you will possibly charge me?
- Can you help me understand over the year the total amount of commissions, fees, and other expenses I will likely incur, including brokerage, custody, fund investment management fees, as well as your advisor fees? Can I get this information in writing from you?
- What is your philosophy about fees? Do you always look to see which funds have the lowest management fees? Why do you think it is that over time, funds with the lowest fees outperformed funds that had lots of Morningstar stars in their ratings?

How to interpret: Here you are looking for how forthcoming the potential advisor is with pricing and cost information. Do you sense any discomfort talking about fees, or how he looks for low Operating Expense Ratio or OER funds? Has he really done his homework in understanding how fees matter to the overall performance?

You want an advisor who is confident in what he is charging but not pompous. It is your money, and you want a capable advisor who can stay cool. After all, at one time or another, you will call on your advisor when you see markets drop somewhere, anywhere, and you want someone who can stay cool, even if you are not.

Question Category 5: The Adviser's Future Plans

- Why did you decide to become an advisor?
- Why did you choose this particular way/firm to provide advice?
- May I ask how old you are?
- How long do you plan to actively run your practice? If something happened to you, do you have a plan for what would happen to my account?
- Are you building succession planning into your practice now by training junior people? Do any of your assistants or coworkers have ownership in your practice? Or an agreement to eventually inherit your business?

How to interpret: Since you are looking for a long-term relationship with an advisor for managing your money, you want to know what the advisor's personal life career plan is. Also, one of the biggest problems in the industry today is advisors who are getting older, working less, and yet won't put a valid process into place for succession. Thus, customers may not get the same level of service they have received in the past. Specifically, is there someone trained with whom you will have some contact, who will eventually take over? When you are 84, do you want an 80-year-old investment advisor? Indeed, this is one of the biggest problems for both the brokerage and the independent RIA industries. Too many RRs and RIAs have not genuinely worked on who will do a good job for their clients when the advisors eventually slow down.

Conversely, the investment business is so difficult that you really prefer to see that your advisor has already lived through a couple of market cycles. The emotional strain of being a responsible person in the investment business during a meltdown, having seen the fear in people's eyes, seeing values that you thought were sacred collapse— this is the best training of all. As I began the book, I offered parallels between karate and investing. One of the most important lessons was that you really don't learn how to fight until you get used to the other guy trying to hurt you. The presence of mind you have to develop to defend yourself before going on the offensive to win is a skill set that is as much emotional training as it is physical training. In investing, until you have lived through a few market crises and seen your assumptions challenged in minutes by collapsing market values—and then having to explain it to investors—you really are not ready to be the senior person advising clients. Thus, as an investor, you really want to see a minimum of 15 years' experience on the senior person advising you. He can be as young as his late 30s, but only provided you verify how many years he has been working full time in the industry. You want the financial advisor equivalent of Captain Sully Sullenberger, the experienced US Airways pilot who back in 2009 kept his cool and knew instinctively what to do as he landed his airliner in the Hudson River. If you were a passenger, you would be glad that he had the quantity and qualities of experiences before he sat in the cockpit of the plane you are seated. The same goes for your advisor. There is no shortcut for decades of deep investment experience when it comes to your portfolio. In earlier chapters, I spelled out ways to safely construct a portfolio that will work irrespective of market conditions and product selections. However, if you can have an experienced and proven financial pilot, a person who knows how to construct and monitor a diversified portfolio, your risk is even further diminished.

Other Intangibles to Look For

One friend of mine calls it the "fit factor." At the end of the discussion with the advisor, you have to ask yourself a few questions:

- Does the advisor bug you? After spending 30 minutes or so, did the person annoy you, or make you feel inferior? More simply, would you prefer not to spend any more time with them?

- Did the advisor really listen to you, or just pretend to listen to you

- Did you find yourself not wanting to share your financial situation with this person? Did something inside your head say, "I don't trust this person enough to reveal my real fears or desires when it comes to financial matters?"

- Was this advisor genuinely interested in what your spouse had to say? If you have a partner or a spouse, one of you is going to outlive the other. Both of you need to feel that the advisor genuinely listens and factors into his analysis what both of you think. The advisor should naturally involve both of you in the questions, the answers, the discussion, and the solution. If either you or your partner is not comfortable with this candidate, you should definitely talk to other advisors.

Conversely, just like with certain doctors or lawyers, some of the best advisors may not have a good bedside manner. But in terms of managing your money and helping you put together a good diversified portfolio, the candidate could be great and have a proven reputation. So, it is important to listen to the substance, and gauge if he/she knows what they are doing.

Another key personality trait you are looking for is whether the advisor has the confidence to respectfully disagree with you when it is the right thing to do and explain why an alternate path might make more sense. After all, you are also paying them to educate you about investing. If all he does is agree with you and do just what you think you want, he is likely doing you a disservice.

THE "YES MAN" AND OTHER FACTORS

Back in the eighties, I was assigned to turn around an investment management subsidiary. Unfortunately, the advisor team was aggressively selling a fund with a high-flying track record, but which was managed recklessly. However, the brand had become dependent on this unpredictable fund; even worse, it was being sold as a low risk fund, which was totally inappropriate. At the advisor meeting, I made it clear this fund was not to be proactively sold to clients, and if any client insisted on buying it, I instructed the advisor to give the client in writing our warning on the fund's high risk level. A few months later, the fund cratered, dropping 40 percent within a few weeks.

The next month, I traveled with one of my advisors to the Middle East. We were in a country that shall remain unnamed and met with the government's minister of finance. I began our presentation by showing him a package of balanced mutual funds in which his citizens could grow their money without taking on undue risk. When I finished my presentation, the minister said, "Your salesman here told me one of your funds had such a great performance record and that the fund was so safe it was almost guaranteed to go up. I bought $200,000 of the fund personally with my own savings, and three weeks later, I lost nearly half my money." I turned to the advisor and he confirmed that he had, indeed, sold the minister the fund despite my previous orders.

I apologized profusely to the minister, but to no avail. It was too late.

That day I learned that ordering an employee not to do something doesn't mean he or she will obey you. The independent compliance oversight process in any advisory firm or institution needs to be firmly in place, and as an investor, you want to verify who is overseeing compliance in the office where you are dealing. Feel free to ask to talk to the compliance manager if you have any doubt about a product or service. Since then, I have met other advisors that are so anxious to please a customer, so anxious to get any kind of sale, they will say "yes" to whatever the customer is asking.

The message to investors is that when you look across the table at the end of your interview of a prospective advisor, you want to have the feeling that the advisor has the confidence to give you the correct advice on products, even if it is not what you would like to hear.

The Gender Factor

Given how critical this issue is, I should highlight the importance of involving both genders in the process of deciding on the advisor and the ultimate portfolio. On average, men die before women. Thus, in the case of the husband, even if your wife says, "I am not interested in investments, you handle it all," both of you still need to be involved. When one of you can no longer manage the advisor, the other needs to have at least a basic knowledge of what the advisor has done to date, and what the continued goals are. You do not want to be in the position my mother was in when my father died.

There is another important dimension to involving both genders. I first saw it when I moved to Schwab. We had a management committee that was fully mixed in terms of gender. At the end of the day, I could see how having both sexes involved in the debate on key issues led to a better decision-making process because more dimensions were considered. Even in countries not known for gender equality, such as Japan, where we had the first female board director, having both genders in the debate yielded more thorough discussions. It is my strong belief that generally, when deciding on the right advisor and portfolio approach, two heads are better than one, and two genders in the discussion are better than one.

The Process for Review after the Interview

Never say yes to the prospective advisor on the spot, especially after only one meeting. You are busy and may not necessarily enjoy this process, but you would ask for a second opinion if it was a life-threatening operation. Do the same for your financial life.

Besides your accountants and attorneys, who else can you involve in evaluating your advisor's answers? Do you have any acquaintances that sit on charitable boards with a reserve fund that needed to be invested for the long haul? CFOs of even small companies can have an interesting perspective.

Above all, make sure to interview at least one other investment advisor, preferably from a different type of firm. Throughout my career, I have been amazed at how much I learned simply by conducting more interviews. Invariably, you will learn new questions to pose to the advisor whom you favor.

Lastly, make sure to review carefully the agreements with the advisor, as well as the account-opening documents of related firms. Take nothing for granted. If you do not understand something, talk to your lawyer.

Ongoing Monitoring

In Chapter 14, we reviewed the process for monitoring the performance of your portfolio. Bring a list of checkpoints with you when you go in (at least on an annual basis) to sit down with your advisor and go over the results of the last year and plan for the next year. On a quarterly basis, you should receive relevant updates on your portfolio from your advisor. I personally like to go over to my advisor's office just to make sure it is still there, and to see if the climate in the office has changed.

As part of your initial review, the advisor should have told you what to expect in information and analysis. Keep what the advisor said to you last quarter, and last year, about his performance and about his prognosis for the future of your account. Then, the next year, see how consistent he is in his story. Has he changed his mind? Is he grabbing at straws and saying whatever is popular now?

On the one hand, just because the portfolio may be down doesn't automatically mean you should fire him. Indeed, he may have done a better job than most in protecting your long-term position. You want to know if he selected the right positions within each asset class, and how they performed versus other similar positions. Did your portfolio not fall as much as the rest of the market? That should be a good sign. But likewise, if the markets were up, and your portfolio did not rise as much, was it due to picking bad stocks or weak funds, or was it due to the advisor doing a good job of minimizing your risk?

You also want your advisor to ask you questions. For instance, are there any changes in your family estate? Do you have any changes in how much you are investing? In how much you plan to withdraw?

And remember, it is worth doing at least a quick review every one to two years with the brokerage firm of the RIA or with the manager of the RR just to make sure that, independent of your advisor, all is continuing to go well.

If you really dislike what you saw and heard, review the situation with others whom you trust; don't be afraid to pull the account if you think it is the right thing to do. I have seen timid investors lose money needlessly. Just because someone was good in past years does not mean they will always be so competent. Your loyalty has to be centered on the health of your portfolio.

Also, if the advisor will let you and if you have much more than the minimum amount of investible funds available, it is wise to first try him out with a smaller portion of your money, even for a brief period of time. Then, after the first review in three to twelve months, you may feel more comfortable with giving the advisor more money. It should be part of your "trickle in" approach to ameliorate your risk. Just make sure that one advisor does not manage all of your Three Pockets.

I may sound overcautious, but it is, after all, your life savings we are talking about.

THE LESSONS LEARNED ABOUT SELECTING THE RIGHT ADVISOR

1. **Take the time to do due diligence and talk to multiple advisors.**
2. **Don't be enamored by the "famous expert."** Make sure you are personally comfortable with your potential advisor. That is more important than what school he went to or how famous he is on TV.
3. **Look for the Naked Advisor.** You want someone who can explain the process and products in an understandable way. If it is still all Greek to you, keep looking.

PART IV
FINAL WORDS
OF ADVICE

CHAPTER 18

THE SEVEN CRITICAL LESSONS

Perhaps you still have some doubts. You may be wondering, What do I do if:

- I end up picking the wrong funds?
- The growth countries run into trouble?
- My adviser disagrees with some of the lessons?
- A global catastrophe or another financial crisis occurs?
- I can't remember all these lessons?

Let's step back and sum up the *BIG* lessons, the key principles I have learned from watching successful investors. Your central goal is to be a safe investor, to build a portfolio that grows more than the savings rate without the risk of losing your money for your later years. If you follow these seven lessons, you will succeed.

LESSON 1: DIVERSIFY YOUR ASSETS

Purchase a broad selection of asset classes—across equities, fixed income, short-term debt, commodities, real estate. Try not to miss any major asset classes. Within each asset class, diversify further by style of investments and by subclasses, by passive investing and, at times, even active investing. Some specific asset classes can be concentrated, so long as you have other investment styles also covering that same asset class. The classes you pick should not only be the popular ones. It is often the most unpopular ones today that will yield you the most tomorrow.

LESSON 2: DIVERSIFY YOUR COUNTRIES

Nations rise and fall. Catastrophes happen. Never be dependent on the fortunes of any single country or region. Diversify your countries by geography, by industry or commodity concentration, by size, and, most important, by stage of development. To get the most growth safely, mix the younger growth countries in with more mature countries.

LESSON 3: DIVERSIFY TIME

Remember tai chi and the sloth. Don't make any sudden moves in your Investing Pocket portfolio. Material impulsive reallocations introduce timing risk, which is one of the greatest risks of all. Instead, practice "trickle in, trickle out" so the power of time will decrease the risk of volatility. Even if global markets are down for years, eventually they come back. In your Investing Pocket, invest small amounts at a time; after you retire, only take out small amounts at a time. The most important step is to *start investing as soon as you can*.

LESSON 4: KEEP THE DISCIPLINE

Don't let fear or greed pull your Investing Pocket into needless danger. If you enjoy trading, or if you must try to time markets or individual stocks or whatever, do it in your Trading Pocket. Conversely, if you panic and want to sell, just sell out your Trading Pocket and put it all in your Savings Pocket. But don't touch your Investing Pocket.

LESSON 5: IT'S DESIGNED TO BE FLEXIBLE

To achieve broad acceptance and use of the Three Pockets approach by investors, a portfolio must be flexible to allow your own ideas about what to buy and to allow you to incorporate a variety of different ideas from your advisers—as long as you keep the above core principles of diversification.

LESSON 6: IT'S DESIGNED TO ALLOW MISTAKES

As we have learned, over a 30- or 40-year period, it just won't matter much if you did not always or did not frequently buy the best-performing funds. In fact, individual fund performance is not nearly as important as following the three above lessons on diversification of Asset Classes, Countries, and Time. Do your homework, but don't worry if you make a mistake. The broad diversity across asset classes and over time will make those fears immaterial.

LESSON 7: DO THE DUE DILIGENCE

Never risk an SPOF—a single point of failure. Never have all your money in one place, under the control of one person, in one institution, or moved as a single transaction. Although in the end you have to trust some key people, make sure—in advance as well as periodically—to independently check them out, no matter who they are.

If you follow these seven lessons, you won't have to worry about any of your doubts. The proper application of the principles of diversity will ensure you can grow your money and be a safe investor.

INFORMATION ON WEBSITE

WWW.TIMMCCARTHY.COM

For your further information, the website has a section dedicated to the book that is organized by chapter and has all the support details for our graphs in an unabridged form. In addition, we have included relevant articles that were helpful in building my recommendations. We look forward to hearing from investors and advisors with any critiques as well as additional information that could be helpful to the investing process.

The website includes:

- Unabridged support information for the book, by chapter.
- The release of the joint research on the Life Expectancy of Funds, conducted by Advisor Partners and myself.
- My ongoing blog on the investing process and related stories.
- Articles and stories from advisors and experts in the financial services industry.
- Detailed descriptions of each asset class and subclass, plus an investment glossary.
- Easy tools to help you with financial planning and asset allocation.
- A list of other relevant investing websites that cover software tools, search tools for advisors, and financial planning software sources.

- Detailed questionnaires to review with your advisor.
- Per Chapter 13, "Beyond Borders," my current views on country classifications.
- A sample of my own personal portfolio weightings of asset classes and country allocation.

IMPORTANT LEGAL INFORMATION: DISCLAIMER

In order to be more beneficial to readers, the author expresses his analyses and opinions in an open and provocative manner throughout the book. However, this book should in no way be perceived as a recommendation, nor should anyone assume that any of the ideas in the book are fail-safe or that there are not valid, opposing opinions available. The author is not acting in any capacity as an investment advisor. All stories are merely as recalled. All data should be checked independently.

NOTES

CHAPTER 2: DIAGNOSES FOR MY DOCTOR

1. In the old ranking system before 2002, Morningstar ranked funds based on performance compared with other funds for periods of at least three years, giving relatively high ranking to the funds invested in high-growth sectors such as technology. For example, a study led by professor Matthew Morey of Pace University concluded that in 2000, Morningstar's five-star class of 1999 lost 15.7 percent, while funds that had one star in 1999 gained 6.9 percent. "Behind Morningstar's Fund Ratings," *CNN Money*, February 13, 2007.

2. In 1999, technology stocks accounted for almost 30 percent of the S&P 500, a more than threefold increase over the proportion six years earlier. Ashwath Damodaran, *The Dark Side of Valuation* (New Jersey: Financial Times Press, 2001).

3. "In 2002, one-third of the US-stock funds with a five-star Morningstar rating had negative returns for the 12 months through February. Three-quarters of the five-star international-stock funds were in the negative column for the same period." Karen Damato, "Stars Alone Don't Illuminate Performance Picture," *Wall Street Journal*, March 22, 2002. "In June 2010, Vanguard published another analysis on predictive value of star systems. The authors analyzed fund statistics for each 36 months following Morningstar Rating: June 30, 1992, through August 31, 2009 on funds found that, on average, only 39 percent of funds with a five-star rating outperformed their benchmarks for the three-year period following the rating, while 46 percent of funds with a one-star rating outperformed their benchmark for the same period. However, based on market feedback, Morningstar unveiled a new rating system in late 2011. This new system sought to avoid 'recency bias' by keeping a long-term perspective and by including qualitative factors on a fund's strengths and weaknesses across five pillars: people, process, parent, performance, and price. It is too early to say how the new rating system has performed." Daniel Solin,

"Problems With Morningstar's New Rating System," *US News*, February 28, 2013, http://money.usnews.com/money/blogs/On-Retirement/2013/02/28/problems-with-morningstars-new-rating-system.

CHAPTER 3: DIETING AND INVESTING

1. *Micronutrient Research for Optimum Health*, Oregon State University, Linus Pauling Institute, May 2013, http://lpi.oregonstate.edu/infocenter/vitamins/vitaminE.
2. Genevieve Shaw Brown, "Chia Seeds the 'It' Food of 2013," *ABC News*, February 6, 2013, http://abcnews.go.com/Travel/eating-chia-seeds/story?id=18296119.
3. Our research on diversification during the period of 1997–2012 shows that including more asset classes can lead to lower volatility in a portfolio. Please see the example on my website: timmccarthy.com. The volatility for a single asset class portfolio is 16.3 percent but for a seven-asset class portfolio the volatility goes down to 11.2 percent. However, volatility and returns for portfolios may change based on selected period and weights of asset and sub-asset classes, and may not always result in lower volatility from diversification.

CHAPTER 5: MY RANDY OLD GREAT-GRANDFATHER

1. According to National Vital Statistics Report 2010, a 60-year-old person can expect to live an additional 23.1 years on average. A 60-year-old male can expect to live an additional 21.5 years while a female can live about 24.5 years. "However, the longest living member of a couple can expect to live another 24 years to age 89. Considering a traditional 30-year retirement duration assumption, for 65-year-olds the probability of surviving another 30 years to age 95 is 6 percent for males, 12.4 percent for females, and 17.7 percent for at least one member of a couple." Michael Finke, Wade D. Pfau, and Duncan Williams, "Spending Flexibility and Safe Withdrawal Rates," *Journal of Financial Planning*, http://www.fpanet.org/journal/SpendingFlexibilityandSafeWithdrawalRates (accessed July 30, 2013).

CHAPTER 6: IT'S ABOUT TIME

1. In the simplest sense, index investing attempts to replicate the performance of a given index of stocks or some other asset class. Since an index fund owns all of the investments in the underlying index, there is no picking of winners and losers. As a result, it involves much less work in managing an index fund, leading to lower costs for the investor.
2. In a wrap account a brokerage manages an investor's portfolio for a flat quarterly or annual fee based on the total assets in the account. Said differently, the various individual funds or securities are "wrapped" into a single account. The advantage of a wrap is that it brings a broker and an investor on the same side;

since brokers only get a flat annual fee, they only trade when it is advantageous to you.

3. The theory was popularized by Burton Malkiel of Princeton University. The theory postulates that stocks follow a random and unpredictable path and it is impossible to outperform the market without assuming additional risk. Burton G. Malkiel, *A Random Walk Down Wall Street: The Time-Tested Strategy for Successful Investing*, (New York: W. W. Norton, 2007).

4. In a study by Massey University, New Zealand, a group of researchers tested a hypothesis on sector rotation over business cycles. The study concluded that even with perfect foresight and ignoring transactions costs, sector rotation would have generated at best a 2.3 percent annual outperformance since 1948. In more realistic settings, outperformance quickly dissipates. Jeffrey Stangl, Ben Jacobsen, and Nuttawat Visaltanachoti, "Sector Rotation over Business Cycles," Massey University–Department of Finance and Economics, New Zealand, August 2009.

5. Tactical funds, those that make frequent and material changes to the weightings of asset classes, have had a mixed record. According to a *Wall Street Journal* article, among funds that invest in a global mix of stocks, bonds, and other assets, over the five years through 2011, an average fund has returned 1.6 percent. In another example cited in the article, the range of 2011 returns for funds with at least $25 million in assets was wide: from positive 10.3 percent to negative 23.6 percent. Karen Damato, "Does Total Freedom Boost Returns? 'Tactical' Funds Offer Some Answers," *Wall Street Journal*, January 9, 2012, http://online.wsj.com/article/SB100014240529702044660045771024 82644384996.html.

CHAPTER 7: HOW AM I DOING?

1. Russel Kinnel, "How Expense Ratios and Star Ratings Predict Success," *Morningstar*, August 2010, http://www.morningstar.co.uk/uk/news/66497/how-expense-ratios—star-ratings-predict-success.aspx.

2. Ibid.

CHAPTER 9: THE REVERSAL OF NATIONS

1. Pär Österholm, "Estimating the Relationship between Age Structure and GDP in the OECD Using Panel Cointegration Methods," Department of Economics, Uppsala University, September 2004, http://www.nek.uu.se/pdf/wp2004_13.pdf.

2. Composed of 35 countries: Australia, Austria, Belgium, Canada, Cyprus, Czech Republic, Denmark, Estonia, Finland, France, Germany, Greece, Hong Kong SAR, Iceland, Ireland, Israel, Italy, Japan, Korea, Luxembourg, Malta, Netherlands, New Zealand, Norway, Portugal, San Marino, Singapore,

Slovakia, Slovenia, Spain, Sweden, Switzerland, Taiwan Province of China, United Kingdom, and United States

3. Based on an analysis of 1994 birth certificates, the National Center for Health Statistics found a direct relationship between years of education and birth rates, with the highest birth rates among women with the lowest educational attainment. "Mother's Educational Level Influences Birth Rate," National Center for Health Statistics, Centers for Disease Control and Prevention, April 24, 1997, http://www.cdc.gov/nchs/pressroom/97facts/edu2birt.htm.

4. Sandra Lawson, Dina Powell, and Lisa Shalett, "Investing in Women," Goldman Sachs, December 11, 2012, http://www.goldmansachs.com/our-thinking/focus-on/investing-in-women/discussion/index.html.

5. OECD members: Australia, Austria, Belgium, Canada, Chile, Czech Republic, Denmark, Estonia, Finland, France, Germany, Greece, Hungary, Iceland, Ireland, Israel, Italy, Japan, Korea, Luxembourg, Mexico, Netherlands, New Zealand, Norway, Poland, Portugal, Slovakia, Slovenia, Spain, Sweden, Switzerland, Turkey, United Kingdom, and United States

6. A Global REIT Fund is a set of publicly traded equity REITs listed in both developed and emerging markets.

7. A unit trust is a regulated investment vehicle consisting of professional managers who issue redeemable securities depicting a portfolio of various securities. It was named unit trust in the UK, while in the United States, we call essentially the same investing vehicle a mutual fund.

CHAPTER 10: THREE POCKETS

1. Charles Mackay did an excellent job in describing a variety of economic bubbles throughout history, including the famous Tulip Mania time in 1636–1637, among the worst financial meltdowns in human history. Even then, the market crashed from February to May 1637 from a price index of nearly 200 to less than 10. However, in November 1636, the price index was only around 10. Charles Mackay, "Extraordinary Popular Delusions," Richard Bentley, London, 1841.

2. Richard Bernstein Advisors conducted research on asset classes returns versus the returns of the average investor during the 1991–2011 period. The analysis concluded that investors typically do not identify bull markets and generate lower returns than many asset classes. Richard Bernstein, "Investors Typically Don't Identify Bull Markets," Richard Bernstein Advisors LLC, April 2013.

CHAPTER 11: THE RISK PRISM

1. From a study by Columbia University Center for Decision Sciences on how often-cautious people change their risk-taking tendencies in different context. Sue Shellenbarger, "What Makes a Risk-Taker," Wall Street Journal, May 22, 2013.

2. A prospectus is a disclosure document that describes a financial instrument for potential buyers. A prospectus includes material information about an investment, such as a description of the company's business, financial statements, risks related to the business, biographies of senior executives, and any other material information. In some countries, this document is called an *explanatory memorandum.*

3. Fund managers are responsible for implementing a fund's investing strategy and managing its portfolio trading activities, including risks involved in portfolio management.

4. Debt service is the cash required for a particular time period to cover the repayment of interest and principal on a debt.

5. The fundamental analysis of a stock and bond involves analyzing financial statements and business aspects to gain insight on a company's future performance.

6. Past performance does not provide useful information about future performance. More likely, a top performer fund would revert to the mean performance. Rick Ferri, "Wishing Upon A Star Manager Doesn't Work," *Forbes*, June 13, 2013, http://www.forbes.com/sites/rickferri/2013/06/13/wishing-upon-a-star-manager-doesnt-work/.

7. Edwin J. Perkins, *Wall Street to Main Street: Charles Merrill and Middle-Class Investors* (Cambridge, UK: Cambridge University Press, 1999).

CHAPTER 12: WHAT'S INSIDE YOUR POCKETS?

1. The Federal Deposit Insurance Corporation (FDIC) website states that it "is an independent agency created by the Congress to maintain stability and public confidence in the nation's financial system by insuring deposits, and examining and supervising financial institutions." http://www.fdic.gov/.

2. MMFs are not insured by the Federal Deposit Insurance Corporation or the National Credit Union Administration.

3. FDIC insurance covers deposit accounts with the same title at the same institution to at least an amount of $250,000 per depositor. Federal Deposit Insurance Corporation, accessed August 10, 2013, http://www.fdic.gov/deposit/.

4. Standard & Poor's and Moody's have a rating system for short-term debt instruments ranging from A1+ to D (S&P) and P1 to NP (Moody's). Ratings from A1+ to A3 (S&P) and P1 to P3 (Moody's) are being considered investment grade.

5. Financial instruments typically with original maturities of less than nine months are considered short-term paper. These instruments are typically issued at a discount and provide a low risk investment alternative.

6. Brokerage firms lend money to investors typically to help them purchase securities. This practice is referred to as margin financing.

7. A market maker is a broker-dealer that quotes both a buy and a sell price in a financial instrument, hoping to make a profit on the bid-offer spread.

8. OTC stocks are traded by broker-dealers who negotiate directly with one another. Originally, OTC, or "over the counter," stocks were known as unlisted stocks because the issuing companies are small, making them unable to meet exchange listing requirements. However, now some of the world's largest and most successful public companies are not listed on exchanges.

9. P/E, or price/earnings ratio, is a valuation ratio of a company's current share price compared to its earnings per share. It is calculated as market value per share divided by earnings per share.

10. A study by Advisor Partners identified the asset classes where active management can make a difference in performance over passive management. The team at Advisor Partners preferred active management in international small-cap equities, emerging markets equities, domestic aggregate bonds, high-yield bonds, international developed-market bonds, and emerging market bonds categories over passive management. Daniel Kern and Gerard Cronin, "Rethinking Asset Allocation and Investment Selection," Advisor Partners, May 2013.

11. Martijn Cremers and Antti Petajistoy, "How Active Is Your Fund Manager?: A New Measure That Predicts Performance," Smith School of Business, University of Maryland, January 15, 2007, http://www.rhsmith.umd.edu /finance/pdfs_docs/seminarspring07/Cremers.pdf.

12. Morningstar published the results of a recent study where expense ratios are considered as strong predictors of performance. In every single time period and investment category tested, low-cost funds beat high-cost funds. Russell Kinnel, "Morningstar: How Expense Ratios and Star Ratings Predict Success," Morningstar, August 2010, http://news.morningstar.com/articlenet/article. aspx?id=347327&page=1#page=1.

Note the weakness in many passive international bond funds that replicate an index weighted most toward those firms that borrow heavily. Since there is no credit screening, there may be more risk in such funds vs. similar actively managed funds.

13. Undertaking for collective investments (UCITS) are forms of collective investment schemes, in which investors pool their money to invest in a variety of assets and securities. Société d'Investissement À Capital Variable (SICAV) is a type of open-ended investment fund where shares in the fund are bought and sold based on the fund's current net asset value.

14. Richard Bernstein, "Historical 5-year Correlation of Selected Asset Classes," Richard Bernstein Advisors LLC, April 2013.

CHAPTER 13: BEYOND BORDERS

1. Quantitative investing applies rigorous and systematic analysis on financial information and ratios to invest in capital markets.

2. "FACTBOX—BRICS emerging powers grow in global strength," *Reuters*, March 26, 2013, http://in.reuters.com/article/2013/03/26/brics-summit-factbox-idINDEE92P09120130326.

3. The MSCI World Index covers large- and mid-cap companies across 24 developed markets. With 1,607 constituents, the index covers approximately 85 percent of the free float-adjusted market capitalization in each country. The FTSE All-World Index also covers large- and mid-cap stocks in 47 countries and covers 90 to 95 percent of the investable market capitalization. FTSE All-World Index provides exposure to 10.9 percent of emerging markets. Both the indexes underrepresent exposure to growth countries but these indexes are changing to represent the shift in macro dynamics and growth patterns of various geographies.

4. The notable research on growth countries is by Blackrock and Goldman Sachs. GSAM Fundamental Equity Team, "Investing in the N-11: Capturing Growth Potential through Local Equity Markets," Goldman Sachs Asset Management, April 2011; Marco Merz, "The Final Frontier," Blackrock, 2011.

5. Results can be viewed at Transparency International's website, www.transparency.org.

6. International dollar is a hypothetical currency with the same purchasing power of goods and services in all countries. Purchasing power parity measures the amount of adjustment needed on the exchange rate between countries to create a measure that is equivalent to each currency's purchasing power.

7. GDP per capita figure is based on GDP figures of 2008 from Yahoo! Finance and population figures from census data. Since census in India happens once in a decade, the latest available data is from 2011. The GDP per capita still provides an indication of disparity that exists in India. Source: http://in.finance.yahoo.com/photos/the-top-15-indian-cities-by-gdp-1348807591-slideshow/the-top-15-indian-cities-by-gdp-photo-1348807048.html (accessed August 10, 2013).

8. GDP per capita is based on purchasing power parity as of 2012. The World Factbook, https://www.cia.gov/library/publications/the-world-factbook/geos/in.html (accessed August 10, 2013).

9. Science, technology, engineering, and mathematics (STEM) enrollments in higher education in Russia was 1.43 million in 2010. Anna Smolentseva, "Science, Technology, Engineering and Mathematics: Issues of Educational Policy in Russia," Australian Council of Learned Academies, 2013, http://www.acolasecretariat.org.au/ACOLA/PDF/SAF02Consultants/Consultant%20Report%20-%20Russia.pdf (accessed August 10, 2013).

CHAPTER 14: WHAT ABOUT YOUR PERSONAL PORTFOLIO?

1. There are a variety of other well-received websites that are also worth Googling, including Motif Investing, Esavant, Personal Capital, Covestor, Foliofn, Wealthfront, and LearnVest.

2. The returns performance is based on S&P total returns index and ten-year treasury data.

3. Total market capitalization of the US market was $18.7 trillion in 2012 compared to $52.5 trillion of global market.

4. MSCI World Index only covers 24 developed markets. However, the MSCI ACWI Investable Market Index has exposure to 24 developed markets and 21 emerging markets countries. In 2012, emerging markets accounted for approximately 38 percent of global GDP (IMF as of January 2012) and emerging market companies contributed 23 percent of global equity market cap (FactSet as of December 2012). Yet, emerging markets only represented approximately 13 percent of global equity market capitalization in MSCI ACWI. Thus, even this index presently under weights the exposure to the Growth Countries and over weights exposure to the mature countries. In this case, investors may be better to select active managers for EM rather than under weighted "all country" index funds in order to garner sufficient EM and Growth Country exposure.

5. Goldman Sachs predicted that emerging markets would contribute 59 percent to global GDP by 2030. Goldman Sachs, http://www.goldmansachs.com /gsam/advisors/education/investment-ideas/emep/index.print.html (accessed on August 11, 2013). IMF predicted 55 percent contribution from emerging markets and developing economies to global GDP based on purchasing power parity. These predictions provide a long-term directional sense of growth of emerging markets; however, as an investor one should check the predictions regularly to understand the shift in macro dynamics.

6. Overbought refers to a situation in which the high demand for a certain asset pushes the price of an underlying asset to levels that are not supported by the fundamentals. In technical analysis, overbought describes a situation in which the price of an asset has risen to such a degree that an oscillator has touched its upper bound. Oversold is opposite of overbought.

7. Fall in AUM (asset under management) can be one of the potential reasons in closing down or merger of funds. Advisor Partners recently analyzed the funds data for the last 15 years ending in December 2012 to figure out the survival rate of funds. The team found that about 69 percent of funds survived five years, 52 percent of funds survived ten years, and only 43 percent of funds survived 15 years. Daniel Kern and Gerard Cronin, "Outliving Your Funds," Advisor Partners, December 2013.

8. GDR (Global Depositary Receipt) is a bank certificate issued in more than one country for shares in a foreign company but trades as domestic shares. The shares are kept by a foreign branch of an international bank and offered for sale globally through the various bank branches. ADR (American Depositary Receipt) is a bank certificate issued by a US bank representing ownership in a foreign stock that is traded on a US exchange. ADRs also trade like domestic shares and are denominated in US dollars, with the underlying asset held by a US financial institution overseas.

CHAPTER 15: WHO IS MOST DANGEROUS?

1. Throughout the book, we use the spelling "advisor" as opposed to "adviser." Investment Advisors that are Registered Investment Advisors normally use the "advisor" spelling. In the broker-dealer community, especially those RRs that are not RIAs, the "adviser" spelling is used, though such distinctions are not always followed by many inside and outside the industry.

INDEX

AAA-rated corporate bonds, 68
AAFM. *See* American Academy of Financial
    Management
AARP, 241
accidental investing, 58–63
    and not picking worst funds, 62–3
    and performance ratings, 60–2
accumulation stage, and personal portfolio,
    211–15
acronyms, 19–20, 101, 128
Active Share Index, 146–7
ADRs. *See* American Depositary Receipt
advanced growth countries, 174, 176,
    186–8, 196, 225, 231
Advisor Partners, ix, xiv, 56, 121, 207, 283,
    292n10, 294n7
Advisor Software Inc., 122, 200, 208
advisors, 6, 26–8, 44–6, 119–28, 131, 199,
    233–75
    and fund managers, 120–1
    and gender, 272
    as "lazy," 44–6
    number one goal of, 6
    and overconcentration, 120–1
    and risk, 119–28, 131
    and scope creep, 119–20
    and selecting the right advisor, 263–75
    See Naked Advisor
    and selecting the right firm, 246–61
    See selecting the right type of firm
    as separate, 257–9
    and single point of failure, 26–8
    and small investors, 259–60
    and succession, 269
    and trading spreads, 128
    and trust, 233–44
    value of, 245–6
    See independent financial advisors;
        registered investment advisors;
        registered representatives

age, xiii, 23, 31–5, 64, 78–84, 113–14,
    198–207, 215–32
    and cognitive tests, 224
    and coming up short, 228–32
    and consumption, 78–81
    and demographics, 79–84
    and health care. *See* health care costs
    and investing for later years, 198–207
    See later years, investing for
    and Investing Pocket, 113–14
    and longevity, 31–5, 79–84
    See life expectancy
    and portfolio allocation, 215–32
    and risk, 113–14
agriculture, 148
alligator flea, story of, 72–6
Alzheimer's, 205–6, 224
American Academy of Financial
    Management (AAFM), 243
American Association Of Retired Persons
    (AARP), 241
American Depositary Receipt (ADRs), 227,
    294n8
American Indians, 111
annuities, 154–5, 211, 219–20
Asia, 16–18, 28, 44–5, 72–3, 86, 89, 120,
    129, 169–70, 175, 179–80, 187, 192,
    194, 227
"Asian barbell" strategy, 73
asset classes, 18, 108–9, 112, 113–15, 121,
    123, 131–65, 279
    and active management, 146
    alternatives, 155–8
    basic, 133–41
    characteristics of, 133–41
    correlation among, 157
    defined, 108–9
    investment vehicles for exposure to,
        150–5
    and returns and volatility, 157

asset classes—*Continued*
  and risk, 113
  and subclasses, 108, 133–4, 145,
    148, 279
  and Three Pockets. *See* Three Pockets,
    contents of
  underperforming, 18
asset classes subclasses, 108, 133–4, 145,
  148, 279
asset-backed securities funds, 138
asset under management (AUM), 215, 294n7
assisted care, 204–6
  See health care costs
astrophysicist's portfolio, 45–6
audited accounting statement, 129–30
AUM. *See* asset under management
Australia, 15, 151, 181, 186–8, 289n2,
  290n5

balance, and risk, 115, 123–6, 131
Bangladesh, 195
Bank of America, 254
bankruptcy, 70, 82
banks, 5, 15–16, 22–3, 27–8, 35, 39, 45, 52,
  64, 70, 73, 82–3, 90–1, 112, 126–30,
  134–9, 162, 177, 190, 201, 214, 218,
  221, 226, 236–44, 246–50
  bank account. *See* savings account
  and selecting the right bank, 253–4
Barbados, 179
BCP. *See* Business Continuation Planning
Benelux, 185
Betterment, 200
blue chip stock, 10–11, 144–5
Bogle, Jack, 41
bonds, 3–7, 21, 24, 42, 60–73, 90–1, 108,
  116–17, 122, 124, 128, 133, 136–42,
  146, 148–50, 154, 156, 160–1, 164,
  168–70, 180, 186, 200, 208–10,
  211–12, 215, 219–20, 225, 227,
  230–1, 251, 258–9, 289n5, 291n5,
  292n10
  and bond market crash, 141–2
  as low risk and high risk, 3–7
  and packaging issues, 139–41
  as short, medium and long-term, 136–7
brands, and firm selection, 247, 251–2
Brazil, 45, 81, 90, 171–2, 179, 181,
  189–90, 193
Brazil, Russia, India, and China. *See* BRICs
  countries
Bribe Payers Index, 178
BRICs countries (Brazil, Russia, India, and
  China), 172
Brightscope Advisors, 264
Broker Check, 240

broker-dealers, 150, 242, 247, 249–53, 255,
  260, 292n7–8, 295n7
Buffet, Warren, 141
Bulgaria, 81, 190
bull markets, 43, 69, 71, 290n2
"bulls surprise you," 69
"bunnies, the snake, and the owl" story,
  197–8
Business Continuation Planning (BCP), 19
business news, xii, 46–7
"buy and hold," 39–40, 43–4

call centers, 89, 111, 255–6
Canada, 167, 185
"cap weighted," 11, 143
capital gains, 67
capital markets dynamics, and risk, 118
Carlyle, Thomas, 83
cash and equivalents, 134
CD. *See* certificates of deposit
Central Registration Depository
  (CRD), 240
certainty equivalent, 23
certificates of deposit (CD), 128, 134–5,
  250, 253
certified financial planner (CFP), 241,
  243, 264
CFA. *See* chartered financial analyst
CFP. *See* certified financial planner
Chad, 174
Charles Schwab Investment
  Management, 50
chartered financial analyst (CFA), 243
chartered financial consultant (ChFC), 243
chartered investment counselor (CIC), 243
Chartered Wealth Manager (CWM), 243
ChFC. *See* chartered financial consultant
chief financial officers (CFOs), 273
Chile, 186, 290n5
China, xiii, 18, 28, 32, 38, 72, 75, 81,
  84, 87–9, 92, 170–2, 179, 181–2,
  187–90, 193–5, 289n2
  as growth country, 188–9
  and US government debt, xiii
CIC. *See* chartered investment counselor
Citi, 254
Citigroup, 254
Clark, Dennis, 232
closed end bond funds, 160
"closet index," 147
CNBC, 112
Code of Hammurabi, 177
cognitive tests, 224
Cold War, 25
college education costs, 114, 199, 217,
  228, 230

Columbia, 194
commissions, 26–7, 138–9, 249–50, 254–5, 268
commodities, 71, 90, 92–3, 125, 148, 155–6, 168, 210–11, 257, 267, 279–80
    defined, 125, 148, 210–11
    and risk, 125
    and sub asset categories, 148
communism, 94, 171–2, 190–1
comparables, 57–8
compliance, 53–4, 129, 170–1, 243, 247, 252, 272
Confucius, 28
constructing your portfolio, 162–4
consumption, and aging, 78–83
corruption, 94–7, 172, 174, 178–80, 188, 190–5
Corruption Perceptions Index, 178
Costa Rica, 89, 111
country allocation, 45, 73, 76, 184–95, 209–10, 225–7, 284
country classifications, 184–95
    See advanced growth countries; emerging growth countries; frontier countries; growth countries; mature countries
country economic ranking, 116, 175–84
    and company domicile versus revenue, 183–4
    and corruption, 178–80
    and GDP and market capitalization, 173
    and infrastructure, 180–1
    and legal/regulatory structure, 176
    and macro-economic metrics, 181
    and natural resources, 181–2
    and political environment, 175
    and population factors, 182–3
    and quality of the companies, 182
country populations, and aging, 79–84
country status, 77–98
    and corruption, 94–7
    and demographics, 77–84
    and foreign shores, 93–8
    and growth countries, 85–93
CRD. See Central Registration Depository
Cremer, Martijn, 146–7
Croatia, 195
Cronin, Gerard, ix, 292n10, 294n7
crowd emotion, 70–1
currencies, 71, 76, 81–6, 90–1, 97, 122–3, 130, 138–9, 181, 183, 188, 191, 193–4, 209–10, 223, 225, 293n6
currency overlay, 138–9
CWM. See Chartered Wealth Manager
Czech Republic, 190
Czechoslovakia, 190–1

debt, xiii, 65–6, 80–3, 85–7, 91–2, 94, 97, 116–18, 122–3, 127–8, 134–7, 141–2, 164, 180–1, 185–6, 188, 191, 220–1, 228, 279, 291n4
    corporate, 137
    crises, 141–2
    and debt service, 291n4
    governmental. See government debt
    lessons unique to, 164
    securities, 65–6, 134–6, 291n4
    short-term, 134, 279, 291n4
    short-term debt instruments, 291n4
    See bonds
declining birthrate, 84
deflation, 123–4
dementia, 59, 204, 205–6, 224
democracy, 89, 175–6
"demographic dividend," 81
demographics, 77–86, 124–5
    and consumption, 78–83
    and declining birthrate, 84
    and government debt, 80–2
    and growth countries, 85–6
    and risk, 124–5
    and "window of opportunity," 81
    See age; later years, investing for; longevity
Deng Xiaoping, 87
dependency ratio, 81
derivatives, 128, 137–8, 148–50, 156, 218, 264
Detroit, 24
Deutsche Bank, 90
dictatorship, 94, 172, 175–6
dieting and investing, 15–18
direct fund company distributors, 256
disaster recovery (DR), 19
discipline, 106, 111, 118, 169, 256, 280
discount brokers, 254–5
diversification
    and asset classes, 108–9
    and assets, 279–80
    and countries, 280
    critical lessons of, 279–81
    and diet analogy. See dieting, and investing
    and fund rating. See fund rating
    and overconcentration, 10–11
    and portfolio investment, 69, 203
    and risk, 114
    and single points of failure, 28–9
    and Three Pockets, 104
        See Three Pockets
    and time, 280
    trickiness of, 9–13, 54–5
    See trickle-in, trickle-out

dividends, 67, 81, 85, 130, 212, 221, 224–5, 227, 230–1
DIY. *See* Do It Yourself
do it yourself (DIY), 161–2, 199–200, 245, 249, 265
doctor's portfolio, 9–13, 53, 162
"dollar cost averaging," 106–7
 See trickle-in, trickle-out
"don't put eggs in one basket," 7, 28–9
 See single points of failure
dot.com bubble, 9–13, 39–40
Dow, xiii, 10, 157, 170
DR. *See* disaster recovery
Dubai, 32, 93, 186–8
due diligence, 51–2, 97, 139–40, 159, 164, 225, 230, 248, 251, 260, 275, 281

E*TRADE, 246, 260
East Germany, 190–1
Eastern Europe, 190–1
Eco Fund, 231
Economic Security Planning, 199
Economist, 89
ED Jones, 252
educating women, 84
EFPA. *See* European Financial Planning Association
Egypt, 195
EM. *See* emerging markets
emerging growth countries, 192–4
emerging markets (EM), 62, 84–97, 146, 153, 171–84, 192–4, 196, 208–9, 215, 222, 290n6, 292n10, 293n3, 294n4–5
 and bond funds, 62, 146
 and company domicile versus revenue, 183–4
 and core investment, 93–7
 and corruption, 94–7, 178–80
 and developed markets, 85
 evaluating, 174–84
 and GDP and market capitalization, 173
 and "good" borrowing, 91–2
 as "growth countries," 85–93
 and infrastructure, 180–1
 and legal/regulatory structure, 176
 lessons about, 97
 and macro-economic metrics, 181
 and natural resources, 181–2
 and political environment, 175
 and population factors, 182–3
 and quality of the companies, 182
 See international markets, investing in
emotions, and investing, xi–xii, 3–7, 17–18, 43–4, 47, 65–76, 104, 110, 112, 128, 142, 222, 228, 270–1, 280–1
 and alligator flea, 72–6

and dieting analogy, 17–18
and emotional management, 72–6, 112
 See Three Pockets
and equities, 65–76
and fear, 47, 65, 71, 104, 110, 112, 270–1
and greed, 71, 112, 280
and lessons, 71–2
and panic, 3–7, 43–4, 104, 110, 112, 128, 142, 222, 228, 280
and patience, xi, 7, 38, 41, 44–7
end of life health care, 203–6
 See health care costs
Ensemble Capital, 147
entrepreneurship, 79, 110–11
equities, 9, 43, 54, 60–1, 63, 65–76, 85, 90, 116–17, 122–3, 125, 133–7, 142–8, 156–9, 164, 173, 179–80, 183, 200, 202–3, 206, 208–9, 211, 216–17, 220–2, 225–7, 230–1, 258, 279, 290n2, 6, 292n10, 295n5
 and bull markets, 43, 69, 71, 290n2
 and emotions, 65–76
 and Three Pockets, 142–8
 value of investing in, 66–8
equivalents, 134
E$Planner, 199–200
ETFs. *See* exchange-traded funds
ETNs. *See* exchange traded notes
European Financial Planning Association (EFPA), 243
evaluating fund and portfolio data, 49–64
 and accidental investing, 58–63
 and being vaguely right, 51–2
 and comparables, 57–8
 and existing performance analysis, 63–4
 and not picking worst funds, 62–3
 and past performance, 53–4
 and performance ratings, 60–2
 and "pie of funds," 56–7
 and precise measurement, 51–2
 and survivor bias, 54–6
 and tiny tracking errors, 50
 and windows, 52–3
exchange-traded funds (ETFs), 11, 42–4, 137, 143–5, 152–3, 163–5, 169, 215, 266–7
 strength of can also be weakness, 43–4
exchange traded notes (ETNs), 159
existing performance analysis, 63–4

FApages.com, 264
FDIC. *See* Federal Deposit Insurance Corporation
Federal Deposit Insurance Corporation (FDIC), 135, 221, 241, 250, 254, 291n1

Federal Savings And Loan Corporation (FSLIC), 241
"fee only" approach, 39
Fidelity, 60, 122, 126, 246, 249, 252, 256
financial catastrophes, guarding against, 19–29
financial cycles, understanding, 37–47
  and customers' impatience, 44–6
  and length of, 40–1
  and mutual funds and ETFs, 43–4
  and the press and the pundits, 46–7
  and the winning spirit, 41–3
Financial Industry Regulatory Authority (FINRA), 240, 242–3, 265
financial institutions, and risk, 126–30
FINRA. See Financial Industry Regulatory Authority
First Republic, 254
fixed income, 61–2, 68, 203, 208–9, 222
Fleming, Robert, 93
flexibility, 146, 151, 161, 198, 220, 280–1
Focus Fund style managers, 147
Ford Motor Company, 170, 227
forest for trees, 51–3
401(k)s, 159, 218–19, 231
"40 Act Funds," 151
Franklin Templeton, 60
French Revolution (1789), 38
frontier countries, 84, 86, 91, 177, 193–5, 219, 221–2, 225, 230
FSLIC. See Federal Savings and Loan Corporation
FTSE, 86, 173, 293n3
Fukushima, 25
fund and portfolio data, evaluating, 49–64
fund managers, 10, 49, 54–5, 116–23, 143–4, 146–7, 157, 168–9, 177, 180, 186, 189, 194–6, 258, 291n3
fund ratings, 10–13, 57, 63

GDP. See gross domestic product
GDRs. See Global Depositary Receipt
GE, 170
Germany, 81, 185, 190–1, 196, 236–8
Global Corruption Barometer, 178
Global Depositary Receipt (GDRs), 227, 294n8
GoalGami, 200
gold, 16–18, 40, 66–8, 84, 93, 115, 148, 207, 210, 227
"gold bugs," 148
Goldman Sachs, 84, 90, 171, 173
government debt, xiii, 80–7, 91–4, 97, 122–3, 141–2
Great Depression, 68, 105, 126–7
great-grandfather. See Richard Sinnott

Greece, 81–2, 178, 185
gross domestic product (GDP), 81–2, 84–5, 87, 172–3, 182–3, 188, 189, 209
growth countries, 85–93, 188–92, 227
  and demographics, 85–93
  and investment, 188–92
  See emerging markets

H&Q. See Hambrecht and Quist
Hambrecht and Quist (H&Q), 70
Harvard Business Review, 89
Hawaii, 31–2, 109
health care costs, xiii, 79, 201–6, 217, 222, 224, 232
hedge funds, 54, 155–8, 227
high net worth investors, 215
high-tech stocks, 9–11, 258
Hong Kong, 72–3, 75, 86, 88, 151, 179–80, 186–7
Hughes, Howard, 238–9

IAPD. See Investment Adviser Public Disclosure site
IBM, 170
IFAs. See independent financial advisors
immigration, and U.S., 31–2, 80
independent financial advisors (IFAs), 39–40, 198
independent verification, 26–8
index ETFs (exchange-traded funds), 42, 143
index fund, 9–11, 42, 50–1, 62, 143–8, 157, 163–4, 169, 195, 211, 212, 266–7, 288n1
  and "Goldilocks," 163
  management of, 143–7
"index huggers," 147
index investing, 39–42, 209, 288n1
India, 25–6, 72, 81, 88–90, 93, 96, 171–6, 179, 181–2, 187–9, 293n7
individual retirement account (IRA), 159, 231, 241
Indonesia, 90, 171, 188, 193–4
inflation, xiii, 35, 47, 60, 66–8, 83, 103, 109, 123–4, 130, 164, 174, 188, 198–201, 210, 221, 225
inheritance, 206, 214, 223
interest rates, xiii, 4–6, 35, 68, 79, 83, 91, 122, 136, 138–9, 160, 188, 194, 221, 224, 250, 259
international markets, investing in, 93–7, 167–96, 209–10
  and breaking rocks, 170–4
  and classifications, 184–95
  lessons for, 196
  as part of core investment, 93–7

international markets, investing
        in—*Continued*
    and rankings, 174–84
    and risk, 169–70
    See country allocation; country
        classifications; country economic
        ranking; country population, and
        aging; country status
Internet brokers, 254–5
investing for long-term. *See* Safe Investor
"Investing in Loss," 111–12
Investing Pocket, 102–4, 106–12, 128,
        139–40, 142, 147–9, 151, 153–5,
        161–2, 180, 196, 200–2, 206–32,
        257, 280
    basic scenario of, 200–2
    and corrupt countries, 180
    and high net worth investors, 215
    and later in life, 207–11
    and minimizing damage, 142
    and number one goal, 147
    sample recommendations for, 222
    as "Tai Chi Pocket," 111–12
    and weightings, 207–11
    See trickle-in, trickle-out
Investment Adviser Public Disclosure site
        (IAPD) (SEC), 240
Investment Company Act (1940), 151
investment vehicles for exposure to asset
        classes, 150–5
    and annuities, 154
    and exchange traded funds, 152–3
    and life insurance, 154
    and mutual funds, 151–2
    and private placement funds, 153
    and real estate, 153–4
IRA. *See* individual retirement account
Iran, 81
Ireland, 31, 33, 185–7, 226, 289n2, 290n5
Irving, Clifford, 238–9
Israel, 186, 289n2, 290n5
Italy, 80–2, 178, 185

J. P. Morgan, 254
Janney Montgomery Scott, 252
Japan, 28, 51, 80–4, 91–2, 97, 123, 167–8,
        172, 174, 179, 185–7, 195, 242, 273,
        289n2, 290n5
Jardine Fleming Unit Trust, 170
Johnson, Chuck, 70
Johnson, Ned, 122

karate, xi, 4, 111, 270
Kern, Dan, ix, 121, 207–8, 292n10, 294n7
"know your customer" (KYC) rule, 243
"knowledge workers," 189

kumite, xi
KYC. *See* "know your customer"

later years, investing for, xiii, 23, 31–5, 64,
        198–207, 215–32
    and basic scenario, 200–2
    and Betterment, 200
    and coming up short, 23, 228–32
    and E$Planner, 199–200
    and GoalGami, 200
    and mid-50s to early 70s, 219–22
    and over 72 years, 223–8
    and personal life expectancy, 33–5
    and portfolio allocation, 215–32
    and strategy, 64, 215
    and up to mid-50s, 217–19
    See health care costs
Laughton, Jim, 104
"leprechaun's green ribbons" approach,
        114–15
lessons, xi–xii
    from around the world, 97
    for building your portfolio, 232
    from diets, 18
    from doctor friend, 13–14
    about emerging markets, 97
    about emotion management, 76
    from existing performance analysis, 63–4
    from great-grandfather, 35
    for international markets, 97, 196
    from Mother's misfortune, 6–7
    for all products including equities, 164–5
    of risk, 131
    and selecting the right investor, 275
    seven critical, 279–81
    about SPOFs, 29
    of Three Pockets, 112
    about time, 47
    and where to go for advice, 261
    and who you can trust, 244
    as unique to debt, 164
licenses, 242–3
life expectancy, 31–5, 67, 79–84
    and longevity, 31–5, 67, 79–84
    personal, 33–5
    of populations, and investing, 79–84
    See later years, investing for
life insurance, 44, 154–5, 256–7
life insurance providers, 256–7
limited partnerships (LPs), 158–9
Lipper, 63, 147
liquidity, 24, 66, 92, 124, 134–6,
        139–42, 146, 150–6, 158, 163, 181,
        225, 228
listening, 72
London Stock Exchange, 183

long-term bonds, 3–7, 136–7
long-term care insurance, 204–6
"long-term investing," 39–40
longevity, xiii, 23, 31–5, 64, 67, 79–84,
        198–207, 215–32
    See later years, investing for
low volatility, 66, 214
    See volatility
LPL Financial, 252
LPs. See limited partnerships

Madoff, Bernard ("Bernie"), 22, 25, 237
Madoff, Peter, 237
Malthus, Thomas Robert, 83
Maquiladora, 195
market crises, 9–13, 39–40, 51–2, 68,
        104–6, 126–7, 137, 141–2, 162
    and Three Pockets, 104–6
    See subprime crisis
"market timers," 69–70
Markowitz, Harry, 41
master limited partnerships (MLPs), 158–9
mature countries, 84, 185–6, 188, 191, 207,
        215, 225, 230, 280
Mauritius, 195
McCarthy, Danny (brother), 3–4, 204
McCarthy, Helen (mother), 3–7, 21, 33, 57,
        65, 78, 115, 204–6, 223, 235, 273
    death of, 204
    and interest rate roller coaster, 3–7
McDonald's, 227
McGraw-Hill, 239
McKinsey, 237
McMahon, James, 197–8
medium-term bonds, 136–7
mergers, 118, 121, 127, 294n7
Merrill Lynch, 126, 252, 254
metals, 148
methodology, xiv–xv, 268, 287–8
Mexico, 89–90, 188, 189–1, 193–5, 290n5
mid-50s to early 70s portfolio allocation,
        219–22
    investing pocket, 218–19
    savings pocket, 217–18
    trading pocket, 219
Middle East, 72, 89, 177, 187, 272
minerals, 148
mining, 210
mistakes, and long-term investing, 7, 10,
        13, 24–5, 37, 44, 51, 64, 65, 71,
        75, 91, 139, 162, 182, 221–3, 246,
        267, 281
MLPs. See master limited partnerships
MMFs. See money market funds
modern portfolio theory, 41
money market account (MMA), 218

money market funds (MMFs), 125, 134–6,
        138–9, 226, 291n2
monitoring your personal portfolio, 211–15
Morgan Stanley, 254
Morningstar, 56, 60–3, 147, 152
Morocco, 90, 194
mortgages, 51–2, 137, 162, 206, 217,
        220, 228
MSCI World, 173, 209
Mumbai, 25–6, 93, 182
mutual funds, 9, 11, 13, 42–4, 49–64, 72,
        121, 151–2, 154–5, 159–61, 196,
        225, 243, 246, 253, 256–8, 272
    and accidental investing, 58–63
    "at risk," 121
    closed end, 152
    and comparables, 57–8
    evaluating, 49–64
    and forest for trees, 51–3
    and "lapping the field," 58–9
    and "not picking the worst," 62–3
    open end, 151–2
    and past performance, 53–4
    and performance ratings, 60–2
    and RIAs, 257–8
    and selection and ratings, 13
    and strength as weakness, 43–4
    survival of, 56–7
    and survivor bias, 54–6
    and tiny tracking errors, 50

Naked Advisor, 263–75
    and basic questions, 265–6
    and clientele, 268
    and fee and compensation, 268–9
    and the "fit factor," 270–1
    future plans of, 269
    key questions for, 264–71
    and ongoing monitoring, 274
    and review process, 273–4
    and substance, 266–7
    and "yes man," 271–5
The Naked Chef (Oliver), 263–4
NASDAQ, 10, 144, 183, 225
"nest egg," v, xiv–xv, 4–5, 32, 35, 47, 59, 64,
        67, 74–5, 206
New York Stock Exchange (NYSE), 143,
        183, 189, 227
New Zealand, 151, 186–7, 289n4, 2, 290n5
Nigeria, 194
Nikko Am, 128, 231
Nikko Asset Management, 51
No Country for Old Men, 80
"no-risk" investment, 6, 23, 35, 73, 105
Notre Dame University, 146–7
NYSE. See New York Stock Exchange

O'Farrell, Bill, 4
OECD. *See* Organisation for Economic
    Co-operation and Development
oil, 93, 105, 125, 148, 194, 211, 227
Oliver, Jamie, 263–4
Operating Expense Ratio (OER), 269
"optimization models," 207–8
Organisation for Economic Co-operation
    and Development (OECD), 92, 94,
    290n5
OTC. *See* over-the-counter securities
other fund vehicles, 158–62
    and do it yourself (DIY), 161–2
    and limited partnerships, 158–9
    and master limited partnerships, 158–9
    and target date funds, 159–60
    and unit investment trusts (UITs), 160
    and wrap accounts, 160–1
over 72 years portfolio allocation, 223–8
    and asset management, 223–4
    and cognitive tests, 224
    and country allocation, 225
    and division of assets, 223
    and driving, 223
    and Investing Pocket, 223–4, 226
    and Savings Pocket, 224, 226
    and Trading Pocket, 225–6
over-the-counter (OTC) securities, 10, 144,
    150, 292n8
overage, 34–5
overconcentration, 10–11, 95–7, 120–1,
    162

P/E ratio. *See* price-earnings ratio
packaging issues with bond products,
    139–40
Pakistan, 32, 193
panic, 3–7, 43–4, 104, 110, 112, 128, 142,
    222, 228, 280
past performance and the future, 53–4
patience, xi, 7, 38, 41, 44–7
pensions, 24, 186, 200, 214
performance analysis, 10, 49–64, 86
    and Asian Tigers (2001–2013), 86
    and high yield fixed income funds, 62
    and NASDAQ vs. Dow (1997–2001), 10
    and performance ratings, 60–2
    and technology funds (1998–2001), 10
    and US equities funds, 61
    and US fixed income funds, 61
    See evaluating fund and portfolio data
personal financial specialist (PFS), 243
personal life expectancy, 34–5
    See life expectancy
personal oversight of risk, 126–30
personal portfolio, 197–232

and accumulation and monitoring,
    211–15
and age, 215–32
and the "bunnies, the snake, and the owl,"
    197–8
and health care, 201–6
and insurance and annuities policies, 211
and key questions, 228–32
and later years, 198–207
    See later years, investing for
and real estate, 206–7
and refining allocation, 215–27
and weightings of your investments,
    207–11
Peru, 194
PFS. *See* personal financial specialist
Philippines, 32, 90, 180, 192–3
"pie of funds," 56–7
"PIIIGS" (Portugal, Ireland, Italy, Iceland,
    Greece, and Spain) countries, 185
PMs. *See* portfolio managers
Poland, 188, 190–1, 290n5
population age, and investing, 79–84
population growth. *See* demographics
portfolio allocation and age, 215–32
    and coming up short, 228–32
    key factors in, 216–17
    and mid-50s to early 70s, 219–22
    and over 72, 223–8
    and up to mid-50s, 217–19
portfolio construction, 162–4
portfolio managers (PMs), 51
Portugal, 82, 185–6, 289n2, 290n5
poverty, v, 84, 92, 181, 191
precise measurement, 51–2
price-earnings ratio (P/E ratio), 85, 144
private client groups, 254
private funds, 155–8
private limited partnerships, 225
private placement funds, 153
probability, 23, 33, 51, 63, 116, 118, 175,
    206, 288n1
product manufacturing, 251
purchase price averaging, 106–7
purchasing power, 23, 82, 201, 221, 293n6,
    8, 294n5

Qatar, 195

"Random Walk Theory," 42
Raymond James, 252
real estate, 24, 90, 92, 110, 121–4, 153–5,
    169, 206–7, 211, 220, 222, 227, 257,
    267, 279
    and direct ownership, 153–4
    and exposure, 211

and long-term planning, 206–7
and property values, 24
and risk, 121–4
See real estate investment trusts
real estate investment trusts (REITs), 92,
    154, 169, 211, 230, 290n6
registered investment advisors (RIAs),
    26, 39, 242–3, 246–9, 251–3, 255,
    257–9, 269, 274, 295n1
registered representatives (RRs), 242–3, 247,
    250–1, 254–5, 259, 269, 295n1, 274
regulators, 26–7, 240–2
REITs. *See* real estate investment trusts
Renaissance, 88
retirement, xii, 9, 24, 32–3, 35, 69, 78–80,
    82, 105, 107–8, 120–4, 159, 199–
    201, 206, 209, 215, 217, 219–22,
    228–31, 240–1, 280
    and spending, 78–80
    and trickle-in, trickle-out, 107–8
    See later years, investing for
"Risk Meter," 240
risk prism, 3–7, 113–31
    and advisors, 119–28, 131
    and age, 113–14
    and "at risk" funds, 120–1
    and balance, 115, 123–6, 131
    and capital markets dynamics, 118
    and commodities, 125
    and company stock, 117
    and company strategy, 118
    and corporate ratings, 116
    and country ratings, 116
    and credit, 116
    and currency, 122
    and deflation, 123–4
    and demographics, 124–5
    and dependencies, 117–18
    and financial institutions, 126–30
    and geographic risk, 121–2
    and high volatility, 120
    and industry deterioration, 125–6
    and inflation, 123
    and interest rates, 122
    and the leprechaun, 15
    lessons of, 131
    and liquidity, 124
    and low risk to high risk, 3–7, 82, 115
    and overconcentration, 120–1
    and past performance, 118
    and personal oversight, 126–30
    and politics, 116–17
    and scope creep, 119–20
    and underlying funds, 116–19
RRs. *See* registered representatives
Rudd, Andrew, ix, 122, 208

Russia, 81, 92, 172, 179, 190, 293n9
Ryan, Greg, 173

Safe Investor, xv, 21–2, 279–81
    critical lessons for, 279–81
    and dieting. *See* dieting
    and diversification. *See* diversification
    and emotions. *See* emotions
    and flexibility. *See* flexibility
    and frequency of investing, 212–15
        See trickle-in, trickle-out
    and international market investing
        See international markets, investing in
    and monitoring portfolio funds
        See evaluating fund and portfolio data
    and personal portfolio. *See* personal
        portfolio
    and the right advisor. *See* Naked Advisor
    and risk. *See* risk prism
    and selecting the right firm
        See selecting the right firm
    and single point of failure
        See single point of failure
    and time. *See* time
    tool for. *See* Three Pockets
    and trusting your advisor. *See* trust, and
        advisors
San Francisco, 4, 32–3, 69
San Francisco earthquake (1906), 32
savings account, xiii, 6, 23, 34–5, 39–40, 64,
    105, 112, 130, 134, 201, 214, 218,
    237, 242
savings habits, 78–84, 110, 199–204, 225–6
Savings Pocket, 102–4, 112, 123, 139, 141,
    217–18, 220–2, 224, 226, 257, 280
Schwab, 50, 60, 116, 245–6, 252, 260, 273
Schwab, Charles R. ("Chuck"), 67
science, technology, engineering,
    mathematics (STEM), 190
scope creep, 119–20
SEC. *See* US Securities and Exchange
    Commission
Securities Investor Protection Corporation
    (SIPC), 240–1, 254
selecting the right advisor. *See* Naked
    Advisor
selecting the right firm, 246–57
    and brands, 247, 251–2
    and banks, 252–3
    and broker-dealers, 249
    and change, 254
    and compliance, 247
    and direct fund company distributors, 256
    and discount/Internet brokers, 254–5
    and flexibility, 249–50
    and independent financial advisors, 246–7

selecting the right firm—*Continued*
  and life insurance providers, 256–7
  and the local factor, 253–4
  and other providers, 257
  and prices, 248
  and private client groups, 254
  and product manufacturing, 251
  and respect for advisors, 250
  and separation of managers, 257–9
separate account manager RIAs, 257–9
seven critical lessons of long-term investing,
  279–81
  and discipline, 280
  and diversification, 279–80
  and due diligence, 281
  and flexibility, 280
  and mistakes, 281
Severeid, Eric, 96
Shanghai Stock Exchange, 170–1
Shelton Green Alpha fund, 232
short-term debt product categories, 134–41
  and bonds, 136–7, 139–40
  and brokerage companies, 136
  and cash and equivalents, 134
  and funds, 137–9
  and MMFs, 134–5
  as not "short term," 140–1
SICAVs, 151
Silicon Valley, 9–10, 187
Singapore, 86, 88, 151, 174, 181–2, 186–8,
  195, 226
single points of failure (SPOF), 19–29, 52,
  73, 110–11, 125, 127, 135, 218, 221,
  237, 281
  and advisors, 26–8
  and alligator flea, 73
  and Bernie Madoff, 22–3
  and certainty equivalent, 23
  and diversification, 28–9
  and due diligence, 52
  example of, 20–1
  and independent verification, 26–8
  safeguarding against, 25–9
  and systematic review, 25
  See "trickle-in, trickle-out"
Sinnott, James ("Jim"), 31–3
Sinnott, Richard (maternal great-grandfather)
  ("Old Dicko"), 31–5, 67, 198
SIPC. *See* Securities Investor Protection
  Corporation
sloths, 111–12, 128
Slovakia, 195
small investors, 259–60
Smith, Adam, 83
Smith Barney, 252, 254
social security, 199–200, 231
South Africa, 191–2

South Korea, 9, 70, 86, 179–82, 186–7
Soviet Union, 190–1
"special" high minimum products, 28,
  139–40
SPOF. *See* single points of failure
Sri Lanka, 32, 93, 195
Standard & Poor's, 9, 11, 291n4
Stannard-Stockton, Sean, 147
STEM. *See* science, technology, engineering,
  mathematics
Stewart, Walter, 205
S&P 500, 11, 105–6, 157, 173, 179, 287n2
subclasses. *See* asset classes subclasses
subprime crisis (2008–2010), 40, 51–2,
  105–6, 137, 141–2, 162
Sullenberger, Sully, 270
Sun Microsystems, 11–12
survivor bias, 54–6
Syria, 174

T. Rowe Price, 60, 249, 256
tactical asset allocation funds, 70
tactical asset allocation (TAA) game, 214
"Tai Chi Pocket," 111–12
Taiwan, 40, 43, 86, 88, 90, 174, 179–82,
  186–9, 192, 289n2
target date funds, 159–60
taxes, 24, 63, 81, 85, 136–7, 144, 151–5,
  158–9, 163, 181, 193, 198–200, 206,
  218, 220–1, 231, 243, 256, 258, 267
TD Ameritrade, 246, 252
Templeton, Sir John, 70
Thailand, 189
Three Mile Island, 25
Three Pockets, 101–12
  contents of. *See* Three Pockets, contents of
  as customer conversation guideline, 102
  and entrepreneurial spirit, 110–11
  inside. *See* Three Pickets, contents of
  lessons of, 112
  and market crises, 104–5
  and Tai Chi, 111–12
  See Investing Pocket; Savings Pocket;
    Trading Pocket
Three Pockets, contents of, 133–65
  and alternatives asset classes, 155–8
  and asset-backed securities funds, 138
  and basic asset classes, 133–41
  and bonds, 136–7, 139–40
  and cash and equivalents, 134
  and commodities, 148
  and constructing your portfolio, 162–4
  and currency overlay, 138–9
  and debt crisis (2007–2008), 141–2
  and derivatives, 148–50
  and equities, 142–8
  and investment vehicles, 150–5

and lessons unique to debt, 164
and money market funds (MMFs), 134–6
and other fund vehicles, 158–62
and packaging issues with bond products, 139–40
and secured instruments packaged into funds, 137–8
and short-term funds, 138
and short-term debt product categories, 134–41
time, 28–9, 37–47, 60–4, 104, 280
    and annual reviews, 38
    and customers' impatience, 44–6
    and diversification, 28, 280
    and financial cycles, 40–1
    lessons about, 47
    and long-term investing, 37–40
        See later years, investing for
    and mutual funds and ETFs, 43–4
    as positive leverage, 47
    and the press and the pundits, 46–7
    and Three Pockets, 104
        See Three Pockets
    and winning, 41–3
    See trickle-in, trickle-out
Time-Life library, 239
tool for managing money and emotions. See Three Pockets
tracking errors, 50
Trading Pocket, 102–4, 109–10, 112, 139, 149, 153, 158, 161–2, 183, 195–6, 217, 219, 222–7, 257, 280
    and derivatives, 149
    and Egypt, 195
    purpose of, 109–11
trading spreads, 128
Transparency International, 178–80, 293n5
"trigger finger" investors, 110
trickle-in, trickle-out, 28, 67, 104–12, 198, 212–15, 275, 280
    and accumulation and monitoring, 211–14
    image of, 108
    and reinvestment of dividends, 67, 212
    and Three Pockets tool, 106–10
trust, and advisors, 233–44
    and Clifford Irving, 238–40
    and friends, 236
    and independent verification, 237
    and licenses, 242–4
    and regulators, 240–2
    and relatives, 235–6
Turkey, 90, 188–9, 191, 193, 195, 290n5
24-hour business news channels, xii, 46
Tyndall, 15

UCITS. See Undertakings for Collective Investment in Transferable Securities

underage, 34
undertakings for collective investment in transferable securities (UCITS), 151
uninterrupted power supply (UPS), 19–21
unit investment trusts (UITs), 160, 259
"unit trusts," 72, 93, 151
United Arab Emirates (UAE), 194
United Nations, 81
UPS. See uninterrupted power supply
US Airways, 270
US Congress, 151
US dollar, xiii
US Securities and Exchange Commission (SEC), 151, 225, 240–2, 251, 265
US Treasuries, 66–7
US Treasury, xiii
USS Boston, 25

Valery, Paul, 37
Vanguard, 41, 60, 249, 256, 287n3
VC. See venture capital
venture capital (VC), 155–8
Vietnam, 179, 195
vitamin E, 16
volatility, 16–18, 41, 66, 68, 72, 83–4, 93, 104–5, 108–9, 113–14, 120, 123, 142–3, 146, 149, 153, 157, 188, 194–6, 202, 208–10, 214, 219, 224–5, 227, 230, 280, 288n3

Wall Street, 5–7, 39, 41, 52, 69, 71, 75, 98, 126–7, 171, 235–6
water, 210
Water Fund, 232
wealth signal, 75–6
website, 49, 86–7, 90–1, 108, 134, 136, 143, 148–9, 184, 206–7, 283–4
weightings of investments, 207–11, 232
    and commodities, 210–11
    and country allocation, 209–10
    and currency, 209–10
    and insurance and annuities policies, 211
    matters, 232
    and ratios of equities versus bonds, 208–9
    and real estate exposure, 211
Wells Fargo Advisors, 254
Wilder, Bill, 51
"window of opportunity," 81
"winning," 41–3, 109, 222
World Bank Green Bond, 232
World War II, 236
wrap accounts, 40, 160–1
    and brokers, 40
    and mutual fund wraps, 161
    and separately managed accounts, 161

Zhou En Lai, 38